AMERICAN EXCEPTIONALISM AS RELIGION

LITERATURE, RELIGION, AND POSTSECULAR STUDIES
Lori Branch, Series Editor

AMERICAN EXCEPTIONALISM AS RELIGION

POSTMODERN DISCONTENT

JORDAN CARSON

THE OHIO STATE UNIVERSITY PRESS

COLUMBUS

Copyright © 2020 by The Ohio State University.
All rights reserved.

Library of Congress Cataloging-in-Publication Data
Names: Carson, Jordan, author.
Title: American exceptionalism as religion : postmodern discontent / Jordan Carson.
Other titles: Literature, religion, and postsecular studies.
Description: Columbus : The Ohio State University Press, [2020] | Series: Literature, religion, and postsecular studies | Includes bibliographical references and index. | Summary: "Identifies American exceptionalism as an emerging form of religion while exploring alternatives to this semi-faith through works by Don DeLillo, Ana Castillo, Thomas Pynchon, George Saunders, and Marilynne Robinson, which delve into the post-secular nexus of religion, politics, and culture"—Provided by publisher.
Identifiers: LCCN 2020003927 | ISBN 9780814214435 (cloth) | ISBN 0814214436 (cloth) | ISBN 9780814278116 (ebook) | ISBN 0814278116 (ebook)
Subjects: LCSH: American literature—20th century—History and criticism. | Religion and literature—United States—History—20th century. | Religion in literature. | Exceptionalism—United States. | Christianity in literature. | Postmodernism (Literature)
Classification: LCC PS225 .C36 2020 | DDC 810.9/382—dc23
LC record available at https://lccn.loc.gov/2020003927
Other identifiers: ISBN 9780814255940 (paper)

Cover design by Larry Nozik
Text design by Juliet Williams
Type set in Adobe Minion Pro

For Dee Dee

CONTENTS

Acknowledgments		ix
Abbreviations of Author Works		xi
INTRODUCTION	American Religion and Its Discontents	1
CHAPTER 1	Unsaying American Ideology: Don DeLillo's Apophatic Approach	25
CHAPTER 2	Faith in the Borderlands: Ana Castillo's Holy *Joderones*	61
CHAPTER 3	The Depth of the Riches: Thomas Pynchon's Spiritual Hybridity	97
CHAPTER 4	Redefining Bountyland: George Saunders and the Gift of Humanity	133
CHAPTER 5	Creeds Fall Away: Marilynne Robinson's Democratic Individuality	167
Works Cited		203
Index		213

ACKNOWLEDGMENTS

I WISH to express my gratitude to all without whom this book would not exist. A generous fellowship from the Baylor English Department afforded me the time and resources to complete this project. I'm grateful to the Baylor folks whose feedback improved my work immensely and whose solicitude kept me going: Sarah Ford, Julia Daniel, Alex Engebretson, Richard Russell, Kevin Gardner, Ralph Wood, and especially Luke Ferretter. Carey Newman put me through the paces and shot me straight. Ana Jimenez-Moreno, Kristen Elias Rowley, and Lori Branch at The Ohio State University Press have been invariably professional and gracious. This book's final form owes much to the careful criticism of two anonymous readers: many thanks to you both. Above all, thank you to Dee Dee Carson for your love, encouragement, and forbearance, and to Porter, Wyatt, and Nolan Carson for being my best motivation and my best distraction.

Portions of chapter 1 appeared in "Transcendence in an Age of Tabloids and Terror: Don DeLillo's Apophatic Approach" in *Religion and the Arts,* vol. 23, 2019, pp. 50–75, https://doi:10.1163/15685292–02301003 (copyright © Koninklijke Brill NV, Leiden, 2019), used by permission.

ABBREVIATIONS OF AUTHOR WORKS

Don DeLillo

C	*Cosmopolis*
FM	*Falling Man*
MII	*Mao II*
UW	*Underworld*

Ana Castillo

G	*The Guardians*
MOD	*Massacre of the Dreamers*
ML	*The Mixquiahuala Letters*
PML	*Peel My Love Like an Onion*
SP	*Sapogonia*
SFG	*So Far from God*

Thomas Pynchon

ATD	*Against the Day*
BE	*Bleeding Edge*
GR	*Gravity's Rainbow*
IV	*Inherent Vice*
MD	*Mason & Dixon*
VL	*Vineland*

George Saunders

BFR	*The Brief and Frightening Reign of Phil*
CWL	*CivilWarLand in Bad Decline*
IPN	*In Persuasion Nation*
LB	*Lincoln in the Bardo*
P	*Pastoralia*
TOD	*Tenth of December*

Marilynne Robinson

DOA	*The Death of Adam*
GL	*Gilead*
GOT	*The Givenness of Things*
H	*Home*
LA	*Lila*
WDH	*What Are We Doing Here?*
WCR	*When I Was a Child I Read Books*

INTRODUCTION

American Religion and Its Discontents

AS NATIVIST MOVEMENTS have become increasingly visible in many Western countries and hate crimes and manifestations of racism continue unabated, I frequently hear variants of this: "I cannot believe that *in 2019* we are still dealing with *this*. . . ." While I share the indignation behind the sentiment, I find this line of thought very unhelpful and a bit baffling. First, it implies a belief that "progress" is linear and inexorable, a sort of natural law. Second, it demonstrates a naïve understanding of how people come to be who they are. "Behind the times" is inadequate as a moral judgment and inane as an explanation. The assumption that everyone simply absorbs the presiding cultural mores ignores the power of ideological commitments to shape people profoundly and thus goes nowhere to address the problem.

In America specifically, many have said that "Make America Great Again" is tantamount to "Make America White Again." Without dismissing the point, we have to admit it's more complicated than that. Plenty of folks who are neither white supremacists nor white want to make America "great again." American greatness is for many Americans a mythological reality, a vision that's spiritual as well as material, and it does not matter to them if by some empirical standard America never has been "great." Norman Mailer pronounced back in 1972, "In America, the country is the religion" (87). Probably few Americans would admit this of themselves: The religiously devout would have to admit it constitutes idolatry, while nonreligious Americans generally don't want to claim a religion. One argument of this book is that Mailer's assessment remains true in many cases but goes unrecognized on account of prevailing notions about religion.

It is just about impossible to cleanly separate politics, religion, and culture, especially given their rhetorical overlap. My contention is that the writers considered in this study help us to think differently and constructively about this nexus by locating politics and culture, as well as organized religion, within the territory of the spirit. Given the normative understandings in this country about the proper sphere of religion, it's permissible to generalize about the lack of spiritual vitality in American culture but unseemly to continue the line of thought to the issue of spiritual discipline. This study focuses on five contemporary American fiction writers—Don DeLillo, Ana Castillo, Thomas Pynchon, George Saunders, and Marilynne Robinson—who engage the nexus of politics and religion to interrogate prevailing understandings of religion and to address the spiritual anemia they consider endemic in American culture. They open out the concept of religion by redefining it primarily in terms of spiritual discipline and practice instead of propositional beliefs. This results not in confusion or dilution but in a better grasp of how individuals actually live out their religious lives. The popular American distinction between church and state often obscures the ways Americans really are religious. By revising the common notion of religion, these writers identify American exceptionalism as an ersatz religion and propose their own religious alternatives.

American exceptionalism may present as a well-worn phrase. The term is generally perceived as toxic in academic circles. There's a prevalent elitism that equates nationalism with ignorance and assumes that those who vocally express love of America are the ones also vocally opposing movements like Black Lives Matter and #MeToo. The assumption that only racists and chauvinists embrace American exceptionalism is itself prejudiced. What's needed is not facile repudiation but greater understanding of American exceptionalism's power and appeal. The rise of globalism has done little to eclipse it, and we dismiss its relevance to our own loss. American exceptionalism has a long history and a range of usages. It's typically understood to have theological and religious origins that have since been shed. However, the authors I examine find warrant for continuing to think of it as a religion, one that shapes individuals in pivotal ways. Let me be clear: I'm *not* offering a thorough genealogy or explanation of nativism. But I do think these authors help us erect a framework for constructively engaging American exceptionalism and the postures that attend it.

For DeLillo, Castillo, Pynchon, Saunders, and Robinson, America is not simply a setting or milieu. They are fiercely concerned with American life—

with the cultural climate and its political, moral, and spiritual tenor. They view contemporary American life as a truncated, diminished thing and understand this to be a spiritual problem. Throughout this book, I maintain that American exceptionalism is a religion. That assertion is, first and foremost, the position of the authors I examine, though I do think it's accurate. This religion is not practiced by all Americans, and not all forms of American exceptionalism are religious. Furthermore, many adherents of this religion do not consciously understand themselves to be practicing a religion. In what sense, then, is American exceptionalism a religion? To address that question, we need more robust accounts of both American exceptionalism and religion.

AMERICAN EXCEPTIONALISM

Cultures, R. W. B. Lewis argues, essentially *are* debates and are therefore distinguished by their particular dialogues (2). John Hewitt shows convincingly that American culture is founded upon dichotomies—including individuality versus community, freedom versus authority, and here versus elsewhere—that leave citizens perpetually ambivalent (236). Yet these debates are never self-contained; they are occasioned by a larger vision and assimilated into a broader consensus. There are always images and narratives that "give direction and impetus to the intellectual debate itself," so that the debate and the story mold and reinforce each other, gradually developing a cultural myth (Lewis 3). American culture fosters a diversity of debates and responses, all of which are absorbed into a larger myth: the myth of election, or American exceptionalism.

This American myth begins with the legacy of the Puritans. Sacvan Bercovitch contends that the Puritans' unique cultural contribution was not religious but rather "lay in the realm of symbology": "The Puritans provided their heirs . . . with a useful, flexible, durable, and compelling fantasy of American identity" (*Rites* 7). The Puritans adopted a "rhetoric of consensus" that gave theological backing to their errand in the wilderness, linked personal identity to corporate endeavor, and gave the enterprise itself an eschatological teleology (*Rites* 32–35). America as sociopolitical enterprise was invested with soteriological significance as they "impose[d] a sacred *telos* upon secular events" (Bercovitch, *Puritan* 52). The rhetoric of consensus was commensurate with the notion of "representative selfhood," which "bound the rights of personal ascent to the rites of social assent" (*Rites* 36). In other words, a reflexive relationship developed between the individual as representative of all Americans and America as an ideal to which the individual conformed. For example, the "self-reliant man . . . [became,] paradoxically, a cultural pattern, the model of a rising nation" (*Rites* 47). According to Bercovitch, to be American was, *essentially*, to be caught up in sacred national destiny; American was "a federal identity not merely *associated with* the work of redemption, but *intrinsic to* the unfolding pattern of types and antitypes, itself a prophecy to be fulfilled" (*Puritan* 88–89). This was the Puritan legacy: America as chosen nation.

This merger of sacred telos and secular aims culminated in the American myth: a conception of America as characterized by liberal democratic values and invested with a sacred destiny. The American way is marked by "freedom, opportunity, democracy, and radicalism itself" and by a remarkable spectrum of "creative energies—enterprise, speculation, community-building, personal initiative, industry, confidence, idealism, and hope" (Bercovitch, *Rites* 19, 8). But the myth of America is most essentially captured by the idea of equality and the notion that the self is freely chosen: "The capacity to choose is at the heart of political freedom as Americans have conceived of it, and the capacity to choose or revise one's own identity is perhaps the ultimate exercise of that capacity" (Howe 257). The ideal of freedom is the heart of the American myth. With the American Revolution, independence became a concrete national goal at both the corporate and individual levels, which was eventually transmuted to the realm of the exchange of ideas and personal liberties. Elsewhere, independence threatened social stability, but in America it became the rhetoric of consensus and the norm for representative selfhood: This "summons to independence magnified the 'pursuit of happiness' from a merely private enterprise into an enterprise that entailed not only the common good but the redemption of mankind" (Bercovitch, *Rites* 42–43).

This American myth offered a sense of spiritual coherence. Bercovitch argues that the dynamics of modernity produced a world of autonomous individuals where no theory of government was compelling enough in its own right to foster community. Even the "pragmatic federalism" proffered by the American Constitution-makers, with its separation of powers, was inadequate because it offered no spiritual coherence. The desire for spiritual integration was not extinguished with feudalism: Americans still needed "some means of consecrating their way of life—a set of metaphysically (as well as naturally) self-evident truths; a moral framework . . . a super-empirical authority to sustain the norms of personal and social selfhood" (*Rites* 40). The lacking spiritual coherence was supplied by the American myth, which "gave the country a past and a future in sacred history, rendered its civic institutions a fulfillment of prophecy, elevated its so-called true inhabitants . . . to the status of God's chosen, and declared the vast territories around them to be *their* promised land. Above all, it grounded the myth in a central symbol, 'America,' that . . . was invested . . . with the double powers of materiality and the spirit" (*Rites* 41–42).

Bercovitch's rhetoric runs away with itself, but *America* is indeed a spiritual as well as material entity. This myth exists today as the all-encompassing ideology of American exceptionalism.[1] Drawing from anthropology, Bercovitch defines ideology as "the web of ideas, practices, beliefs, and myths through which a society . . . coheres and perpetuates itself" (*Rites* 13). This is not ideology in its more pejorative sense—the medium of demagogues and pundits. Ideology as Bercovitch uses it is inherently conservative but not static, both constraining and creative, marking "the interaction between levels of experience and belief (religious, intellectual, political, technological, aesthetic), reinforcing, modifying, redefining, and challenging each other in a volatile fusion" (*American* xv). In this sense, American ideology permits and even induces dissent as a source of vitality, so long as the dissent seeks a better, "truer" America. American ideology imputes to *America* (as cultural symbol) a history and a future telos that conflates sacred and secular: "As the myth's dominant symbol, interchangeably sensory and ideological, 'America' came to signify both self-gratification and the self-evident good, the most pragmatic of communities and the most abstract of ideals" (*Rites* 42). To be clear, this ideology isn't simple nationalism; it is belief in a consecrated national destiny.

One need not accept every tenet of Bercovitch's analysis to agree that this myth/ideology ratifies a transcendent "America." Terry Eagleton offers an apt description of how the nation can assume the role of the divine: The nation "is an ideal to be honoured by solemn rites, and gives birth to a pantheon of saints, martyrs, venerable patriarchs and totemic heroes. The nation is incomparably greater than any individual, rather as God transcends his own Creation; yet it also lies at the core of personal identity, which is also true of the Christian deity" (*Culture* 84–85). Today, many Americans no longer consider America to be a "light unto the nations" or the "city on a hill" (though some do). But many continue to see America *functionally* as a form of the transcendent. The American way still functions for them as *the* true path. Americans (including politicians) thus speak of the *meaning of America,* in a way that is uncommon if not unique among nation-states. This meaning has altered over time but has historically been understood as sacred.

When I refer to American exceptionalism as a religion, I do not have in mind the American civil religion of Robert Bellah's (in)famous 1967 essay.[2]

---

1. According to Bercovitch, "'America' (as a cultural symbol) bridges the antinomies that are often used by political scientists to distinguish between myth and ideology" (*Rites* 41).

2. In fairness, it should be noted that Bellah moved away from the term *civil religion*. Even in 1967, his concern was the morality and welfare of the civic community and its political practice. By *Habits of the Heart* (1985), Bellah no longer advocated a civil religion but rather a strengthening of the secondary modes of discourse that sustain civic community.

However, conceiving of religion in terms of spiritual discipline (which I establish below) illuminates the transition from the latter to the former. Bellah, drawing from Rousseau, defines civil religion as the "set of beliefs, symbols, and rituals" by which the "public religious dimension is expressed" (42). So conceived, civil religion is properly the domain of neither state nor church. It is the means by which Americans from various cultural and religious perspectives collectively understand America in light of the "universal and transcendent religious reality" (49). In *Varieties of Civil Religion*, Bellah's coauthor Phillip Hammond explains the genesis of civil religion:

> (1) The condition of religious pluralism prevents any one religion from being used by all people as a source of generalized meaning, but (2) people nevertheless need to invest their activity with meaning, especially when that activity brings together persons of diverse religious background. Therefore (3) a substitute meaning system is sought and, if found, the people whose activities have been facilitated by it will tend to exalt it. (Bellah and Hammond 121–22)

On this idealized account, the aim (more zeitgeist than conscious intention) is a generalized meaning system constructed of transcendentals common to citizens of all religious commitments. According to Hammond, "Civil religion depends for its existence upon circumstances allowing persons and institutions to be 'religious' and 'political' at the same time. The heavenly sphere of theology must blend with the worldly sphere of the civil" (Bellah and Hammond 78). Implicit here is the assumption that religion is properly a private affair. Civil religion, then, functions as a control mechanism, determining *what* content from the "heavenly sphere of theology" may be acceptably expressed in the public sphere. American civil religion, however, was marked by two pivotal developments that Bellah and Hammond do not adequately acknowledge. First, it evolved into a religion that competed with other religions instead of accommodating them, and second, it remained invisibly Christian in significant ways.

Bellah defends civil religion as a necessary "point of articulation between the profoundest commitments of the Western religious and philosophical tradition and the common beliefs of ordinary Americans" (Bellah 52). Civil religion is characterized here as a mediating space, normative only by virtue of deriving from other normative traditions. However, civil religion was not compatible with all established religions as Bellah insisted, but rather proceeded to rival and in cases supplant them. Instead of serving as a point of articulation, civil religion exerted a "common-denominator homogenizing effect" that produced "not a coalition of faiths but a new religion, significantly different from each of the particular traditions it claim[ed] to transcend and to fuse" (Yoder 3). Indeed, Bellah promotes civil religion to a status and conceptual essence that *cannot* but compete with the "private" forms of religion that supposedly sustain it. At times, Bellah implies that American civil religion *is* a robust religion in its own right, capable of exerting influence upon its parent traditions. His description of it as "a genuine vehicle of national religious self-understanding" is a case in point (46). His ambiguous phrasing leaves it unclear whether this self-understanding is first and foremost religious or political. Elsewhere Bellah conjectures (either naïvely or smugly) that "perhaps the real animus of the religious critics has been not so much against the civil religion in itself but against its pervasive and dominating influence within the sphere of church religion" (50). Evident in his surmise is that civil religion has become a threat to church religion. The crux of this threat was not that the tenets of civil religion were objectionable; the threat was to the normative force of doctrinal commitments. As stated in Hammond's definition (cited above), civil religion is a meaning system that sustains allegiance by facilitating people's activities; in other words, this "new religion" entailed its own rituals and practices. And as John Howard Yoder explains, differences of doctrinal commitment had to be ignored if the resources of the civil religion were "to have the desired supportive effect without being undercut by narrow 'sectarian' definitions of loyalty and identity" (3). In effect, any doctrinally grounded political critique is marginalized, emptied of real public influence. Civil religion ironically enabled secularization by appearing to deny its entrenchment. Religious differences were duly demoted to "folklore" status. As such, they became "sources of ethnic identity and cultural belonging rather than metaphysical, universal claims or required religious practices" (Douglas 31). America becomes the object of greatest allegiance. This "new religion" remained subtly Christian in key ways, however, passing as generalized and universal because the American population remained largely Christian.[3]

The most significant way American civil religion remained Christian was its eschatological tenor. It was rooted in the ideology of election. Hammond summarizes the original, particularly American alliance of religion and politics: "(1) There is a God (2) whose will can be known through democratic procedures; therefore (3) democratic America has been God's primary agent in history, and (4) for Americans the nation has been their chief source of identity" (Bellah and Hammond 41–42). Bellah and Hammond readily concede

---

3. See Douglas 28–32 for a detailed account of the latent Christian character of American civil religion.

that an ever-decreasing minority of Americans would affirm all four tenets, especially the second and third. Bellah states that the "obligation, both collective and individual, to carry out God's will on earth" is the legacy of a Puritan covenantal theology that is "now implicit rather than explicit" (Bellah 42). Hammond (a decade later) goes further, triumphantly proclaiming that the specifically Christian theological trappings of civil religion have sloughed off. But these elements don't just go away; they become, as Tracy Fessenden says, "unmarked."[4] I contend that the religion of American exceptionalism prevalent in the last few decades—the phenomenon described by the authors analyzed in this book—is the heritage of a civil religion that has largely dispensed with God yet retained its "unmarked" Protestant character.

Bellah insists that American civil religion is not only distinct from (yet compatible with) institutional religion but also distinct from idolatrous nationalism: "American civil religion is not the worship of the American nation but an understanding of the American experience in the light of ultimate and universal reality" (54). What Bellah implies but doesn't acknowledge is that "the American experience" *is* normative for that "ultimate" reality. The legacy of covenant theology (which Bellah mentions earlier in the essay, then tries to bury) abides. The "reality" here is that America *is* an ultimate reality. And when the covenantal logic at the heart of American exceptionalism largely disappears from public perception, America becomes for many Americans *the* ultimate reality. A religion of American exceptionalism is, according to Bellah and Hammond, a perverted or regressive form of civil religion. I submit that it's more accurately understood as civil religion's logical conclusion, given America's changing religious and political landscape over the last half century. Bellah warns (presciently, it turns out) that "without an awareness that our nation stands under higher judgment, the tradition of the civil religion would be dangerous indeed" (Bellah 54). This is precisely what has transpired. The civil religion that Bellah describes has lost normativity over the last half century for various reasons. One is that the version of the American dream attached to Bellah's civil religion perished for many Americans in the 1960s and 1970s, as they became disillusioned by Vietnam and Watergate and periods of economic turmoil. Another reason is that America became more religiously and ethnically diverse, which, as Christopher Douglas has shown, resulted in heightened awareness of the Protestant elements of civil religion that had become invisible to much of (white, Protestant) America. A resurgent evangelical population, on the other hand, rejected civil religion

---

4. See Fessenden, *Culture and Redemption* for a compelling and robust explication of American culture's "unmarked" Protestant character.

as not nearly Christian enough.[5] And yet, as civil religion foundered, and as the belief in America's divine mandate lost currency, the need to sanction and legitimate the nation state—the "chief source of identity" for many Americans—remained. The notion that America is *sacred* thus remains pervasive. Even as Americans have increasingly relinquished the notion that the nation stands under divine judgment, palimpsestic traces of election persist in the popular imaginary through American exceptionalism. *America* endures as a mythical entity both material and spiritual. American civil religion ends in worship of the nation itself.

RELIGION

Religion remains ubiquitous enough in America that many have never had cause to specify its particulars. It is part of the air we breathe (even if one considers that air toxic) and yet commonly understood as a private matter. For many, religion is probably one of those things you know when you see it. One argument of this book is that this is not the case: We *don't* always know it when we see it. This argument is implicitly corroborated by the fact that the so-called secularization thesis enjoyed decades of ascendency (at least in academic discourse) before Charles Taylor and others pointed out that religion has diversified rather than disappeared.

The twenty-first century has seen renewed attention to religion in many disciplines. In literary studies, John McClure's *Partial Faiths* made a seminal case that religion remains a serious concern for many of America's literary luminaries. Building upon Gianni Vattimo's notion of "weak religion," McClure argues that postsecular fiction is typified by "partial faiths": "forms of religiously inflected seeing and being" that are "at once critical of secular constructions of reality and of dogmatic religiosity" (ix). He focuses on conversions that "tend to strand those who experience them in the ideologically mixed and confusing middle zones . . . through which the conventional protagonist passes with all possible haste, on his way to a domain of secure religious dwelling," and he highlights that characters manage to occupy this middle zone without seeming overly anxious to move on (4). McClure makes an important argument, but I find his terminology problematic. "Partial faiths," like "weak religion," is susceptible to misapprehension and is laden

---

5. Douglas cogently and provocatively establishes significant correspondence between the right-wing Christian resurgence and the multicultural movement of the 1970s, arguing that both rejected "the vaguely religious liberal consensus on civil rights that preceded them and both sought to reenergize specific religious traditions" (25).

with conceptual baggage belonging to the secularization thesis it aims to subvert. McClure's term implies that religion that wavers, flags, or departs in its orthodoxy is not fully religion, as if religiosity has never been a bumbling and erring, if sincere, business. (Taking examples just from the Christian and Hebrew Scriptures, the Israelites at times literally couldn't keep the covenant to save their lives, and Paul had to publicly remind vigorous young men that stepmothers were off-limits.) Only in theory has religiousness ever been an unfaltering mode of life. I think McClure exaggerates the distance between "middle zones" and "domain[s] of secure religious dwelling." In contrast, Liliana Naydan's study of post-9/11 fiction identifies "counterfundamentalist work" that comprises examples of religious faith that allow for ongoing "negotiations between secularism, atheism, faith, fundamentalism, and fanaticism" without intellectually, ideologically, or spiritually "strand[ing] anyone" (*Rhetorics* 15). In other words, there are forms of religion that are no weaker for being exploratory, under revision, or hybridized. I posit that the relative strength of religion is best measured not by commitment to certain fundamentals but by how strongly religion serves as the ground and guide for behavior, morality, sociality, and politics.

I am defining religion as *the set of practices by which one makes present the transcendent or divine.*[6] It's a bit clunky as definitions go, but I've retained it for reasons explained below. There is no universally accepted definition of religion. Only relatively recently have we needed one. For most of human history, religion has been studied from within a particular tradition and considered primarily in terms of truth and falsehood, orthodoxy and heresy. A momentous shift in cultural imaginary preceded the notion of religion as a thing existing in plurality and open to academic study. Religion remains notoriously difficult to define in a way that is both specific enough to be useful and broad enough to be inclusive. The task is complicated further by its vexed relation to spirituality and by disagreement over the greater centrality of belief or practice.

Essentialist definitions are concerned with what religion *is* and functionalist definitions with what it *does*.[7] Theologians tend toward the former, while

---

6. In *Religion*, Christian Smith defines religion primarily in terms of practice as well but opts for "superhuman powers"—instead of *transcendent, divine,* or other popular terms—on grounds of inclusivity. I include *transcendent* alongside *divine* for the same reason, understanding it analogously to Smith's "superhuman," which he defines as that which is "(believed to be) able to influence or control significant parts of reality that are usually beyond direct human intervention" (22). While some may disagree, I understand *transcendent* to be inclusive of nontheistic and animistic religions.

7. There also exists a smaller third class called polythetic definitions. Influenced by Wittgenstein's work, these rely on a family resemblance approach. This approach, too, makes it hard to separate religion from culture (Cusack 20).

nonconfessional disciplines, especially sociology and anthropology, tend toward the latter. Anthropologist Clifford Geertz seminally defined religion as "a system of symbols which acts to establish powerful, pervasive, and long-lasting moods and motivations in men by formulating conceptions of a general order of existence and clothing these conceptions with such an aura of factuality that the moods and motivations seem uniquely realistic" (90). This approach sees religion as a way of making sense of the world, identifying and concretizing ultimate meaning through ritual and symbol. Some reject this approach for rendering "a wide range of apparently nonreligious phenomena . . . religiously significant" and thereby making religion difficult to distinguish from culture (Mazur and McCarthy 4). This objection implicitly posits a cultural consensus about what qualifies as religious. I would argue that one such common conception is articulated by William James, who famously defined religion as "the feelings, acts, and experiences of individual men in their solitude, so far as they apprehend themselves to stand in relation to whatever they may consider the divine" (36). James's definition specifies that religion, whatever its profile, happens *in solitude*, reflecting the common assumption that religion is a private, discretionary affair. If a thing is *essentially* private then it is in some way distinct from what we generally think of as culture, which is shared.

Must we separate religion from the broader category of culture? The devoutly religious may favor the distinction as a way of affirming the transcendent truth of their faith, while committed secularists may favor the distinction as a way of separating rational fact from superstition and delusion. If declining to separate them means conceiving of religion as *merely* a personal choice or set of popular habits internalized osmotically, then I would insist that there needs to be a distinction. However, there is certainly significant overlap between religion and other facets of culture and good reasons for thinking about them together. First, we can affirm that religion involves a unique mode of experience without separating it from culture. (If it were easy to distinguish religion by experience alone, would idolatry be a perennial problem?) Second, the very attempt to separate religion from culture carries implicit assumptions about the proper and distinct spheres of the secular and religious. Recognizing the overlap helps us identify and interrogate some of these assumptions, especially the issue of intentionality. Some scholars cite intentionality as the only distinguishing factor between popular religion and popular culture that functions as a religion (Mazur and McCarthy 2).

Does a religion have to be so recognized by participants in order to *be* religion? I posit that it does not. Consider the phenomena that fit the following definition: "a set of markers that are suggestive of religious meaning . . . includ[ing] the formation of communities of shared meanings and values, the presence of ritualized behaviors, the use of language of ultimacy and transcendence, the marking of special, set-aside 'sacred' times and spaces, and the manipulation of traditional religious symbols and narratives" (Mazur and McCarthy 6). This definition *can* include basketball and the Daughters of the American Revolution alongside Buddhism and Baha'i. (Of course, basketball is not *intrinsically* religious.) One can reasonably argue that a definition this broad is useless. I don't believe it is, and I'll offer a basic example to show why. It's common parlance to say that baseball (or food or comics) is someone's religion. We accept such remarks as facetious, but rarely are they made *entirely* in jest. The implication, even if unconsciously made, is that the person in question has become obsessive, perhaps alarmingly so. Forms of popular culture *do* become religious for some individuals, and we dismiss such talk with possible moral risk. Sometimes the "religion" in question has become the principal orienting engagement of that individual's life, entailing corresponding practices and rituals we are disinclined to subject to moral scrutiny because they are not *actually* (i.e., apparently) religious. Yet, such practices may be spiritually and morally formative in ways we neglect to acknowledge.

Normative notions about religion can obfuscate our understanding of how ostensibly secular practices and orientations may be religious. Bruno Latour poses a provocative question that applies here very well: "Why not say that in religion what counts are the beings that make people act, just as every believer has always insisted? That would be more empirical, perhaps more scientific, more respectful, and much more economical" (235). Latour's question sidesteps, for the moment, the matter of transcendent truth and propositional beliefs, not because they don't matter but because they aren't the very heart of religion. On the one hand, we are all engaged in practices and allegiances that are not usefully called religious. My participation in recreational soccer is not religious, even if the game entails a set of practices and even if a superb goal is described in religious rhetoric. On the other hand, there are "beings that make people act" that are not typically considered in a religious context but should be, because they inspire acts and practices that amount to a spiritual formation. *America* is one of those beings.

This book considers American exceptionalism as a religion—religion defined as the set of practices by which one makes present the transcendent or divine. This definition accommodates but does not privilege the role of belief and doctrine and does not confine religion to the solitary realm. To *make something present* entails both a practical and an experiential dimension. Religion has always had to do with the soul or spirit, which is rightly linked to human experience. But I want to distinguish between religion that privileges spiritual discipline and a spirituality characterized by individual feeling.

RELIGION, SPIRITUALITY, AND PRACTICE

Spirituality has become a buzzword, a serviceable term for a religious impulse directed (if anywhere) toward outlets either unorthodox, non-Western, or noninstitutional. It's become commonplace for individuals wishing to distance themselves from a particular religion to repudiate organized religion categorically. Unlike religion, spirituality doesn't exclude or oppress anybody, or so it is thought. This assumption is not confined to millennials or to popular culture; academics are guilty as well. Tracy Fessenden has cautioned scholars to tread carefully around schemas of "good" and "bad" religion, warning that "as a term for all that's good in religion, 'spirituality' too easily functions in scholarship as shorthand for good religion—good insofar as it is spiritual, spiritual insofar as it is good—all the while seeming to float free of its own normative power" ("Problem" 165). In this context, spirituality becomes an ally of the secularization thesis, a cipher for "progressive" or rational religion as opposed to superstitious or antiquated forms. Certainly the distinction can be overdone and each term has considerable semantic range. But I'm eschewing the term *spirituality* and retaining *religion* to encapsulate the phenomenon described by the writers I examine in the following chapters. I've chosen the term *religion* to stress the role of discipline and practice and to distinguish it from spirituality, especially the connotation of vulgar eclecticism that has gained normative cultural force.

The current dichotomy between religion and spirituality is not new, although it's perhaps more calcified today. As Leigh Eric Schmidt has compellingly shown, America has a robust history of restless spirituality. The "spiritual but not religious" position well preceded the 1960s counterculture and later New Age movement; it's new only in the lack of seriousness more common now. *Spirituality* originally signified the facet of Christianity concerned with personal piety. Only after a protracted extrication from Protestant piety did the term "begin to refer to 'direct mystical experience' and 'an individual's solitary search' for 'the absolute or the divine'" (Schmidt 3–4). Schmidt traces this disengagement, which hit full stride with the transcendentalists. Chafing at the rigid, unreflective conventionalism of American Protestantism, these spiritual seekers began reconsidering religion. Octavius Frothingham, seminal chronicler of the American Renaissance, insisted that discerning religion's true essence was *the* exigency of his generation. Believing religion had become bloated and constricting, Frothingham and his contemporary seekers sought to redeem it by freeing it from the shackles of its Latin etymology and insisting that, *essentially*, religion was not a set of forms and precepts but "the universal human search for meaning, and its archetype . . . [was] the individual seeker" (Schmidt 228). This search for meaning was less a metaphysical pursuit than a spiritual union with the divine, the enlightenment of the soul. For these seekers, liberation was the hallmark of authentic religion.

The rise of the seekers provoked a new struggle over the bounds of religion's flexibility: "Was the point precisely the *freedom* of spiritual seeking? Or was the real point to find a well-marked path and to submit to the disciplines of a new religious authority in order to submerge the self in a larger relationship to God and community?" (Schmidt 184). This inherent tension of seeker spirituality persists today, compounded over the last fifty years by a cultural shift toward greater individual autonomy. Seeker spirituality, when cut loose from all tradition and authority, easily becomes consumer spirituality wherein the goal is the expression of individual personality. Consumer spirituality is "marked by eclecticism and its advocacy of the position that all religions [are] equally valid and that an individual [is] only required to find his or her 'truth'" (Cusack 17). Spirituality becomes a commodity that the seeker conspicuously consumes. Schmidt's *Restless Souls* aims to redeem a sincere, pious seeker spirituality from the consumer spirituality that reflects the worst of American culture. What distinguishes Schmidt's noble "restless souls" from dallying or sybaritic seekers is an earnest quest for spiritual fulfillment—for enlightenment or salvation—and disciplined commitment; for them, the freedom to seek is not an end in itself.

Along similar lines, Robert Wuthnow distinguishes authentic spirituality as rooted in practice rather than in individual identity and choice. As practice-centered, Wuthnow's spirituality has key characteristics that hold for my definition of religion as well. One is that spiritual practices are inevitably social because they are, somehow and at some level, embedded in or derived from institutions. Second, practices have a moral dimension, meaning that they entail "rules that constrain a person's behavior . . . [and] these rules are built into the practice itself: following them is morally binding because they are accepted as the way to conduct the practice" (Wuthnow 185). In other words, practices constrain the practitioner and demand commitment. It is this moral dimension that decidedly differentiates "authentic spirituality" from consumer spirituality. Third, practices involve reflection about who one is, understood in narrative terms. Finally, because they are specific activities, spiritual practices become deeply interlaced with other parts of one's life. My definition of religion is not identical to Wuthnow's practice-centered spirituality, but his account helps demonstrate just how informative and revealing an account of a particular practice can be. Wuthnow's account is perhaps idealized in implying that practice-centered spirituality is intrinsically good. Religious practice, by my account, is neither inherently good nor bad, moral nor immoral, constructive nor destructive. But these practices shape who we are, and they are embedded in social networks.

When discussing religious practices, I characterize some as *spiritual disciplines*. These terms are not quite synonymous: All spiritual disciplines *are* practices, but the reverse isn't always true. A spiritual discipline is a formational practice or complex of practices that trains us to see the world in a certain way and shapes our values. Thus, while spiritual disciplines rely on "constructed forms, the original underlying emphasis is on the transformation of life rather than on mastery of the forms" (Frohlich 76). A practice may be performed inconsistently, but a discipline is executed routinely over a period of time and results in evident change. Spiritual disciplines are typically engaged in consciously. However, I maintain that an individual may engage in spiritual disciplines without identifying them as such, in which case one may be transformed in unanticipated ways. This is one implication of my argument that some ideologies and commitments generally understood as secular are constructively considered religious territory. Cultural rituals and practices can become spiritual disciplines.

Transcendence

What marks a practice as religious is its orientation to some kind of transcendence. In postsecular studies, there is often in view a form of religion that rejects traditional notions about the transcendent. My understanding of *transcendence* (and its cognates) derives primarily from Louis Dupré's work. According to Dupré, "transcendence is not merely what lies beyond the world, but first and foremost what supports its givenness" (*Passage* 251). Transcendence is not synonymous with the supernatural or divine, although it can include either, but is primarily our source of ontological grounding. Nor is *transcendent* synonymous with *sacred*, especially not *the sacred* (to which I'll return) as commonly understood today.[8] The transcendent is a core component of what Dupré calls the "ontotheological synthesis." This tripartite synthe-

---

8. Although Dupré never explicitly engages Mircea Eliade's work, he seems to have *The Sacred and the Profane* in mind when discussing common views of the sacred.

sis of the self, the transcendent, and the cosmos (or natural world) sustained Western culture to the Middle Ages. Dupré explicates its breakdown, beginning with the rise of nominalism and continuing through the Renaissance and Enlightenment. The sieve of modernity totally disbanded the synthesis, and its three components now stand autonomously.

If the transcendent is what supports the world's givenness, this idea of givenness is contravened by the Cartesian notion that the self is the locus of meaning and value. According to Dupré, "the notion of transcendence lost much of its meaning when the mind itself had to define what, by its own description, totally surpassed it" (*Religion* 15). When meaning and value are understood to be located in the human mind, rather than encountered directly from nature or the divine, all extra-mental reality becomes objectified. When the mind becomes merely the source of objectivity, there is nothing left of substance; selfhood then lacks content and the capacity for inwardness. The upshot, for Dupré, is that the collapse of the ontotheological synthesis has impoverished selfhood. He contends that "the nature of selfhood is that the self is *essentially* more than a mere self, that transcendence belongs to its nature as much as the act through which it is immanent to itself, and that a total failure on the mind's part to realize this transcendence reduces the self to *less* than itself" (*Selfhood* 104). (I contend that this is a conviction of all five writers I consider in this book.) All three components of the synthesis are necessary for an integrated self, and this integration is crucial for human flourishing. A nonintegrated self cannot realize its potential: "With its scope thus limited freedom itself becomes jeopardized. Within such a restricted vision any possibility of meaning beyond the directly experienced is excluded" (104). The reduction of the self to immanent experience has led to dissatisfaction and even dehumanization. The transcendent shapes the moral life, and Dupré insists (anticipating Alasdair MacIntyre's *After Virtue*) that a wholly immanent moral code lacks foundational support and is thus ineffective and potentially oppressive.

The role of direct experience returns us to the place of the sacred. The sacred functions to integrate the self with the transcendent. With the breakdown of the ontotheological synthesis, the transcendent has come to be viewed as unprecedentedly distant and the world as increasingly secular: "As man discovers the control over his universe to reside within himself, the need to relate each aspect of existence to a transcendent principle ceases to be felt urgently" (Dupré, *Selfhood* 22–23). The traditional role of the sacred is then extraneous. The sacred has traditionally denoted a type of direct experience of the transcendent, which the modern self with its privatized spirituality is no longer capable of. Because the world is no longer perceived as intrinsically sacred, the sacred becomes a category of interpretation rather than experience: "If anything is 'sacred' to the modern believer, it is only because he *holds* it to be so by inner conviction and free decision, not because he passively *undergoes* its sacred impact" (29). This modern conception of sacred departs radically from its traditional, religious sense. Formerly, "verbal revelation and ecclesiastical institutions determined the inner experience, [whereas] today it is mostly the inner experience which determines whether and to what extent outer symbols will be accepted" (29). For Dupré, this inward movement of piety is irreversible; the sacred will always be mediated. The key, then, is to relearn to recognize the transcendent, which Dupré worries we are no longer capable of doing. Lacking the sacred, we lack integration, but sacralization depends upon one's capacity to acknowledge and recognize transcendence.

One of the animating tenets of postsecularism is that the lack of integration Dupré describes has not gone unfelt in secular societies. The fragmented and often dislocating nature of a completely immanent framework has precipitated the search for a new synthesis. These searches are not necessarily efficacious: "Even if we grant that modern man's spiritual need forcefully reopens the question of transcendence, it does not follow that the question itself places life in a transcendent perspective and, even less, that it constitutes a return of the sacred" (*Selfhood* 24). Some, like Ernst Bloch, have attempted to recapture the sacred (as integrating symbol) from a thoroughly secular, immanent framework. Dupré calls this "progressive secularization," defined as a "more radical (and more sophisticated) effort to be secular by expanding the immanent world view so as to include even the *religious experience*" (25). These attempts, born of an experienced "need for that other dimension which neither enlightenment nor scientism nor even the new social activism can provide," refuse to accept "a commitment to the transcendent as to *another* reality" (25–26). Charles Taylor in *A Secular Age* describes several such attempts to imbue an immanent existence with the aura of the sacred and achieve a greater sense of self-integration. Such attempts include humanitarian work as well as collective events like concerts and raves. Such events are "fusions in common action/feeling, which take us out of the everyday . . . [and] often generate the powerful phenomenological sense that we are in contact with something greater, however we ultimately want to explain or understand this" (Taylor 517–18). For Taylor, the motivation for such events lies in a desire to experience the transcendent. Ultimately, for Dupré and Taylor, these purely immanent attempts at integration only highlight the continuing need for true transcendence, which is not *chosen* but experienced. This view is affirmed by the authors considered in the following chapters.

Religion and Belief

What, then, becomes of belief in my account of religion? Practice-focused does not mean that belief is irrelevant or elective. Beliefs are important, and we cannot do without them. Defining religion as the practices by which one makes present the transcendent assumes some sort of belief about the transcendent. However, the American tendency to make belief the litmus test of religion is insufficient for several reasons. First, it places inordinate emphasis on individual choice, which, as Robert Orsi explains, isn't reflective of actual religious life:

> To "believe in" a religion means that one has deliberated over and then assented to its propositional truths, has chosen this religion over other available options, a personal choice unfettered by authority, tradition, or society. What matters about religion from this perspective are its ideas and not its things, practices, or presences. This is not necessarily how Americans actually are religious of course, but this account of religion carries real normative force. (18)

When religion consists in an individual's choice to believe, it remains largely a private matter, which insulates it from public scrutiny. Moreover, as Talal Asad reminds us, the practice of typifying religion by belief *is* an outcropping of a Christian framework (48), making it especially unrepresentative of how non-Christians are religious.

Another problem with identifying belief as the core of religion is the installation of ideas as the essence of religion. Religion is then really about meaning-making, which is again not reflective of how most individuals are religious. A view of religion as meaning-making generally translates to religion as meaning *made*. Orsi states, "Religious theories that emphasize meaning focus on the end-product, a story that is said to link heaven and earth, but the solidity and stability of this dissolves if you focus instead on the processes of religious meaning-making" (144). Certainly meaning is important, but accepting a proposition is no guarantee of spiritual fulfillment. Exclusive emphasis on individual assent ignores the influence not only of cultural factors that are doubtless present but also of divine encounter and experience. Orsi provocatively confesses, "Belief has always struck me as the wrong question, especially when it is offered as a diagnostic for determining the realness of the gods" (18). Meaning-making is an insufficient definition because the ways that the transcendent enters into the immanent present may explode meaning and create uncertainty rather than clear, comprehensible meaning. Or, as Adam Miller says, "The one thing that isn't allowed is for religious objects to speak on their own behalf" (124).

In a similar vein, the centrality of belief commonly contributes to a monolithic view of religion. As the index of orthodoxy, belief is typically perceived as rigid and binary. So when belief "declines" (or evolves), orthodox religion is said to decline, a source of alarm for believers and smug gratification for zealots of secularism. But anxious defenders of orthodoxy and gloating secularists unwittingly join forces in "inventing another kind of past, namely, the past of religion as a monolithic edifice gone to ruin, a singular and once robust, now depleted guarantor of meaning, order, and spiritual plenitude" (Fessenden, "Problem" 162). This influential, purportedly historical, developmental model in fact ignores history. While there's been a real shift in cultural imaginaries, the assumption that religion was ever so uniform is simply unfounded. It ignores historical divergence and development within particular religious traditions as well as historical examples of pluralism. Rather than some fossilized tradition adhered to by legions of drones, religion is a vital thing. One shouldn't focus on inquisitions to the exclusion of the councils. The tenets of various orthodoxies, now seen as timeless propositions, emerged after centuries. Seen from a wide view, belief is always under revision. As Fessenden has highlighted, postsecular studies is not innocent of this homogenizing tendency. When scholars find a religious impulse expressed in an unorthodox or apparently secular context, then insist upon identifying it not as religion but as some other thing (like "spirituality" or immanent transcendence), they participate in the ahistorical construction of a once-grand religion now fragmented and languishing into obsolescence. It's just as fallacious to pretend that hybrid and unorthodox religions emerge ex nihilo as it is to relegate institutional religion to a calcified historical past. Even "partial" faiths "have histories, [and] their conditions of possibility open up along particular trajectories that mobilize and constrain us in particular ways" (Fessenden, "Problem" 162). Even as they constrain us, religions are sites of human becoming, loci of ongoing determination, and practices constitute the means and register of that determination.

Defining religion in terms of encounter or mystical experience, instead of belief, would be another option. (Schleiermacher is often seen, somewhat unfairly, as reducing religion to emotional experience, and some transcendentalists, his avid readers, favored this approach.) But this approach is subject to a homogenizing tendency of a different kind, assuming in its more obtuse versions that all religion aims toward the same inarticulable, ineffable thing.

Invoking the presence of the transcendent is then reduced to a particularly strong form of awe or contact. This assumption—that there exists a form of experience that is the common denominator of all religion—underwrites the sacralization of dimensions of secular life (Dupré's "progressive secularization"). These efforts seek the feeling of transcendence without having to answer for claims it might make upon one's life. Here, sacredness is correlated with the strength and quality of feeling induced, and religious experience is narrowly understood as individual feeling. The upshot is that the specific activity or event is unimportant so long as it produces this phenomenological sense of being drawn out of the self into a larger force. "Whooshing up" is the designation Dreyfus and Kelly give it in *All Things Shining*, which looks to Western literature as a lens for locating meaning of a quasi-transcendent sort in a secular age. In a withering appraisal, Fessenden highlights the book's gross decontextualization, derisively noting the authors' denial of any difference between the feeling experienced in worshipful connection to the Christian God and the feeling inspired by a good football game. This denial ignores not just the context that elicits the feeling, but also the constraints that attend the context. Recovering a sense of enchantment is not necessarily synonymous with or directly correlated to spiritual fulfillment. Working with Doctors Without Borders, attending the Super Bowl, and participating in a Native American sweat lodge may all produce a phenomenological sense or *feeling* that is not *essentially* different. But the rituals, practices, and motivations involved differ vastly. The issue of moral and spiritual formation has been abandoned here. Dreyfus and Kelly assume that radiance is immediately accessible through some particular activity, neglecting to consider that fulfillment might be the product of disciplined practice. Fessenden conjectures that shirking claims upon the self is perhaps exactly the point: "What end is served in abstracting the glimmer of numinosity, the summons to awe, perhaps even the neural or chemical charge identified with the sacred from its place in particular histories, institutions, communities, struggles? Perhaps to mute the various claims, these may otherwise make on us by locating the sacred squarely at the level of individual *feeling*" ("Problem" 162). The sacred things that give us this feeling are sacred only because we allow them to become so, and thus Dreyfus and Kelly's approach underwrites a consumer spirituality. This is weak religion, indeed. Religion, as I'm defining it, *is* experiential, but it is not reducible to personal *feeling*. Any heady sense of oneness or mystical connection is situated within a broader ambit of experience. (The Exodus was an experience, but encounter and covenantal relation is not what most people mean today by religious experience.) Thinkers from Karl Barth to Bruno Latour have emphasized encounter as central to religion, but setting aside instances of theophany and the miraculous, encounter is often the fruit of practice.

POSTSECULAR BUT NOT ADRIFT: LITERATURE AND RELIGION

I believe it is no accident that the account of religion I've developed here has much in common with "lived religion" scholarship in sociology. This scholarship proceeds from the premise that "religions are as ambiguous and ambivalent as the bonds that constitute them, and their effects cannot be generally anticipated but known in practice and experience" (Orsi 2). On this view, religions are best described in narrative rather than doctrinal terms. Focusing on practices honors the dynamic nature of religion. As David Hall describes it, practice "encompasses the tensions, the ongoing struggle of definition, which are constituted within every religious tradition. . . . Practice thus suggests that any synthesis is provisional. Moreover, practice always bears the marks of both regulation and . . . resistance" (xi). Practice is the alembic of belief, the medium by which it is both expressed and interrogated. Religious practices may be provisional and exploratory or express dogmatic conviction; they may be borne of hope, despair, gratitude, rage, or subversion. Christopher Douglas has criticized lived religion scholarship for "tend[ing] to avert its eyes from the destructive dimensions of American Christianity" and for focusing unduly on practice to the extent that beliefs are put "off-limits to public scrutiny, discussion, and evaluation" (113). But this is a criticism of execution rather than methodology. A thorough and nonpartisan attention to religious practices *is* a way of subjecting religion to public scrutiny: Religion is brought out into the open, and the *effects* of religious belief are available to evaluation.

I'm not proffering my definition of religion as a candidate for transdisciplinary normativity. First and foremost, it reflects how the authors I examine conceive of and depict religion. But I do contend that this definition has its advantages. One benefit is that "thinking of religion as relationships between heaven and earth with the specific shapes that relationships take in particular times and places . . . frees us from any notion of religious practices as *either good or bad*" (Orsi 2). It is by attending to the effects and consequences of religious practices—considering the kinds of individuals they produce—that we can begin to evaluate religion. It is not only scholars of lived religion (sociologists) who think about religion this way. Theologian Rowan Williams concurs:

> A religious life is a material life in a particular place, marked by particular material patterns and rhythms. Its goal is for the place it inhabits to be a place in which certain realities become visible. It takes responsibility for the appearing of God; in doing so it equally embodies responsibility to God. It makes a bid to be fairly "tried" as a narrative among others; and what it has to show is that it is indeed a distinctive place. (319)

This is not a definition of Christianity alone; it applies to all religions, even, if we substitute for God an Ultimate or higher reality, nontheistic traditions. We have much to gain by thinking about the religious lives of all Americans as material, imbricated, suggestive of realities they seek to make visible with their lives. By thinking about material realities as also territories of the spirit, we will better understand what is lost when we confine religion to the realm of private choice.

The way religion has been theorized and purportedly privatized in this country has prevented us from critically engaging secular ideologies that are experientially lived as religions. An approach to religion centered on practices opens out the definition of religion to include modes of devotion that are nonreligious or secular by prevailing views. This approach allows, on one hand, that ostensibly secular modes of being may be no less rich, vibrant, and formative than traditionally religious ones; it also insists, on the other hand, that these same modes may be as destructive as any narrow, militant religion. My hope is to temper any triumphalism and model an approach to religion marked by respect *and* the willingness to critically engage it.

Literature, specifically narrative literature, is a fruitful resource for considering the nature and role of practice. As Fessenden parses it, Amy Hungerford's work suggests that "American literature post-1960 reconciles us to our spiritual condition post-1960, which is to be ever orbiting the twin poles of desire for conviction (the pole of belief) and assent to the indeterminacy of belief (the pole of meaninglessness)" ("Problem" 159). I want to suggest that there's another way to look at recent American literature, which urges us to consider that religion is not strictly about dogmatic belief or religious feeling but also spiritual and moral formation. In the last few years, scholars like Lori Branch have tried to shift the conversation away from theorizing the relationship between religion and secularity and onward to the ways individuals encounter this dichotomy, to the "range of practices and experiences that has to do with the *real construction* of selves and meaning" (26). Just as scholars like Robert Orsi find themselves using recourse to narrative—plain old stories—as the best and, really, only way to convey the texture and contours of "lived religion," so "literature takes us into the tangle of human feeling, behavior, and value creation that accompanies secularity" (D. Coleman 521). Individuals are religious *in time*; the performance of practices and the consequent personal development are constrained by rules of narrative time. In other words, practices are a becoming, and literature is an ideal vehicle for a view of that becoming. This book is not, or at least not primarily, an effort to index and evaluate signs and vestiges of religion or the secular. I'm not out to prove the resurgence or enduring vitality of religion in America. (The writers discussed take for granted Taylor's view that secularism is best understood in terms of the diversification, rather than decline, of religion.) First and foremost, this book is about spiritual discipline and formation, emphasizing that it matters not only *what* assumes the mantle of transcendence but also *how* human beings seek to commune with and manifest the transcendent.

Each of the following chapters examines two facets of a single author's work. First, I demonstrate that each author portrays American exceptionalism as a compelling but corrupted religion that comprises both an object of belief and a set of disciplines. These writers aim to divest "America" of its claim to transcendence and reveal America for what it is: a place and a way of government, a set of nontranscendent but worthy ideals, a place of freedom but also of oppression, not wholly evil but also not a chosen nation. This book is not intended as a rejection of American culture. My aim is not simply to delineate the ways these writers criticize America and the particular evils and excesses they impute to the nation. Dissent, after all, is nothing new, and America, as an ideological entity, actually depends upon it. "American jeremiads," as Bercovitch calls such dissenting voices, serve a ritual function in American culture, excoriating aspects of contemporary life by appealing to traditional, *truly* American values or policies. Rather than arguing on behalf of a *true* America, these writers show American exceptionalism to be a religion, a powerful and formative set of rituals and practices dictated by a certain vision of the good.[9] Even so, the aim in each case it to improve American life rather than destabilize it.

The second component of each chapter is an analysis of each writer's depictions of specific religious practices and their yield: how these practices shape individuals morally, spiritually, emotionally, and aesthetically. By focusing on spiritual disciplines and practices, I reveal these authors' respective depictions of the human construction of identity and meaning and the role of religion within that process. Primarily through close readings of the authors' works, I identify how the religious practices depicted in their works shape individuals and I place those practices within the moral framework established in the text. To this end, I draw upon theologians and scholars of religion to describe the authors' religious outlooks. Excepting Robinson and to some extent Saunders, the writers in focus are not widely considered religious. I aim to revise this

9. This is not to say that these authors have achieved a viewpoint of complete objectivity from which to comment on American life. There's no escaping ideology (as defined by Bercovitch). It shapes even America's sharpest critics to some degree, even as they shape it. There is simply no escaping one's situatedness. But it is possible to narrate (if not escape) ideology, and, as Bercovitch exhorts, exposing the limits of ideology is itself a necessary, salutary, and feasible task. Exposing these limits functions to uncover the deficiency of "America" as symbol for truly integrating the self and as the object of religious devotion.

general perception by showing that all five authors hold spirituality to be a vital part of human flourishing. Without insisting rigidly upon orthodox traditional forms, these writers aver that spiritual fulfillment results from discipline and formation and not from pop psychology, indiscriminate mysticism, or noncommittal belief in belief.

Each author also presents a religious alternative or set of alternatives. I am not advocating any one of these over another. Of primary importance here is the way these authors define and engage religion. But at some point evaluation is necessary, especially as the benefit of approaching religion as practice-focused is the attention to spiritual formation. One must finally decide what vision of human flourishing, and indeed salvation, is most compelling. However, the religious turn has seen instances of affirmative engagement with religion that border on the utilitarian. These sometimes make a *use* of religion, coopting it to advance a political agenda or subjecting it to evaluative frameworks that are, ironically, rooted in a secularist view of knowledge. We must tread carefully. Attending to practices at some point returns us to belief and to the notion of transcendental truth. But hopefully we return to that concern more enlightened and attuned after considering the practices beliefs inspire.

These writers seek the integrated life, for which the recognition and experience of the transcendent is foundational. According to Dupré, with modernity the three elements of the ontotheological synthesis (self, cosmos, transcendent) achieved autonomy. However, he does not see this as necessarily deleterious. Only when one element comes to dominate and diminish or relegate one or both of the others is this disastrous. For Dupré, the requisite for our era is that we achieve a new synthesis of these elements. This is both possible and necessitated by the way modern thought has "opened up a gap in the very nature of the real that will never be closed again" (*Passage* 252). Dupré argues that "the spiritual discovery of the moderns consists in understanding the active relationship of mind to cosmos as one that changes the nature of the real" (252). The notion of transcendence has been under revision since the fifteenth century and the "search for an adequate conception of transcendence appears far from finished" (252–53). This rethinking of transcendence will undoubtedly continue in what many call our postsecular age. But according to the writers in this study, American exceptionalism, in spite of its long tenure, is a poor substitute, one that must be supplanted by a richer notion of transcendence.

CHAPTER 1

Unsaying American Ideology

Don DeLillo's Apophatic Approach

FROM HIS earliest novels, Don DeLillo has been concerned with how individuals construct identity and seek spiritual fulfillment in an American culture marked by consumer capitalism, media manipulation, and warring ideologies. In *End Zone* (1972), characters employ various (ineffectual) means of "self-actualization" or "self-realization." *Players* (1977) opens this way: "Motels. I like motels. I wish I owned a chain, worldwide. I'd like to go from one to another to another. There's something self-realizing about that" (3). DeLillo's characters confirm what philosophers such as Louis Dupré and Charles Taylor have long stressed: The longing for transcendence does not dissipate with the decline of organized religion. The question is not whether but how religiosity will be expressed. "When the Old God leaves the world," observes a character in *Mao II*, there will always be "unexpended faith" (7). Disciples of traditional religions tend to fare poorly in DeLillo's fiction: Religion subsumes rather than integrates them as selves, or organized religions come to eerily resemble power structures.[1] Many of DeLillo's characters are spiritual vagrants, for whom the "Old God" is not a viable object of faith, in search

---

1. There are several exceptions: the Sufism of Brutha Fez (*Cosmopolis*); Father Paulus, Sister Gracie, and to an extent Sister Edgar (*Underworld*); the qualified endorsement of glossolalia in *The Names*; and, perhaps, the Buddhism of Levi Blackwater (*Running Dog*). DeLillo's portrayal of organized religion has become more favorable over his career, and criticism of certain expressions of religion does not constitute principled opposition to religion as such.

of a new grounding of identity. DeLillo gives credence to Dupré's postulate (discussed in the introduction) that the self must be integrated through some form of "ontotheological synthesis," in which the self finds mooring through a dual relation to the transcendent and the cosmos or material world (*Passage* 3).[2] Disaffected or aggrieved by traditional religion, many of DeLillo's pilgrims unavailingly attempt such a synthesis through either political ideology or vague mysticism. In chronicling the damage wrought by misplaced faith, DeLillo enjoins us to reconsider our understanding of religion, shifting the focus from belief to practice.

Religion is an elastic concept, probably unequaled in its capacity to polarize scholars, who cannot agree on its definition. Among the American populace, at least, religion is most commonly identified with, and by, belief. This conception contributes to two problematic notions: the specious notion that religion can be effectively privatized, and the unwarranted assumption that ideologies that do not directly invoke the divine are in no way religious. DeLillo doesn't dismiss the question of belief but depicts it as too malleable and provisional to be either the defining factor in distinguishing the religious from the secular or the guarantor of spiritual fulfillment. For one thing, according to DeLillo, we're *all* believers, if not in God, then in a god that may go by myriad other names or go unacknowledged.[3] For another thing, belief finds too many ready objects, and many of them are called God. In DeLillo's disquietingly recognizable world, God has become the watchword of terrorists and the catchphrase of admen—the term stretched and co-opted to the point of vacuity—so that it communicates insufficiently little to say that one believes or disbelieves in God. DeLillo heightens our awareness of the susceptibility of language, especially religious language, to manipulation, in order to underline the frequency with which religion is co-opted and the real difficulties of speaking meaningfully about the transcendent.

---

2. We must distinguish between Dupré's "ontotheological synthesis" and the "ontotheology"—the conception of the divine as Being—that's been attacked by philosophers and theologians such as Martin Heidegger, Emmanuel Levinas, Jacques Derrida, and, more recently, by Jean-Luc Marion and John Caputo. William Franke has argued that one may accommodate their concerns without a wholesale rejection of ontotheology, but the salient point is that it's possible to conceive of an ontotheological synthesis that includes an understanding of the divine or transcendent that differs from the God of classical theism. For example, Dupré, identifying the need for new forms of ontotheological synthesis, cites as a possible exemplar Nicholas of Cusa, who has also been invoked by Marion and others.

3. This is not an entirely outlying view. DeLillo finds company in thinkers from Charles Taylor to Slavoj Žižek. See Taylor's *A Secular Age* and Žižek's *The Puppet and the Dwarf*.

DeLillo exposes the common conception of religion (private and distinguished by belief) as not only inadequate but also dangerous. Focusing predominantly on the question of belief in God blinds us to ideologies and systems that also operate as religions yet are understood to be secular. Given the ubiquity and exploitability of belief, DeLillo establishes practice as the hallmark of religion. What one believes certainly matters, but in DeLillo's novels it is the exercise of disciplines and practices that really shapes individuals morally, spiritually, and aesthetically. In other words, one's practices disclose where one's faith actually lies and therefore provide an effective means of identifying sources of spiritual and moral degeneration.

DeLillo's work abounds with religious language and that unruly guest, mystery, employed so as to trouble the easy dichotomy of religious and secular. The concrete exercises by which individuals channel spirituality: *That* is religion for DeLillo, and such an accounting reveals what individuals truly hold as the ultimate concern. DeLillo opens out the notion of religion to confront America with its true gods. Americans speak facetiously of sports as a religion, of Fenway Park as a temple and praying to the football gods. In characters like *Underworld*'s Marvin Lundy, DeLillo shows that this is not a joke but a reality, humorous only in the darkest sense. Most threatening are secular ideologies parasitic upon religious language. DeLillo reveals one prevalent American religion to be Americanness itself: a religion of American exceptionalism inflected with salvific language, in which the orienting object of faith is America itself. In identifying religion by practices, DeLillo depicts the ways that religions shape individuals, inclining some to charity and gratitude and others to solipsism and violence.

DeLillo not only chronicles the spiritual aridity of American culture. He also intimates a way forward for his failed pilgrims by drawing upon the apophatic tradition. Ultimately, DeLillo exposes the gods' clay feet in order to facilitate a more authentic engagement with the transcendent. This chapter examines DeLillo's depiction of ersatz religions before turning to his circumspect intimation of a religious alternative. While DeLillo looks to disciplines as the stamp of religion, these cannot occur in a vacuum but are rooted in some notion of the transcendent. DeLillo nullifies neither the possibility of belief in nor meaningful speech about the divine. Joseph Dewey rightly says that throughout his career DeLillo comes to "a bracing confidence that the material world cannot bear to be simply what it is" (*Beyond* 11–12). DeLillo is not simply attempting to reenchant the world, however. His focus on spiritual and moral formation subverts easy enchantment and vague mysticism. Apophatic discourse—discourse that points toward that which is beyond language—is not merely a means of highlighting language's limits but a way of approaching the Ultimate that results in personal transformation. DeLillo appropriates the apophatic tradition as a means of approaching the transcendent in the age of tabloids, terror, and Trump.

AMERICAN BELIEVERS

DeLillo's characters often pursue self-realization through some version of the American dream. DeLillo has said that his first novel, *Americana*, was his own "journey—into America," which has become his primary subject ("Don DeLillo"). DeLillo's upbringing has given him both an insider's and outsider's perspective on American life. The son of Italian immigrants, DeLillo watched his father vigorously pursue the American dream. DeLillo doesn't eschew this pursuit; he claims that in his own way he followed his parents' footsteps ("Don DeLillo"). Yet while he has never denied the glittering potentialities that attend American life, he has always been interested in the shadows they cast as well, seeking to explore this subterranean America and trace to its source the discontent seething below the surface. DeLillo's work reveals that the myth of the American dream is artificially bolstered by a confluence of political ideology and consumerism that entices Americans with the dual promise of spiritual and material fulfillment. Some critics have denounced DeLillo as exploitatively apocalyptic and even labeled him a bad citizen, but his critical depiction of the American way(s) of life emanates from a keen attunement to its spiritual cost.[4]

DeLillo's spiritual drifters find political ideology so compelling because it offers a clear-cut conception of the good and a putative transcendence. In an interview with *PEN America*, DeLillo offered his take on religion in America today and its role in his work in light of his Catholic upbringing:

> The Latin mass had an odd glamour—all that mystery and tradition. Religion has not been a major element in my work, and for some years now I think the true American religion has been "the American People." The term quickly developed an aura of sanctity and inviolability. First used mainly by

---

4. George F. Will first accused DeLillo of being a bad citizen (and betraying literary ethics). Will complained that "conspiracy addict" DeLillo offered a baseless, lunatic theory to advance left-leaning political sentiments. Jonathan Yardley and Bruce Bawer accused DeLillo of penning political tracts rather than novels and espousing an excessively apocalyptic view of American culture. Others, like Frank Lentricchia, have taken Will's charge as a badge of honor and sign of authentic cultural engagement.

politicians at nominating conventions and in inaugural speeches, the phrase became a mainstay of news broadcasts and other more or less nonpartisan occasions. All the reverence once invested in the name of God was transferred to an entity safely defined as you and me. But do we still exist? Does the phrase still soar over the airwaves? Or are the American People dead and buried? It seems the case, more than ever, that there are only factions, movements, sects, splinter groups, and deeply aggrieved individual voices. The media absorbs it all. ("An Interview")

Organized religion is not a major preoccupation of DeLillo's work, but religiosity certainly is. DeLillo's assessment here of the "true American religion" accords with Bercovitch's account of the "Puritan origins of the American self": Sacred and secular aims are conflated, as innate spiritual longing is translated "safely" to a political collective. America or "the American People" becomes both reality (physical populace) and ideal, a first-person identity and a third-person identity. As a unified entity, "the American People" really exists only as a media figment, but this powerful idea is hardly "dead and buried." Even as it becomes pure simulacrum in the media's hands, its alluring aura perdures. The phrase of course comes with its implicit associations: "The American People" stand for a certain set of principles, living free and proud as the progenitors and protectors of democracy; they are an exceptional lot. Even a hyperreal image can retain mythic appeal.

The proliferation of buzzwords like *transnationalism, globalization,* and *global citizen* may tempt one to conclude that the corporation has trumped the nation-state, and that American exceptionalism belonged to the twentieth century. While the notions of globalization and transnational capitalism (ideologies in their own right) regularly appear in DeLillo's later works, DeLillo quashes the notion that American exceptionalism has faded into the glowing cyber-matrix of a global age. America's response to 9/11—both officially and unofficially—has demonstrated the tenacity of that ideology. The War on Terror, while opposed by a significant sector of America, is certainly an American mind-set, a reinscription of "Us." Though the "Them" is far more abstract and diffuse than in the Cold War, the "Us" of American ideology persists.[5] American exceptionalism is alive and well, according to DeLillo, and it is not simply an outsized form of nationalism. It is a religion, albeit one parasitic on

---

5. Joseph M. Conte suggests that American rhetoric now ultimately serves globalizational ends, claiming, "It is disconcerting to regard how representative democracy, or 'freedom on the march,' has subsequently been employed as a shill for globalization in the war in Iraq" (187). Conte's argument warrants consideration, but for my purposes—in terms of how American ideology functions, and how DeLillo treats it artistically—it changes little.

Christianity, complete with its own spiritual disciplines and embraced by a wide swath of Americans, to their spiritual impoverishment.

DeLillo portrays the continuing pull of this ideology in *White Noise*. Immersed in consumer culture, character Jack Gladney frequently recurs to American mythology as a grand narrative by which he situates his life. Stacey Olster has pointed out how in the opening scene, Jack observes students returning to college from their summer break and regards the scene as "an ode to Manifest Destiny, with station wagons evoking covered wagons on their journey through the west campus, and saddles, sleeping bags, and bows and arrows taking pride of place among the students' belongings" (81). Jack's categorization of the students of the "College-on-the-Hill" by economic class "is deliberately framed . . . to recall the theocratic 'City vpon a Hill' in which spiritual election was a function of its Puritan settlers' visible economic prosperity" (Olster 81). Even though Jack is postmodern enough to grant a mystical dimension to his daughter's recitation of "Toyota Celica" in her sleep, he cannot dispense with American myth as a source of spiritual community and continuity. Similarly, DeLillo's *Underworld* characters wax nostalgic for the Cold War. *Underworld* depicts a clear Us versus Them mentality, describing the competing headlines in the *Times* proclaiming the Giants' remarkable win (baseball being the all-American sport) and the news of the USSR exploding an atomic bomb (668). As the novel weaves achronologically through the latter half of the twentieth century, characters confess decades after the Cold War to missing the sense of security and the clear division of right and wrong furnished by the conflict.

As *White Noise* shows, this American dream of security and identity doesn't end with the Cold War; political ideology finds consumer culture thoroughly hospitable. In *Americana*, David Bells tells us, "To consume in America is not to buy; it is to dream. Advertising is the suggestion that the dream of entering the third person singular might possibly be fulfilled" (257). DeLillo links the genesis of the American myth and the genesis of television. The crux of both is the dream of becoming the "universal third person." A character quips that television came to America on the *Mayflower*, his point being, as Frank Lentricchia observes, this possibility of entering the third person: "It is *that* [the universal third person] which 'came over on the Mayflower,' the person we dream about from our armchairs in front of the television, originally dreamt by the first immigrants, the pilgrims on their way over, the object of the dream being the person those pilgrims would become, could the dream be fulfilled: a new self because a new world" (193–94). Lentricchia eloquently captures the logic of Bercovitch's representative self—that American self in which the first and third person become inextricably and reflexively tied. This longing for a third-person self is the American legacy, easily exploited by advertising. The third person becomes a means of integrating the first person: "To be real in America is to be in the position of the 'I' who would be 'he' or 'she,' the I who must negate I, leave I behind in a real or metaphoric Europe" (Lentricchia 195). The American dream has always been a third-person sensibility, even as the desire for independence: The independent and free individual is a new "he" or "she" for which the "I," in seeking, sheds its old self. Possibility and opportunity furnish America its cachet. America's mythical exceptionality rests upon its fostering conditions favorable for becoming the desired third-person self. In other words, "the distinction between the real and fictional cannot be sustained; its undesirability is the key meaning, even, of being an American.... [F]or America to be America the original moment of yearning for the third-person must be ceaselessly renewed" (Lentricchia 194–95). This yearning is a profoundly religious impulse, a hankering for the transcendent. The new self dreamt of by Pilgrims was thoroughly religious in nature, informed by theologically grounded consensus, and this yearning for the third person remains religious, even as the person we dream of becoming enters the domain of individual choice and is no longer subject to theology or consensus. As the "person we want to become" is emptied of definite content, the subjectivity of the American dream renders it susceptible to manipulation, especially by those on Madison Avenue and in Washington, DC.

While the third-person self "invented" on the *Mayflower* may have been spontaneous, borne of earnest belief of participating in divinely sanctioned destiny, DeLillo shows how the universal third person becomes a means of ideological manipulation.[6] In *Point Omega*, Richard Elster, a "defense intellectual" during the second Iraq War, divulges the exploitative attempts by the American government to rationalize and represent the war:

> "There were times when no map existed to match the reality we were trying to create."
>
> "What reality?"
>
> "This is something we do with every eyeblink. Human perception is a saga of created reality. But we were devising entities beyond the agreed-upon limits of recognition or interpretation. Lying is necessary. The state has to lie. There is no lie in war or in preparation for war that can't be defended. We went beyond this. We tried to create new realities overnight, careful sets of words that resemble advertising slogans in memorability and repeatabil-

---

6. Bercovitch argues in *The Puritan Origins of the American Self* and *Rites of Assent* that it is precisely the religious foundation of this third-person sensibility that allowed it to become tied to individual identity. Even as the religious roots withered, the sensibility persisted.

ity. These were words that would yield pictures eventually and then become three-dimensional. The reality stands, it walks, it squats. Except when it doesn't." (28–29)

David Cowart points out that this dialogue is not the easy shot at the Bush administration that it may appear. Rather, by painting Elster as gradually and begrudgingly becoming a "defense intellectual," the novel reminds us how we are all prone to error because of the third-person dreams we harbor ("Lady" 42). DeLillo conveys how this yearning can lead even to the complete immolation of the first person. *Underworld* contains the most unsettling example of such immolation in character Richard Henry Gilkey, the "Texas Highway Killer." Gilkey becomes a serial killer not out of misanthropy but because he can only perceive himself as a self in the third person, through a deadly form of triangulation. Gilkey has "to take everything outside, share it with others, become part of the history of others, because this was the only way to escape, to get out from under the pissant details of who he was" (*UW* 266). He lives vicariously through his victims' lives. He calls a reporter live on air and feels, as he talks to her and watches her on the television talking back to him, that he is being reified. Seeing her and hearing his voice on the TV makes him real to himself.

Consumer culture thrives on such triangulation, which may be spiritually lethal, even if not physically so. DeLillo concludes his remarks about the splintering of "the American People" (quoted above) by saying "the media absorbs it all." This portentous last line warrants scrutiny. DeLillo implies that though the American People no longer (if ever) exists as a material reality, it abides as a spiritual entity kept in circulation by the media. With the media driving consumerism, an integral connection develops between ideology and consumerism. This connection is explored by William Cavanaugh, who elucidates the potency of consumerism as a spiritual discipline that instructs consumers how to see and live in the world. Cavanaugh describes two ways that consumerism constitutes a spiritual discipline. First, it inculcates a form of false transcendence by distancing us from material things and inciting "a restlessness that constantly seeks to move beyond what is at hand" (Cavanaugh 48). Consumers are removed from the production process and often from a product's natural use, so that the thing itself cannot satisfy and must be accompanied by a mythology or ideal. Consumers buy a product not for its utility, but for its associations, its third-person promises. Purchasing a material good becomes an end in itself rather than a means to its use and enjoyment, and the quest for transcendence is continuously redirected immanently through consumption.

Such specious transcendence is offered by national ideology, or even by waste, the inevitable by-product of all production and consumption. In *Underworld*, Nick Shay muses about the worship of waste: "We feel a reverence for waste, for the redemptive qualities of the things we use and discard. Look how they come back to us, alight with a kind of brave aging" (809). Nick watches the recycling process: A farrago of castoffs and leftovers comes in, then leaves repackaged and rebranded as a story of redemption and recovery. This mystery of redemption even draws its own pilgrims; families and school groups come to Nick's facility:

> Gas keeps rising from the great earthen berm . . . [and] it produces a wavering across the land and sky that deepens the aura of sacred work. It is like a fable in the writhing air of some ghost civilization, a shimmer of desert ruin. The kids love the machines, the balers and hoppers and long conveyors, and the parents look out the windows through the methane mist and the planes come out of the mountains and align for their approach and the trucks are arrayed in two columns outside the shed, bringing in the unsorted slop, the gut squalor of our lives, and taking the baled and bound units out into the world again, the chunky product blocks, pristine, newsprint for newsprint, tin for tin, and we all feel better when we leave. (*UW* 810)

The passage's lyricism enacts the way that the process described is engineered to console and inspire. The "pilgrims" experience recycling as a process of repristination, even salvation. Sacred work is going on, affording visitors the reassurance that this "desert ruin" is not their own doing, or, if it is, that they are making it all new again. As fellow recyclers, the pilgrims feel the pride of contribution, which typifies the second way that consumerism forms a person spiritually: through the offer of community. In *Consuming Religion*, Kathryn Lofton suggests that consumerism in a neoliberal economy is manifestly religious in its "efforts to mass-produce relations of value" (2). "Whatever else religion might be," Lofton writes, "it is a way of describing structures by which we are bound or connected to one another. Religion is therefore also a way of describing structures by which we distinguish ourselves from others, often by uniting around things that claim universal interest" (5). (Recall my assertion that religious practices are always socially embedded.) Our consumption also distinguishes our community from others. This offer of community may materialize as solidarity with a protest movement through buying a music album or becoming a fan of a baseball team by buying team gear. Or, as in *Underworld*, it may mean backing the American Cold War effort by supporting the companies making the weapons that symbolize American dominance. Even the most well-intended consumption contributes to the replacement of concrete political action with virtual solidarity.

DeLillo exposes the symbiotic relationship in America between political ideology and media-driven consumerism, especially in his depiction of the Cold War climate. In a section of *Underworld* titled "Better Things For Better Living Through Chemistry" (an actual DuPont slogan), characters buy into product slogans as they buy into ideological stances. The Deming family—tellingly named Rick, Erica, and Eric—prove themselves consummate consumers and patriots. Their names reflect how homogenous and derivative their identities are. The links between commodities and nationalistic ideology proliferate as DeLillo describes the Demings' domestic life. Erica makes "strontium white" Jell-O chicken mousse and cleans with a "satellite-shaped" vacuum cleaner (*UW* 516, 520). While Rick and Eric drive out to a field to spot the newly launched Sputnik, Erica exhibits paranoia, feeling "a twisted sort of disappointment. It was theirs, not ours" (*UW* 518). The Demings' consumption is both a means of celebrating their *American* preferences (spurious political activism) and an attempt at self-realization. Erica does "things with Jell-O that took people's breath away" to stave off a nagging gloom she can't quite place (*UW* 513–14). Her compulsive need for openness and visibility reveals this gloom to issue from a deep-seated dread of the secret and opaque, a dread manifest in her conflation of a deep mistrust of Russian clandestine activity and a puritanical view of sexuality as inherently shameful. This section of the text is interspersed with various product warning labels repeated catechetically, demonstrating how consumer goods shape the lives of these characters.[7] As the novel describes the Demings' lives, the underlying fear and malaise that attend such an ideological posture emerge, as well as parallels between ideological orientation and religion. While Erica dons kitchen gloves at the thought of her pubescent son's developing sexuality, Eric himself is secreted away in his room, pleasuring himself while wearing a condom he likes "because it had a sleek metallic shimmer, like his favorite weapons system, the Honest John, a surface-to-surface missile" (*UW* 514). Eric is fantasizing about this very weapon, its "infallible flight," its "precision so saintly and sun-tipped," and "the way the fireball haloes out above its column of smoke and roar, like some nameless faceless whatever. It made him want to be a

---

7. Phrases like these are interspersed between paragraphs of narration: "Do not reuse this bottle for storing liquids; Do not puncture or incinerate; Flush eyes with water and call physician at once; To avoid suffocation keep out of reach of small children" (*UW* 513–17).

Catholic" (*UW* 514–15). Eric's fantasy exhibits the religious feeling that ideological authority can evoke.

When Eric later reenters the novel, now in his thirties, he is a "bombhead" who works in nuclear weapons development and delights in spreading ghastly rumors about the mutational effects of weapons testing on "downwinders" (*UW* 403–6). Eric enjoys approaching his coworker Matt Shay and whispering things like, "Your child is born with eyes that are pure white. No discernible pupil or iris. Just a large white eyeball. Two if you're lucky" (*UW* 420). Eric insists he doesn't believe these rumors, and when Matt asks why he spreads them, Eric answers, "For the tone, of course.... The bite. The existential burn" (*UW* 406). The detachment from material goods inculcated by consumerism results in two concomitant effects: the possibility of attaching any narrative or value to a product, and an ignorance of the effects of production methods and of possible nefarious uses of the product. Younger Eric's enchantment with American weaponry has only amplified. Matt narrates Eric's mind-set: "The bombheads loved their work but weren't necessarily pro-bomb, walking around with megadeath hard-ons. They were detail freaks. They were awed by the inner music of bomb technology.... They carried an afterglow of sixties incandescence, a readiness to give themselves compulsively to something" (*UW* 404). Eric has internalized the detachment from material goods and their production even as he participates in their creation. He is so enthralled with the "inner music of bomb technology" that he fails to engage his work's moral ramifications, even though he knows, theoretically at least, what can happen to "downwinders." Elsewhere in the novel, the rumors Eric likes to spread for the "existential burn" become realities, not only in the US, but also in the former USSR: Matt Shay's brother Nick, a waste management executive on a business trip, finds himself in a literal museum of mutants, victims of radiation poisoning. DeLillo structures the novel to suggest that it is but a short step from Eric Deming to Richard Henry Gilkey, the aforementioned "Texas Highway Killer." For both men, the identity or community sought is third person, never second person; it is impersonal, devoid of interpersonal encounter and vulnerability. Eric loves the aura of mystery; Gilkey loves the details of his victims' lives. Both seek to order their lives through indiscriminate consumption. Gilkey kills directly, Eric indirectly. Matt Shay is more aware than Eric of his place in the system but faces the same issue. A Vietnam veteran, Matt struggles after the war to distinguish mundane goods from military ones: "How can you tell the difference between syringes and missiles if you've become so pliant, ready to half believe everything and to fix conviction in nothing?" (*UW* 466).

DeLillo links not only political ideology and consumerism, but also political allegiance and religious devotion. In drawing this connection, DeLillo refrains from reducing religion to a power structure. His point is rather, as John McClure notes, that political entities may project an air of mystery and thus evoke the awe traditionally ascribed to the divine (*Partial* 71–72). DeLillo's comparison of political and religious beliefs speaks to the character of current political organizations and the innate human attraction to mystery. Political bodies maneuver themselves into the priestly role of secrets-keepers, inspiring awe by shrouding themselves in mystery while also promoting a discernable telos: namely, the flourishing of the sacred nation and its citizens' security. In *Libra*, a CIA operative's wife views the CIA as "the best organized church in the Christian world, a mission to collect and store everything that everyone has ever said and then reduce it to a microdot and call it God" (260). Secrets bestow power; to disclose them is to risk loss of authority. The Bomb, too, possesses this kind of power, inspiring a beguiling complex of fear and security. DeLillo's fictional J. Edgar Hoover believes "there is the secret of the bomb and there are the secrets that the bomb inspires" (*UW* 51). As Mark Osteen claims, "The Bomb engendered underworlds—not only the secrets of powers and dominions, but also the private fears of Americans and the remedies sought to quell them" (220). The Bomb promotes an epidemic of paranoia, and this fear throws people back upon the state as the source of reassurance. Power is taken for probity, as the "desire for absolute security readily mutates into a rigid form of dualistic thinking in which absolute good battles absolute evil" (Osteen 220). This role of security amounts to playing God, inspiring what one character calls "the faith of suspicion and unreality. The faith that replaces God with radioactivity, the power of alpha particles and the all-knowing systems that shape them, the endless fitted links" (*UW* 251). McClure articulates the nature of this relationship between paranoia and religion: "Conspiracy explains the world, as religion does, without elucidating it, by positing the existence of hidden forces which permeate and transcend the realm of ordinary life" ("Postmodern" 103). The Bomb, and the ever-growing nuclear stockpile of the Cold War, becomes the Alpha and Omega, an article of faith in the religion of America exceptionalism. When America becomes the object of faith, the purported source of security and blessing, untold disciplines may be urged upon citizens as measures necessary for preserving the nation that will, in turn, preserve them.

Ultimately, DeLillo shows American exceptionalism to be a compelling religion in its own right. In *Underworld*, Sister Edgar, a committed if jaundiced nun, finds that while she never loses her Catholic faith, another, subtle and pernicious faith ascends to rival it. As Cold War strictures fade, Edgar registers the degree to which the adversarial wartime ideology has structured her life. She finds "the serenity of immense design is missing from her life, authorship and moral form" (*UW* 817). Edgar believes "all terror is local now," which tests her faith because she is accustomed to giant, cosmic forces (*UW* 816). She realizes, "It is not a question of disbelief. There is another kind of belief, a second force, insecure, untrusting, a faith that is spring-fed by the things we fear in the night, and she thinks she is succumbing" (*UW* 817). The security and moral conviction that have buoyed her have come as much from political assurance as from her Catholic faith, and it becomes clear how damaging this reliance on American ascendancy has been. Though she is routinely out serving derelict sections of the Bronx, Edgar is exceedingly misanthropic. Her treatment of pupils borders on abuse. She is also a severe germophobe and seeks security in latex gloves that embody for her a confluence of grand narratives: "Safe, yes, scientifically shielded from organic menace. But also sinfully complicit with some process she only half understood, the force in the world, the array of systems that displaces religious faith with paranoia" (*UW* 241). Edgar faintly perceives that ideologically driven consumerism only perpetuates the psychological fragility that makes individuals gravitate toward reductive accounts of the world and demand palpable sources of security, be it gloves or bombs. But the gloves stay on: Ensuring physical cleanliness is more easily accomplished and empirically verifiable than looking to the cleanliness of her soul and reevaluating how she treats others.[8]

American exceptionalism engenders an adversarial outlook that's domestic as well as international. Edgar's fraught faith in American dominion feeds her misanthropy, but her lack of sympathy is generally indiscriminate; she's an equal opportunity offender. Other characters in *Underworld* prove the American dream to be fundamentally exclusionary. Baseball, America's pastime, appears to transcend race—allowing black youth Cotter Martin to befriend older white Bill Waterson during a Giants-Dodgers game—until Cotter comes out of a scramble in possession of a historic home-run ball. Bill immediately assumes a kind of white privilege, trying to convince Cotter the ball really belongs to him. That night, while Cotter sleeps, the ball is pilfered by his own father, Manx, who hocks it for a fraction of its worth because no one fully trusts the word of a marginalized black man as to the ball's legitimacy. Manx finally sells the ball by appealing to family legacy, inspiring the buyer to dream of passing the ball, along with the history it signifies, down to his son. Manx, having stolen the ball from his own son, will never pass

---

8. Throughout there are clear and damning parallels between Sister and another Edgar—J. Edgar Hoover.

on any American legacy. He has no share of the American dream to pass on, even if his son does forgive him for stealing the ball. Even *Underworld*'s paratextual elements indicate the Martin family's marginalization: Each of the three short sections narrating their lives is separated from the larger text by blank black pages.

DeLillo repeatedly draws attention to the effects of religious devotion: the ways that characters develop morally and spiritually. For Sister Edgar, it is finally a religious vision that spiritually rejuvenates her and compels her to do what her "other faith" could not: embrace those around her without reaching for latex gloves. The vision produces in Edgar "an angelus of clearest joy," as "everything feels near at hand, breaking upon her, sadness and loss and glory and an old mother's bleak pity and a force at some deep level of lament that makes her feel inseparable from the shakers and mourners, the awestruck who stand in tidal traffic—she is nameless for a moment . . . pouring into the crowd" (*UW* 823). The joy and newfound empathy inspired by Edgar's vision are undeniably salutary, yet DeLillo injects ambiguity as to the veracity of the vision. This ambiguity is instructive, encouraging us to question not simply Edgar's credulity but the criteria by which we evaluate religious experience. Edgar carries with her the memory of the vision and the "fellowship of deep belief" it inspired, but she dies soon after, foreclosing any glimpse of the vision's lasting impact. The reader is left to wrestle with a question: How susceptible has Edgar become to seizing upon *any* thrum of transcendence? Edgar embodies the coexistence of two human drives: the fascination with mystery (a desire for transcendence) and the need for stability. Humans seek the transcendent as a means of ordering their lives. But Edgar has exhibited a proclivity for placing her faith in easily assimilated sources of transcendence, mysteries ultimately answerable to human will. Edgar's religious vision reforms her in ways her ideological faith never could, inspiring her to what McClure calls a "sacramental mode of being" ("Mystery" 167). The sacramental is hazardous territory, however, for religious aura may be an *ignis fatuus*, drawing the undisciplined off the path into the bog of false transcendence. DeLillo conveys the true difficulty of authentic religious faith in the information age, when everything is connected: "The intersecting systems help pull us apart, leaving us vague, drained, docile, soft in our inner discourse, willing to be shaped, to be overwhelmed—easy retreats, half beliefs" (*UW* 826). "Easy retreats" and "half beliefs" are all-absorbing yet personally undemanding. In a culture in which political and religious rhetoric are often conflated, DeLillo focuses attention on the effects of devotion, encouraging readers to consider religion more in terms of practices than belief.

THE HAZARDS OF BELIEF WITHOUT CONTENT

"How human it is to see a thing as something else," muses *Underworld*'s Nick Shay (64). A baseball, a pair of gloves, a bomb: Products from the mundane to the extraordinary transcend the fact of their production and acquire mythical resonance. Human beings, avers DeLillo, have an inherent fascination with mystery. This fascination is not necessarily salutary, however. Near the end of *Underworld,* Nick, now a grandfather with a successful career in waste management (which he sees as a form of transcendence) and an ordered life, confesses a longing for some other form of mystery: "I'll tell you what I long for, the days of disarray, when I didn't give a damn or a fuck or a farthing.... [for] the breach of peace, the days of disarray when I walked real streets and did things slap-bang and felt angry and ready all the time, a danger to others and a distant mystery to myself" (806, 810). The fact that Nick misses the violent and aimless days of his youth reveals how corrupted his horizons have become and how deficient his attempts at self-actualization are (McClure, *Partial* 94). Mystery of any kind generates appeal, and a few critics have accused DeLillo of artfully exploiting human fascination by generating "esoteric" mystery for the sake of affect.[9] But as McClure points out, "DeLillo's work urges the reader to perform a discrimination of mysteries" ("Mystery" 167). DeLillo aids the reader in this discrimination through exploring the damaging effects of misplaced religious devotion.

In *Mao II*, DeLillo dramatizes the dangers of indiscriminate mysticism through Karen Janney, an ex-Moonie who has found no satisfactory replacement to fill her need for an absolute authority figure. Karen is described as a

---

9. DeLillo's handling of mystery has occasioned many treatments of paranoia in his work. James Wood argues that "*Underworld* reads as if complicit with the paranoia it describes," proliferating into endless connections when it should be offering the reader a means of navigating such a web (11). Peter Knight argues that DeLillo both exposes the costly toll that pervasive paranoia exacted on the America public during and after the Cold War and tracks the shift to a new variety of paranoia tied to the insidious web of multinational capitalism ("Connected" 828–30). Knight sees DeLillo's treatment of paranoia as diagnostic, intended as a means of resistance. Glen Scott Allen contends that DeLillo rejects the "paranoid strategy for postmodern survival" endorsed (Allen claims) by Pynchon in favor of "an almost romantic return to the sovereign powers of the individual" who is capable of resisting paranoia (116–17). According to Allen, DeLillo depicts paranoia as a rational coping mechanism for the postmodern alienated subject—for whom the choice between art and terrorism is virtually random—but insists we need not become such alienated paranoiacs. The element of paranoia has fascinated critics, but such attention risks unjustly marginalizing DeLillo as a conspiracy theorist. Lentricchia argues, regarding *Libra* especially, that it is a mistake to use "paranoia" to describe DeLillo's work because it diverts attention from the novel's critique, allowing one to dismiss its critical thrust (205).

consummate believer, though the object of her belief is rather inconsequential: "If it's believers you want, Karen is your person. Unconditional belief. The messiah is here on earth" (*MII* 69). Amy Hungerford has suggested that Karen's "capacity to believe" is portrayed as exemplary, and more important than the content of her belief, because it reflects an aptitude for imagination (64). Yet while the novel affirms the recognition of mystery, it also undermines "unconditional belief" by revealing how Karen's indiscriminate mysticism precludes her from developing a coherent sense of self. Karen's speech has been syntactically formed by her cult history, and Hungerford suggests "that the fractured quality of her language . . . demonstrates what it would mean to find a language commensurate to imagination, commensurate to the mystery that Karen honors in all that she encounters" (64). Karen's encounters, however, are *all* mystery. She prowls derelict lots of New York, absorbing and attempting to parrot the "vernaculars" of the slum culture, all the while "telling them about a man [Rev. Moon] from far away who had the power to alter history" (*MII* 172). She tells "familiars in the park . . . how to totalize their lives according to the sayings of a man with the power" (*MII* 176), yet she herself is only trying on vernaculars with no cohering principle.

Karen embodies a crowd mentality that the novel censures. Mystery remains for her a source of shallow fascination. She never achieves communion; she fears real contact with others:

> Contact could be dangerous. . . . She was learning how to alter the way she walked and sat, how to hide her glances or sort of root them out. She remained in the deep core. She walked within herself, did not cross the boundary into the no-man's-land of a glance, a fleeting ray or recognition. Like I'm a person and you're a person, which gives you the right to kill me. She formed a picture of people running in the streets. (*MII* 176)

Karen's imagination is devoid of true engagement. Hers is the world view of the crowd, the nonself who recognizes alterity only as curiosity. Her language may be fruitful for imagination, but it also discloses a lack of selfhood: Dewey notes that "as she moves through the harrowing night-world of Manhattan's homeless . . . she feels 'all drift and spin.' . . . The narrative voice appropriately flatlines into non sequiturs and disjointed observations, childlike syntax and diction, garbled fragments and clichés" (*Beyond* 110). Karen drifts in search of a new home for her ample belief. She glimpses one possibility as she watches the news on television (notably, without sound) and sees the implacable surging crowds at Ayatollah Khomeini's funeral. Karen responds by telling herself that surely no one else nearby is watching or people would be filling the streets: "If others saw these pictures, why is nothing changed, where are the local crowds, why do we still have names and addresses and car keys?" (*MII* 191). Belief without content leads to encounter without engagement. Others do not register with Karen as autonomous individuals. Suffering is unreal to her: She watches the crush of contained people in an internment camp and mentally compares it to a religious painting of suffering.

Vija Kinski in *Cosmopolis* further exemplifies DeLillo's wariness of any attempt to co-opt religious authority. The reader first encounters Vija emerging from a Catholic church. And as chief theorist to financial titan Eric Packer, she translates the aura of awe and mystery from Catholicism to the notion of wealth as existing for its own sake. Stepping into Eric's mobile office—a titanic, futuristic limousine—she remarks, "Oh and this car, which I love. The glow of the screens. I love the screens. The glow of cyber-capital. So radiant and seductive. I understand none of it" (*C* 78). Her lack of understanding, accompanied nonetheless by awe, mirrors the mystery that Hungerford suggests DeLillo intends to transplant from religion to literature. The thrust of *Cosmopolis*, however, is precisely that blind enthrallment with aura bars the way to self-understanding. Aura becomes mere spectacle:

> [Eric] knew what [Vija] was thinking. Never mind the speed that makes it hard to follow what passes before the eye. The speed is the point. Never mind the urgent and endless replenishment, the way data dissolves at one end of the series just as it takes shape at the other. This is the point, the thrust, the future. We are not witnessing the flow of information so much as pure spectacle, or information made sacred, ritually unreadable. The small monitors of the office, home and car become a kind of idolatry here, where crowds might gather in astonishment. (*C* 80)

DeLillo has spoken pointedly of the perilous divorce of ritual from the world. Of the fictional cult he portrays in *The Names*, DeLillo said, "My interest was the way in which a mind centered on ritual can so easily slip off into violence. I thought that ritual stripped from the world becomes dangerous, becomes violent. It loses its connection" ("Writing"). *Cosmopolis* reveals that the same danger threatens when information is divorced from the world. Vija watches stock tickers and sees only the pulsing glow, while the world outside the buffered limousine surges with violence. She is a kind of anti-saint: She emerges from the Church of Saint Mary the Virgin in simple dress, gray-haired yet youthful, and she likes to sit in the seat of power in Eric's limousine and speak "ex cathedra" (*C* 100). She fancies that her market theorizing carries the weight and subtlety of Catholic casuistry, but the abstract tenuousness of her ideas becomes apparent when she encounters the exigencies of nondigital, extra-limousine life. Violence fails to trouble Vija so long as she can theoretically rationalize it. Thus, she postulates the source of the well-being that Eric experiences upon hearing of the murder of his friend and rival Nikolai Kaganovich: "He died so you can live" (*C* 82). Vija dilates about market totality and the reabsorption of violence and revolution, but she cannot rationalize a man who has set himself on fire in protest. Eric thinks, "A man in flames.... What did this change? Everything.... [Vija] had been wrong. The market was not total.... This was a thing outside its reach" (*C* 99–100). Vija is dejected; her only rebuttal is to snivel about the man's unoriginality. When Eric challenges her, she "sharply" replies, "That was theory. I deal in theory" (*C* 95). Like Karen, Vija is a soulless spectator: "She talked. This was her job.... But what did she believe? Her eyes were unrevealing . . . bright at times but only in the flush of an insight or conjecture. Where was her life? . . . Give her a history and she'd disappear" (*C* 104–5). Vija fades from the narrative, defeated, a cautionary tale reinforcing Nick Shay's quip in *Underworld*: "What was Latin for if you couldn't reduce the formal codes to the jostled argot of the street?" (107).

Karen and Vija are not isolated cases: Throughout his novels, DeLillo depicts an environment where self-mystification is endemic. In perhaps *Underworld*'s grimmest scene, waste disposal experts Viktor Maltsev and Nick Shay stare at malformed fetuses preserved in a literal museum of mutants in post-Soviet Kazakhstan. Before these deformed dead, Viktor tells Nick that the atomic bomb and its radioactive aftermath became a reality as soon as it became a possibility: "'Once they imagine in the beginning, it makes everything true,' he says. 'Nothing you can believe is not coming true'" (*UW* 801–2). When the unimaginable becomes reality, when cyclopes leave the pages of Homer and enter the quickened world, nothing seems impossible. Self-mystification becomes rampant, as Viktor's next words reveal: "An interesting thing. There is a woman in Ukraine who says she is second Christ. She is going to be crucified by followers and then rise from the dead. Very serious person. Fifteen thousand followers. You can believe this? Educated people, look very normal. I don't know. After communism, this?" (*UW* 802). Something so utterly fantastic, when measured against the irradiated realities floating in jars of ether, is less easily dismissed. Because the need to believe finds so many readily available objects, DeLillo cautions against uncritical enthrallment with mystery.

Mystery remains not only a subject but also a feature of DeLillo's work. DeLillo commented in an interview on the place of mystery in his writing: "I think my work has always been informed by mystery; the final answer, if there is one at all, is outside the book. My books are open-ended. I would say that mystery in general rather than the occult is something that weaves in and out of my work. . . . Possibly it is the natural product of a Catholic upbringing" ("Outsider" 55). Hungerford posits that DeLillo preserves a mystical experience divested of content and foundation, and she is rightly concerned that this is a dereliction of writerly responsibility, as such ambiguity "insulates religious assumptions from individual and communal thought, and from individual and communal response" (133). But this doesn't hold for DeLillo's work. DeLillo directs the reader toward critical engagement by counterbalancing an evocation of ambiguously rendered mystery with withering depictions of promiscuous mysticism.

The contention that DeLillo usurps religious authority to gild literature with prestige, thus offering belief without content, overlooks the fact that DeLillo makes it abundantly clear how destructive belief without content can be. As Cowart claims, DeLillo seeks to restore to language cultural authority, yes, but also the capacity to invoke the numinous that transcends language (*Physics* 174). Ambiguity functions constructively to obviate false statements about the Ultimate and the idolatry that becomes a mask for coercion. Hungerford is right that, like the Latin Mass, DeLillo preserves some "lack of transparency" (56). But DeLillo aspires to more than aura. He is conscious of writing in an age when terrorism has become an ostensibly rational response to the world, and he aims not to install literature as the medium of religious experience, but to point toward a mystery that transcends both the possibility of media absorption and co-optation by terrorist groups. When religion and politics are conflated, when transcendence is on offer everywhere one looks, how can one speak meaningfully of ultimate things? Addressing a culture in which he believes the primary religion turns out to be the American people, a thoroughly image-bound and hypermediated culture, DeLillo is compelled to find new, often oblique or negative, ways to invoke the transcendent.

DeLillo attempts to carve out a space for the transcendent through his appropriation of the apophatic tradition. The apophatic tradition acknowledges the limits of language while confirming its power to access the Real. DeLillo makes it clear that numerous entities that exude an aura of sacramental mystery only prove themselves sources of anguish. Other mysteries, however, which seem to be authentic (in the sense of benign and redemptive) lead to spiritual fulfillment and communion with fellow human beings. A distinction emerges in DeLillo's work between a fascination with mystery and the spiritual exercise of seeking to access the transcendent at the limits of human language and comprehension. Mysticism is validated insofar as it proves redemptive, spiritually and morally enlightening. Apophasis entails both a way of speaking about the ultimate and a spiritual discipline that results in individual transformation.

LANGUAGE AND LAST THINGS

Language is, for DeLillo, both subject and medium, philosophical problem and theological concern. Critics have written voluminously about DeLillo's language, questioning if his work is truly postmodernist and if it can achieve any authentic critical purchase on the late capitalist culture he writes about.[10] Peter Knight asks if DeLillo's "writing [is] a symptom, a diagnosis, or an endorsement of the condition of postmodernity" ("Postmodernism" 27). I maintain that it is not only diagnostic but also prescriptive: In light of Fredric Jameson's seminal work, many scholars have insisted that art and criticism must seek new forms to effectively forestall commodification, and DeLillo's approach to language absorbs this insight. Cowart has cogently demonstrated how DeLillo both adopts and challenges the insights of deconstruction and poststructuralism.[11] DeLillo's use of apophasis further proves Cowart right: DeLillo grants the limits of language while retaining belief in its power to make meaningful statements about the transcendent that cannot be co-opted by the market, the media, or violent ideologies.

DeLillo clearly aims to speak meaningfully about Last Things.[12] Yet in spite of the copious analysis of DeLillo's language, his incorporation of the apophatic tradition has gone overlooked. Understanding DeLillo's use of apophasis, which is both a narrative subject and a performative dimension of his fiction, further elucidates his use of language as well as the role of religion in his work.[13] DeLillo subverts the notion that language itself is sacramental but

---

10. For arguments for DeLillo as modernist, see Gleason 130–39; Parrish 87; Nel 14; and McClure, *Partial* 65. For DeLillo as postmodernist, see Knight, "Postmodernism" 27; Johnston 268; Keesey; and DeCurtis. Regarding language, Dennis Foster uses Kristeva's work on prelinguistic speech to argue that "disregard of the referential dimension of language" produces disastrous consequences for DeLillo's characters (168). On the other hand, John Frow aligns DeLillo with Deleuze for glorying in postmodern "play" as liberating, and Steven Kellman (72–73, 76) and Paula Bryant (157) argue that DeLillo upholds the permanent divorce of signifier and signified as an expedient of liberation.

11. Cowart argues that DeLillo seeks to restore to literature a measure of its lost authority, "leav[ing] open the possibility that a relationship persists between the linguistic and the divine," without making a "prison-house" out of language (*Physics* 177–78).

12. See interview, "Dangerous Don DeLillo."

13. Especially with *Underworld* (1997), the religious dimension of DeLillo's work has gained more attention. Indeed, Joseph Dewey suggests that only its undercurrents of spirituality and its assumption of a "vertical" dimension of experience afford authenticity to DeLillo's work (*Beyond* 11). For sustained treatments of religion in DeLillo's work, see Hungerford; McClure, *Partial*; and Kavadlo.

affirms that language remains the site of access to the transcendent. The insufficiencies of language contribute to the promiscuity of belief among DeLillo's characters, who "desire transcendence but struggle to find a language in which to express that desire, to say nothing of realizing it" (LeMahieu 11). According to Michael LeMahieu, "DeLillo's novels mediate what can be said and meditate on what must be passed over in silence" (7). And yet, the very limits of language for speaking of the transcendent offer a fruitful form of spiritual discipline. DeLillo presents the apophatic tradition as a gainful means of navigating the struggle for transcendence. The tensions, negations, and dynamic dialectical form of apophatic speech forestall ossification of the relationship between the linguistic and the divine. Apophasis operates by a dialectical form of absorption and denial that reveals truth gradually and incrementally, offering provisional moments of enlightenment while denying ultimate closure.

At its most basic, "the apophatic is the linguistic strategy of somehow showing by means of language that which lies beyond language" (Turner qtd. in Franke 152). The roots of the apophatic tradition, as its Greek extraction suggests, lie in ancient Greece. For Plato and Aristotle, apophasis simply signified a negative statement or denial. Plotinus first appropriated apophasis to develop a truly original metaphysics, which inspired "the search for a mystical experience of the One, that is, of oneness and of union with the supreme principle in silence" (Franke 10). Plotinus's Neoplatonic school culminated in the work of Proclus, then fully entered the Christian tradition at the beginning of the sixth century through the work of Pseudo-Dionysius. For the latter, not the Neoplatonic One but the Christian God transcends human language.

In some Christian texts, apophatic negation is used as a means of denying one affirmative claim in order to prepare the way for a second, higher-order affirmative statement. This is how apophasis typically appears in Aquinas (*via postiva, via negativa,* then *via eminentiae*), as well as in some of the early Alexandrian and Cappadocian Patristic fathers (Clement, Gregory of Nyssa, John Chrysostom). Other Christian works, however, follow the Neoplatonists in "distinguish[ing] between the kind of negation which, in denying an affirmative proposition, takes over its claim to truth, and a kind of negation which denies the accuracy of both whatever affirmative proposition is at stake, and its contradictory" (J. Williams 4). Patristics scholar J. P. Williams maintains that only the latter are truly apophatic statements, and it is this latter form of negation that I have in view when discussing DeLillo's work.

Apophatic mysticism reached full flower in the medieval era, beginning with John Scotus Eriugena's *Periphyseon* and finding mature expression in Meister Eckhart. Apophatic discourse also flourished within the Jewish and Islamic traditions during the later Middle Ages. The Kabbalah and Sufism both adopt complex symbolisms for conveying the ineffability of the divine. A parallel apophatic tradition (under different appellation, of course) developed spontaneously within the Buddhist tradition, which shares with the Christian apophatic tradition an insistence "on the simplicity or nonduality of the divine or the ground of being" (Williams 7).

Especially when it comes to analyzing fiction and engaging literary theory, we must distinguish between apophatic theory and apophatic discourse. Unlike apophatic discourse, apophatic theory offers a normative statement "affirm[ing] the ultimate ineffability of the transcendent . . . without turning back upon the naming used in its own affirmation" (Sells 3). Apophasis may be misleadingly conceived as a second-order discourse that concerns not a discursive subject but discourse itself and its limitations. But, as William Franke insists, "then apophatic discourse is presented as having no bearing on extra-linguistic reality, no ontological import," when actually the ontological "realm is redefined by apophasis as the mystery of the real upon which discourse opens at the limits of what it is able to articulate—as what it cannot formulate and determine in terms of itself" (152). Apophatic discourse possesses an ontological dimension, placing demands on the individual "speakers." I am concerned in what follows with this latter form of apophatic discourse—specifically, theological discourse—rather than apophatic theory.

Apophasis is a way of approaching some mystery or mystical experience that has made an indelible personal impact but for which language is finally inadequate. Apophatic texts and approaches emerge out of specific traditions, signally when a tradition finds itself stagnating or decaying. Williams cites, for example, Buddhist schools that adopted apophasis to combat moral quietism resulting from skewed notions of freeing oneself from attachment. Apophatic discourse is a potent way of resisting the human proclivity to bend truth to human order and co-opt divine authority for human establishment. Apophasis points to the reality that language can never fully encapsulate the Real.

Apophaticism, for all its unyielding insistence on fallibility, is not a complicated form of agnosticism. It offers a means of "unsaying" or "unknowing" ostensibly absolute statements that fall short of the full reality, without stagnating into mere cynicism (Franke 199). Apophasis assumes some form, or limit, of experience, but it does not induce "discursive rest"; rather, each successive attempt to speak about the divine (or Real), even as it is incomplete, leads to greater knowledge and spiritual development in the individual. And it is through this recognized partial failure that apophasis engenders its fruitful tension. Apophatic discourse is never simply an intellectual endeavor, for it entails an acknowledgment of the failure of "human intellectual resources" and thus requires an "existential commitment" from the outset (Williams 190). Williams states that "apophasis is in some sense a validation of the soteriological need to speak of the divine, coupled with a repeated recognition that each attempt so to speak is not entirely successful" (5). This need to speak, combined with the failure of language to adequately capture experience, "flushes the human need for icons of the ultimate out of the epistemological arena into a wider existential ground" (Williams 9–10).

The "existential" ramifications of apophasis include a social dimension. Apophatic discourse serves to affirm and preserve a degree of pluralism. While no religious system or understanding of truth can exist without kataphatic (affirmative) statements, apophatic discourse fulfills a monitorial function by insisting that all kataphatic statements remain incomplete and that no one party possesses *the* truth. Because apophatic thought creates a space for the truth-beyond-language rather than producing affirmations, "methodologically it can play a key regulatory role, given the pluralistic situation of philosophy today, by offering a theory as to why this pluralism of discourses is necessary in the first place" (Franke 149). Such recognition fosters humility and magnifies social awareness. Williams asserts a direct connection between apophasis and the recognition of alterity: the process of shattering one's own images and affirmative statements about the divine (or absolute) results, on the one hand, in a shattering of the self for whom those were absolutes/truths, and, on the other hand, in "encounters with the 'other' who subverts our self-sufficiency" (223). Because of this encounter with the other, there is an "essential connection" between the apophatic activity of union with the transcendent and compassionate care of one's fellow creatures (Williams 192). Apophatic discourse *demands* practical activity. The very acknowledgment of that which is beyond language reveals its claim upon one, even if that claim cannot be easily defined. Or as Franke puts it, "For consciousness to conceive of what it cannot define or say is for it to transcend itself in its very act of conceiving and saying. Such a significance ... can be vouched for only by the effects it inspires in human beings, and it can be given a definite content not in itself and as such but only by human action and emotion, and perhaps devotion" (30).

DeLillo clearly has some familiarity with apophatic writings. The Catholic tradition in which DeLillo was raised includes a corpus of eminent apophatic texts.[14] The fourteenth-century mystical text the *Cloud of Unknowing* appears in both *Underworld* and *White Noise*. His prose—from sentence structure to arrangements of chapters—often employs techniques used by apophatic writers, including the creation of spatial relationships in the text and drawing

---

14. DeLillo has been untypically forthright about his Catholicism. Though by all accounts "lapsed" as an adult, DeLillo self-identifies as Catholic and has repeatedly stated how formative his Catholic childhood and education have been for his world view and his writing. (For example, see his 2010 interview with Robert McCrum in the *Guardian* ["Don DeLillo"].)

attention to aporia (felt absences) in the text.[15] Cowart has pointed out DeLillo's penchant for creating verbless paragraphs that force the reader to contemplate the relation of the words. The most salient characteristic of apophasis in DeLillo's work is its effect on the individual. Apophatic discourse is not simply a way of (not) speaking about the divine or Real but also, and fundamentally, a mode of spiritual and moral self-formation. Apophasis is part of DeLillo's Catholic tradition, but it also exhibits a natural affinity for the postmodern milieu because it recognizes the dynamic nature of truth while also fostering spiritual development:

> What apophasis has to receive from the postmodern consciousness is a reinforcement of its own insight that what is at stake here is not merely changing human perceptions but changing human perceivers, and not merely developing apprehensions of an unchanging truth, but apprehensions of a truth that is itself both unchanging and dynamic. What apophasis has to contribute to the postmodern consciousness, is a sense of the celebration of that dynamic, and a rich tradition of negotiating its organization into a *paideia* or anagogy which effects human liberation. (Williams 219–20)

DeLillo's apophatic techniques constitute a form of unsaying that offers the potential for new insight and urges a vision of compassion and communion with others.

Christopher J. Knight, in his work on modern apophaticism, argues that "the post-Jamesian artist or intellectual has made it something akin to a practice to imagine the work as incomplete, except as this completion is understood as taking place in a realm outside of, or invisible to, common understanding. As [Henry] James . . . writes, 'The pearl is the unwritten'" (5). For DeLillo, "unwritten" has two senses: that which is outside the text, as he avers the final answers are, and that which he explicitly unwrites in his work. Any work that is incomplete, pointing toward something outside the text, must preserve mystery in some fashion. DeLillo's use of apophatic techniques preserves mystery while insisting on the discriminatory principle that mystery must engender a recognition of alterity and never abandon the world. In this

---

15. For example, Liliana Naydan points out how *Point Omega* juxtaposes a slowed-down representation of violence in the film *Psycho* with the complete absence of the representation of (implied) violence in the main narrative of the novel ("Media"). The effect of this is twofold, (1) exhorting readers to consider how representations of violence are received and appropriated by audiences, and (2) drawing readers' attention to the potentially influential role of absence (aporia)—what (possibly or probably) occurs off-screen yet profoundly shapes what is on-screen. Naydan interprets *Point Omega* as DeLillo's attempt at a counternarrative to the kind of fundamentalism that can inspire terrorism.

way, DeLillo maintains an opening toward the transcendent while "unsaying" ideologies and esoteric mysteries that would parade as ersatz objects of religious devotion.

For DeLillo, mystery—the unsayable, the unknowable—properly demands contemplation and, in turn, engagement. Apophatic discourse is not to be reduced to a means of affirming the notion of *deus absconditus*, the hidden God. Divine hiddenness is a recurring trope in DeLillo's work, through which he distinguishes between a disciplined apophatic approach to the transcendent and the attempt by characters like Nick Shay to exploit mystery for coercion. In *Underworld*, Nick recounts his reading of *The Cloud of Unknowing*, an apophatic text by an anonymous Catholic mystic. Nick explains, apparently indifferent to the deviance of his interpretation, "It made me think of God as a force that withholds himself from us because this is the root of his power" (*UW* 295). For Nick, the pursuit of God is an erotically charged fascination with negation and secrecy, an attempt to penetrate a darkness that Nick understands to be the source of power: "This is what I respected about God. He keeps his secret. And I tried to approach God through his secret, his unknowability. Maybe we can know God through love or prayer or through visions or through LSD but we can't know him through the intellect. *The Cloud* tells us this. And so I learned to respect the power of secrets" (*UW* 295). The viciousness of Nick's reading eclipses its irony. Nick's entire life is driven by the need for order and mastery, and he divorces the pursuit of transcendence from morality. Acknowledging that love, prayer, and visions may offer alternative means of insight, Nick spurns them all. He further elaborates his take on *The Cloud* to Donna, a woman he meets in a hotel where she is attending a swingers convention with her husband:

> We approach God through his unmadeness. . . . How can we attempt to know such a being? We don't know him. We don't affirm him. Instead we cherish his negation. . . . And we try to develop a naked intent that fixes us to the idea of God. *The Cloud* recommends that we develop this intent around a single word. Even better, a single word of a single syllable. (*UW* 295)

Ironically, it is Donna who proposes the word *love* as the focal term for approaching the divine. But the word itself is insignificant. Nick entirely misses the point: The meaning of the focal word doesn't matter because the point is to move past the word. He tells Donna that as a twenty-year-old he agonized over which term to use, finally landing on the phrase *todo y nada*, which is itself laden with theological import, borrowed from St. John of the Cross. Now middle-aged, Nick remarks to Donna that this same phrase describes sex. Tellingly, as the pair have sex following their discussion, Nick narrates their lovemaking in terms similar to those with which he describes his attempt to know God. Nick scrutinizes her before, during, and after intercourse, so intently that she asks him to stop. Nick's thoughts disclose what amounts to conquest in the fullest sense:

> I raised up and saw how small she looked, naked and abed, how completely different from the woman of the movietone aura in the hotel lobby. She was near to real earth now, the sex-grubbed dug-up self, and I felt close to her and thought I knew her finally even as she shut her eyes to hide herself.
>   I said her name. (*UW* 300)

Nick's respect for secrecy as a source of power is rooted in his desire to exert power. Unable to penetrate the divine mystery, he forces Donna into the role of surrogate, intent upon knowing her through and through to the point of mastery. He presses until no part of her remains a mystery to him, but in the end, it remains "bleak bargain sex" that Nick knows will only result in guilt and further secrecy (*UW* 294).

Nick's reading of *The Cloud* altogether misses its point. Authentic apophatic discourse does not leave a person unchanged. Nick evinces a notion of the hidden that evokes only a galling fascination and a desire for power, whereas the apophatic tradition is distinguished from vague mysticism and simple negation by the fact that it engenders personal spiritual development and precipitates compassionate action in the world (Williams 187–88). Nick refuses the kind of contemplation that would inspire engagement rather than conquest.

TRANSCENDENCE IN AN AGE OF TERROR: *FALLING MAN*

DeLillo has demonstrated a prescient understanding of the growing power of terrorism, first taking up the subject in *End Zone*, which preceded 9/11 by nearly three decades. This milieu has shaped DeLillo's artistic handling of the transcendent, especially in his post-9/11 novel *Falling Man*. As much terrorism is, ostensibly at least, religiously motivated, DeLillo's apophaticism preserves mystery in a way that gainsays fundamentalist certainty without foreclosing the possibility of transcendence. The apophatic tradition has long been a way of unsaying substantialist conceptions of the divine that have become either oppressive or rote and deflated. Mystery is a "key component of mysticism in apophatic writings. . . . neither a set of abstruse doctrines to be taken on faith nor a secret prize for the initiated. Mystery is a referential openness onto the depths of a particular tradition, and into conversation with other traditions" (Sells 8). Because apophatic writings rely on tensions, juxtapositions, and negations, any enlightenment "is glimpsed only in the interstices of the text, in the tension between the saying and the unsaying. Yet as elusive as it is, it is in principle accessible to all. The decision to write takes the discourse out of the immediate control of its author and opens it to readers beyond any particular group or school" (Sells 8). In *Falling Man*, DeLillo suggests that apophasis is really a means of stripping away barriers to the transcendent, while sustaining the value of mystery in inspiring greater awareness of one's world.

In *Falling Man*, the shifting narrative focus creates a central juxtaposition of Hammad, a fictionalized version of one of the 9/11 hijackers, and Lianne, a New Yorker whose semi-estranged husband is a survivor of the attack. The spiritual lives of both are explored throughout the story, revealed through internal monologues. Hammad's ideological fervor leads him to become increasingly enthralled with death, while Lianne's spiritual quest provokes a fuller engagement with the world and comfort in her own identity.[16]

The religious motivation of the attacks causes Lianne to critically examine her own spirituality and the essential validity of religious belief. Recollecting her youth, she remembers her nominally Catholic father telling her, "Human existence had to have a deeper source than our own dank fluids. . . . There had to be a force behind it, a principal being who was and is and ever shall be. She loved the sound of that, like chanted verse, and thought of it now, . . . and something else as well, the existence that hummed in the words themselves, was and is" (*FM* 231). Even as Lianne finds this possibility of transcendence compelling, the prospect of fanaticism ruptures her captivation. Her friends read the Koran to be more informed about Islam, and Lianne is disturbed to learn the first line is, "This book is not to be doubted." She agonizes that religious devotion will cancel out the world: "God would consume her. God would de-create her and she was too small and tame to resist. That's why she was resisting now. Because think about it. Because once you believe such a thing, God is, then how can you escape, how survive the power of it, is and was and ever shall be" (*FM* 235). Lianne fears the kind of "unconditional belief" shown by Karen in *Mao II*, who could watch with awe as the crowd surges toward the coffin at Khomeini's funeral and wonder why individuals still have driver's licenses. Lianne begins attending Mass, which ignites a flickering belief that she hesitates to kindle and examine: "She didn't believe this,

---

16. DeLillo is not Islamophobic or categorically dismissive of Islam. Other works include sympathetic Muslim characters, such as Brutha Fez in *Cosmopolis*.

the transubstantiation, but believed something, half fearing it would take her over" (*FM* 233).

Lianne offsets her spiritual insecurity by seeking empirical signs of health. Exhibiting no discernible malady, she requests a battery of medical tests, all to confirm that she has "normal morphology." Normal morphology becomes a form of identity in which Lianne seeks solace and affirmation of well-being. Yet her confidence in her physical condition proves insufficient; she feels the desire for transcendence, for ontological grounding:

> She had normal morphology. She loved that word. But what's inside the form and structure? This mind and soul, hers and everyone's, keep dreaming toward something unreachable. Does this mean there's something there, at the limits of matter and energy, a force responsible in some way for the very nature, the vibrancy of our lives from the mind out, the mind in little pigeon blinks that extend the plane of being, out beyond logic and intuition. (*FM* 232)

Lianne continues to mull over this question, to believe and to doubt. She worries that belief opens into fanaticism, that the truth will consume her so that there will be no escape. The reader perceives that Lianne's fear has already come true: Her ceaseless internal wrestling confirms that there is no escape; she is consumed already. Belief here is an ongoing process, a form of apophatic discourse with no terminus in view. In accordance with DeLillo's penchant for ambiguity, Lianne never exactly settles for herself the question of God. Her final spiritual reflection:

> She thought that the hovering possible presence of God was the thing that created loneliness and doubt in the soul and she also thought that God was the thing, the entity existing outside space and time that resolved this doubt in the tonal power of a word, a voice.
> God is the voice that says, "I am not here."
> She was arguing with herself but it wasn't argument, just the noise the brain makes. (*FM* 236)

Lianne's thoughts combine apophatic and kataphatic statements about God that threaten to undo one another, the tension allowing for productive reflection: God is not present, yet God speaks. If God is not "here," is God elsewhere? Spiritual insight remains steeped in ambiguity. Each of Lianne's intimations of transcendence invokes a dismissive rationalization, and each potential spiritual insight may also be nothing more than the ticking of physiological processes. Gradually, DeLillo establishes a reflexive connection between the physical and spiritual so that transcendence and immanence are not easily separated. While Lianne finds it possible to dismiss her internal arguments about God as "noise the brain makes," it is by directing her attention toward the "hovering possible presence of God" that she perceives how the question bears upon human lives. This is the true fruit of apophatic discourse:

> A major motivation for turning our attention toward what cannot be said is that only in this domain, if at all, is it possible for truth in its (always only virtual) wholeness to be touched and brought into contact with life. Though Truth, especially in its wholeness or totality, is presumably forever beyond our comprehension, discourses on what cannot be said bear witness to how it bears upon us and thus to how we can live in relation to and in acknowledgment of this perhaps divine (im)possibility. (Franke 33)

The felt absence of God, this longing for divine presence, draws Lianne out of herself and into her life and into communion with others. Her attendance of Mass corresponds with an increasing sense of fellowship and spiritual fulfillment:

> She was stuck with her doubts but liked sitting in church. She went early . . . to be alone for a while, to feel the calm that marks a presence outside the nonstop riffs of the waking mind. It was not something godlike she felt but only a sense of others. Others bring us closer. Church brings us closer. What did she feel here? She felt the dead. . . . It was a comfort, feeling their presence. . . . They brought intimacy and ease. (*FM* 233)

While the communal nature of church directs her attention otherward, there is a concomitant movement in the opposite direction: "But isn't it the world itself that brings you to God? Beauty, grief, terror, the empty desert, the Bach cantatas. Others bring you closer, church brings you closer, the stained glass windows of a church, the pigments inherent in the glass, the metallic oxides fused onto the glass, God in clay and stone, or was she babbling to herself to pass the time?" (*FM* 233–34). The two movements prove reflexive: Others bring one closer to God, and the pursuit of God brings one closer to others. Lianne thinks that "it is not something godlike" she feels but a sense of community. Yet she feels there is something in that sense of communion that gestures at the transcendent. Furthermore, the content of her descriptor, "godlike," is left open-ended. The closest DeLillo comes in the novel to defining "godlike" is to suggest that it *is* this very capacity to inspire communion with others and investment in dailiness. For DeLillo, the world may bring us to God, but God must bring us to the world.

In the novel, it is just after Lianne reflects, "God is the voice that says, 'I am not here,'" that she reaches a point where she is able to get on with her life after the attacks. Lianne's revelation has the sacramental effect of restoring her to her own life and history: "She was ready to be alone, in reliable calm, she and the kid, the way they were before the planes appeared that day, silver crossing blue" (*FM* 236). Contemplation here leads to engagement. She comes to a sense of wholeness, a sense of bodily self that is more than simply physical:

> It was just her, the body through and through. It was the body and everything it carried, inside and out, identity and memory and human heat. . . . It was something she'd always known. The child was in it, the girl who wanted to be other people, and obscure things she could not name. It was a small moment, already passing, the kind of moment that is always only seconds from forgetting. (*FM* 236)

Apophatic discourse is precisely a means of referring to "obscure things she could not name"; it points toward that which cannot be said because it is rooted in transient experience. *This* sense of bodily existence—as one who stands in some relation to that which cannot be said—is then offered as Lianne's revised, final definition of "normal morphology."

In contrast to Lianne's productive engagement of mystery, Hammad's fideistic "faith" is depicted as a form of escape, a deluded, misanthropic, and world-denying attempt to vault himself into eternity. The novel offers brief snapshots of Hammad's life. He pursues flight training in Germany. He is a marginal member of a radical jihadist group. He fears the group's senior members, one of whom shames him for his lack of chastity and proclivity to glut himself on street food. Hammad's devotion to the group strengthens as he is chastened, resulting in a gradual repudiation of the world. This rejection is no traditional askesis, however, for there is no spiritual change in Hammad but only a resignation to a collective will. Hammad is impressed foremost by the strength of their conviction that there is no greater glory than death. This conviction "is the truth he has always looked for without knowing how to name it or where to search," and the hijacking plan "shapes every breath he takes" (*FM* 176). While the contemplation of mystery opens up the world for Lianne, the all-encompassing devotion to plot narrows the world for Hammad: "They felt the magnetic effect of plot. Plot drew them together more tightly than ever. Plot closed the world to the slenderest line of sight, where everything converges to a point" (*FM* 174).

Hammad's ideological commitment is more accurately called thanatological than theological. He believes people "need to be ashamed of their attachment to life," that worldly commitments are "empty space" (*FM* 177). Hammad's desire to "spread his arms and walk right into" a storm he sees coming in off of the gulf suggests that even the method of death is not of real importance to him (*FM* 177). Hammad is seldom given to contemplation, never dwelling on the purpose of the plot: "He didn't think about [it]. All he saw was shock and death. There is no purpose, this is the purpose" (*FM* 177). One of the novel's last scenes, its most chilling, conveys Hammad's final thoughts as the plane they have hijacked nears the World Trade Center:

Forget the world. Be unmindful of the thing called the world.
   All of life's lost time is over now.
   This is your long wish, to die with your brothers. (*FM* 238)

Hammad is "wishing for death" and focused on "eternal life" (*FM* 239). At this point, he takes comfort from a story that was initially told to him as a tale of horror by a fellow Muslim. The man had told Hammad about the child suicide brigades used during the Iran-Iraq War, detailing how thousands of children were sent to their deaths as a military tactic. As Hammad nears death, he recalls this story: "He took strength from this, seeing them cut down in waves by machine guns, boys in the hundreds, then the thousands, suicide brigades, wearing red bandannas around their necks and plastic keys underneath, to open the door to paradise" (*FM* 238). It is the zealous certainty of Hammad's death wish that gives Lianne pause in her spiritual pursuit, the notion of God that can overcome someone to the extent that she commits acts of terror. Significantly, Hammad's thoughts are always about death, Paradise, and ritual and *never* about Allah. Hammad never contemplates the divine nature, never pursues divine mysteries, never learns humility or compassion.

The apophatic approach assumes an individual's pursuit of communion with the transcendent. Union or integration, never immolation, is the intention, and discourse about the unsayable is rooted in some form of experience of the unsayable. Hammad has no such experience. He is convinced by a zealot's impassioned speech that "sounded like philosophy" (*FM* 176), and unlike Lianne, he never wrestles with the possibility of One who "was and is and ever shall be" (*FM* 235).

DOMINUS VOBISCUM: PERFORMING APOPHASIS IN *UNDERWORLD*

DeLillo's insistence that his "books are open-ended" and that "the final answer, if there is one at all, is outside the book" anticipates, even expects, readers' willingness to struggle toward enlightenment, if not a final answer. DeLillo's invocation of mystery does not offer a coherent theological or spiritual vision. The reader must pursue that outside of the book. But DeLillo confirms that the problems of our age are spiritual and thus require spiritual answers, and he insists that any authentic spirituality must result in worldly action. In *Underworld,* DeLillo directly challenges the reader to a pursuit of mystery and to worldly engagement. In *Falling Man,* DeLillo depicts apophatic speech; *Underworld* enacts it, drawing the reader into the experience of dynamic negation.

In its first line and again some 800 pages later, *Underworld* directly addresses the reader. The novel begins ambiguously, with the polysemic line: "He speaks in your voice, American, and there's a shine in his eye that's halfway hopeful" (*UW* 11). The antecedent of "American" is intentionally open; it may refer to either shared language or national identity. The direct, second-person address resumes at the novel's end, brilliantly integrated into a section where DeLillo blends traditional third-person omniscient narration with the conceit of web-browsing. The section is framed so that web navigator suddenly becomes "you." "You" are present as Sister Edgar experiences the miracle referenced above, the miraculous appearance of Esmeralda that results in Edgar's embrace of those around her. After the miracle ceases, "you" are charged with judging its veracity:

> And what do you remember, finally, when everyone has gone home and the streets are empty of devotion and hope, swept by river wind? Is the memory thin and bitter and does it shame you with its fundamental untruth—all nuance and wishful silhouette? Or does the power of transcendence linger, the sense of an event that violates natural forces, something holy that throbs on the hot horizon, the vision you crave because you need a sign to stand against your doubt? (*UW* 824)

The answer is yes; both responses find textual backing, and "you" are stuck with a tension. The apparent insufficiency of both options guides the reader in a further intellectual ascent toward the nature of Ultimate reality. As Osteen states, "What matters is not whether the apparition is 'real' (it resides in a fiction, after all), but that each reader be forced to decide if such things are possible, and what they mean if they are" (258). The ambiguity here is not intended merely to mystify but to augment: "DeLillo's narrator-authority liberates the contemporary reader into complexity, offers not essential truths for the reader to grasp but rather the essential, sustaining truth of grasping itself, the reader as invested in and as rewarded by the text as the writer" (Dewey, *Beyond* 124). As the image of Esmeralda flickers into view, even Sister Edgar's fellow nun, Gracie, expresses skepticism, saying, "It's just the undersheet.... A technical flaw that causes the image" (*UW* 822). Yet in spite of, or perhaps because of, its ambiguity, it is enough to change Edgar's perception of things and her relation to those around her; the mystery impels her to a new level of engagement.

As *Underworld* closes, DeLillo evinces a clear connection between the apophatic approach (or "discursive unrest") and the "existential" plane. As "you," the internet surfer, click through links, concluding with a perusal of the etymology or "tunneled underworld" of the word "peace" (*UW* 826), "your" attention is drawn from the glow of the screen to the radiance of the immediate physical world:

> And you glance out the window for a moment, distracted by the sound of small kids playing a made-up game in a neighbor's yard, some kind of kickball maybe, and they speak in your voice, or piggyback races on the weedy lawn, and it's your voice you hear, essentially, under the Glimmerglass sky, and you look at the things in the room, offscreen, unwebbed, the tissued grain of the deskwood alive in light, the thick lived tenor of things, the argument of things to be seen and eaten, the apple core going sepia in the lunch tray, and the dense measures of experience in a random glance, the monk's candle reflected in the slope of the phone, hours marked in Roman numerals, and the glaze of the wax, and the curl of the braided wick, and the chipped rim of the mug that holds your yellow pencils, skewed all crazy, and the plied lives of the simplest surface, the slabbed butter melting on the crumbled bun, and the yellow of the yellow of the pencils, and you try to imagine the word on the screen becoming a thing in the world, taking all its meanings, its sense of serenities and contentments out into the streets somehow, its whisper of reconciliation, a word extending itself ever outward, the tone of agreement or treaty, the tone of repose, the sense of mollifying silence, the tone of hail and farewell, a word that carries the sunlit ardor of an object deep in drenching noon, the argument of binding touch, but it's only a sequence of pulses on a dullish screen and all it can do is make you pensive—a word that spreads a longing through the raw sprawl of the city and out across the dreaming bourns and orchards to the solitary hills.
>
> Peace. (*UW* 827)

Pensiveness, as described at the passage's end, takes on the connotation of quietism, which would make of peace only a velleity. But the rueful tone and ostensible pessimism of the last few lines are a challenge to "you," the reader, a summons to engagement rather than resignation. As one attempts to penetrate that which is beyond comprehension and the mystery of how it might enter the world, one becomes more attuned to the world. In the cited passage, the mundane becomes refulgent. DeLillo has spoken in an interview of "radiance in dailiness" ("Outsider" 63), but no one has noticed how DeLillo literally enacts that phrase in this scene. The physical objects in the room surrounding "you" are described in terms that suggest radiance, images of light and the color yellow: Ordinary things like pencils and pastries are "alive in light," "glazed," "reflected," "yellow," "the sunlit ardor of an object deep in drenching noon." Here is DeLillo's discriminatory principle for differentiating among mysteries: It must impel one toward a "becoming in the world." This radiance provokes one to transcend mere pensiveness, to become more than "pulses on a screen" or ink on a page. The passage above sends the reader back to the novel's first page when, as "you" look out the window and glimpse children playing, "it's *your voice you hear,* essentially, under the Glimmerglass sky" (my italics). By hearing one's voice in others, one communes with them, however momentarily, and this draws one out of cyberspace into the "argument of things to be seen and eaten" and "the argument of binding touch."

David Cowart observes that in *The Names*, "cultist and terrorist are manifestations of a need for stable meanings. . . . Each turns to violence in a desperate attempt to restore a vanished center to life" (*Physics* 171). This desire for "stable meanings" supersedes all other concerns, so that their aims lose all contact with daily life. The arguments of the visible and tangible no longer exert influence on the terrorist or cultist. The need for stable meanings is not limited to terrorists and cultists, but their refusal to acknowledge any sense of mystery leads to a ready acceptance of violence. DeLillo wrote in a post-9/11 reflective essay, "It is the presumptive right of those who choose violence and death to speak directly to God" ("Ruins" 38). For DeLillo, there must be a connection between mystery and the mundane, and it is the "argument" of mundane life swirling all around us that tempers the use of violence.

DeLillo imputes the spiritual and moral enervation endemic in America to the practice of ersatz religions, which regularly go unrecognized as religions, and urges us to rethink the secular/religious binary and expand our understanding of what it means to be religious. Louis Dupré claims that "the nature of selfhood is that the self is *essentially* more than a mere self, that transcendence belongs to its nature as much as the act through which it is immanent to itself," and the failure to find mooring in transcendence "reduces the self to *less* than itself" (*Selfhood* 104). DeLillo reminds us of the curious case of human beings: We crave stable meanings and yet cannot resist mystery. The danger is that we are willing to be shaped in vicious ways for the sake of security and stability or for the thrill of the numinous mystery. No DeLillo character who places her faith in ideology, commodity, or conspiracy finds fulfillment. DeLillo's use of the apophatic tradition combats the easy co-optation of religious language and imagery for ideological agendas. In "unsaying" these idols, DeLillo creates a felt absence. In *Falling Man,* a German character, Martin, expounds his view that America, especially in the wake of the 9/11 attacks, is losing its place of ascendancy and its international influence. According to Martin, "There's an empty space where America used to be" (*FM* 193). To this, an American character responds, "Ask yourself. What comes after America?" (*FM* 192). DeLillo suggests that America is a poor object for one's ultimate faith. By showing how our culture has made of cipher of God, and opening out the concept of religion, DeLillo recovers a fuller sense of religion and highlights the necessity of finding new (or forgotten) ways to speak authentically of the divine in a culture given to hyperreality. He employs apophatic discourse in a way that refers beyond the text, challenging the reader to discern what must come after.

CHAPTER 2

Faith in the Borderlands

Ana Castillo's Holy Joderones

ANA CASTILLO'S WORK demonstrates that *the* "American self" does exist, but only as an ideal. There are, of course, many American selves. However, the fact that the American self is but an ideological construct makes it no less influential. The pressure to embody this ideological self, to assimilate into the dominant culture, deprives many Americans, especially Chicanxs, of a coherent identity. As a Chicana, Castillo offers a perspective on American exceptionalism that is unique among the authors considered in this book. *Chicana*, as Castillo defines it, signifies a Mexican American woman with a borderlands consciousness, one who feels at home neither in her country of residence (the US) nor in the land of her ethnic heritage (Mexico).[1] This borderlands state is also called *nepantla*, a term theologian Miguel De La Torre describes as being in the middle, "that situation in which a person remains suspended in the middle between a lost or disfigured past and present that has not been assimilated or understood" (74).[2] *Nepantla* results from the process of *mestizaje*: the "cultural, political, religious, social, and physical 'mixing' birthed from the pain and anguish of continuous conquest" (De La Torre 74). Castillo describes her own experience of such homelessness: "Today, in my own

---

1. *Chicanx* generally refers specifically to Mexican Americans, but Castillo sometimes employs the term more inclusively, closer to *Latinx*.
2. For a fuller explication of *nepantla*, see Anzaldúa's *Borderlands/La Frontera*, a work heavily influential for De La Torre.

nation of birth and citizenship, as a mestiza born to the lower strata, at best, I am often mistaken for an immigrant, at worst, as a nonentity. Moreover, this occurs not only in the United States, the country of my birth, but also in European countries. In Latin America, including México, I am taken for a foreigner" (*MOD* 17–18). Whereas Marilynne Robinson has written a book entitled *Mother Country,* Castillo as a Chicana has no mother country at all.

Castillo imputes the borderlands state of Chicanxs today to the lamentable history of US-Mexico relations and the process of Manifest Destiny. Castillo recalls that in the nineteenth century, the US annexed half of Mexico, suddenly situating a sizeable Mexican population on the American side of the border. These Mexicans were not immigrants yet found themselves culturally as well as geographically dislocated: "Assimilation into the fabric of the WASP American Dream had been the rule of thumb for all immigrants," but "Chicanos for the most part were also not immigrants" (*MOD* 2–3). Without moving, these Chicanxs arrived elsewhere, in a country they had not intended to inhabit and with no wish to assimilate. Castillo describes the cultural disparity: "Unlike the white, Anglo-Saxon Protestant, whose Puritanism shaped a democracy founded on capitalism, the Mexican comes from, in the words of Octavio Paz, 'a Catholic world of Mexican viceroyalty, a mosaic of pre-Columbian survivals and baroque forms'" (*MOD* 91). Reductive as Castillo's account may be, it points to the cultural morass experienced by Chicanxs today: caught between two cultures and marginalized by the dominant expressions of both. Deborah Madsen explains that Chicana subjectivity is shaped by a cultural milieu that includes "not just the cultural imperialism of the United States, expressed in a history of military aggression, conquest, annexation, and ongoing cultural and economic humiliation, but also the cultural imperialism of Mexico and Latin America from the perspective of which Chicanos/as are defined as mestizo, mongrel, Anglicized, and bastardized" (21–22). For Chicanxs, the US both is and is not their homeland, yet, driven by the desire to realize an authentic identity, they attempt to embrace this land as theirs.

In spite of her alienation, Castillo feels a connection to the US, the land of her birth, that stirs her desire to be here rather than elsewhere. She explains that if she retreated elsewhere, "the core of my being would long for a return to these lands. The collective memory that I share with other *indigenas* and mestizos and mestizas makes me yearn to claim these territories as my spiritual homeland" (*MOD* 18). Castillo feels that her spiritual homeland lies here, yet her cultural heritage makes assimilation contingent upon rejecting that heritage. Castillo maintains that while it is possible for Chicanxs to forge an authentic self-identity in America, the means many Chicanxs adopt—

especially attempts at assimilation—are spiritually and psychologically crippling. Nevertheless, the American dream continues to entice many Chicanxs.

Castillo asserts that any notion that might be called the American self is *essentially* noninclusive of Chicanos and, especially, Chicanas. Her work discloses prolonged exposure to the American dream; she has witnessed its allure while also experiencing its marginalizing effects. Her characters, mostly Chicanxs, negotiate life in America as men and women who cannot feel at home there, however keenly they wish to. They pursue the American dream with abandon, but their pursuit often yields only dislocation and disenfranchisement. This sociopolitical dimension of Castillo's work has been informed by her own experience as an activist. As a participant in el Movimiento Latino in the 1970s, she witnessed the intractable influence of American ideology on Chicanxs. She recounts the impotence of the movement's "efforts to bring unity and courage to the majority of our people" and its poor reception by Latinx communities:

> Among the factors contributing to this [lack of receptivity] were the desire to succeed, the consumer fever that overrides people's fundamental needs, and the competitive American premise that encourages individual versus community efforts. The temptations of the rewards of assimilation and the internalization of racism by the colonized peoples of the United States remain devastating. Society has yet to acknowledge the trauma it engenders. (*MOD* 22)

Castillo renders this trauma in her work, showing it to be physical, psychological, and spiritual. She insists that the only way for Chicanxs to overcome it is to realize its spiritual essence and to embrace an alternative religion.

Castillo insists that American exceptionalism, with its concomitant notion of the American dream, is best understood not simply as a political ideology but as a religion with formative rituals and practices. Its influence is far-reaching, extending beyond the ballot and passport to the very soul. Any system that wields such influence is never morally neutral. Castillo asserts that discerning the religious resonance of American ideology is distinctly imperative for Chicanas.[3] Though the hallmark of the American dream is that *anyone* who works hard and believes in it can avail herself of America's opportunities, this is utterly impossible for Chicanas who hope for a coherent identity

---

3. This aspect of Castillo's thought holds for Chicanxs of any gender. However, much of her work, especially her essays, focuses on Chicanas, who are subject to further marginalization on account of being female. Thus, while much of the content of this chapter speaks to the situation of all Chicanxs, I focus largely on Castillo's depiction of the situation of Chicanas.

encompassing their cultural heritage. For Castillo, failure to descry the spiritual complexion of American ideology results not only in an anemic spiritual life but also in disenfranchisement; Chicanas must pursue a spiritual life that affirms them both as women and as "Mexic Amerindian," combatting the dual marginalization Chicanas face in America.[4]

Castillo believes it is possible for Chicanxs to live a gratifying and stable life in America. But this requires a religious life that draws from non-Western, indigenous symbols and beliefs as well as *selectively* from dominant cultural systems. This hybrid religion grants Chicanas both greater awareness of the American milieu in which they live and the self-definition with which to live in it. Castillo believes all spiritual truths to be contextual and upholds individual subjectivity while also emphasizing the role of communal interpretation. Castillo's spiritual vision culminates in a Chicana expression of what theologian Miguel De La Torre calls an "ethics *para joder*," a trickster ethics intended to harass and destabilize regnant power structures.

WRITING *MESTIZAJE*: THE TECHNIQUES AND VISION OF CHICANA LITERATURE

Castillo is one of a cadre of Chicana writers for whom art and theory are not easily separated. As Madsen states, "In important ways the subject of Chicana writing *is* the Chicana subject: feminine subjectivity in a Mexican American context is the primary subject matter of Chicana literature" (5). Castillo describes Chicana literature as a response to the mainstream, predominantly white feminism that, however unintentionally, has perpetuated racism by focusing on white women within a predominantly white cultural milieu. Earlier feminism(s), she says, failed to transcend white privilege: "Most renowned white feminists came from privileged backgrounds. Their place in society could not be excluded from their understanding of it" (*MOD* 4). As a result, Chicana feminists have had to shoulder the double burden of advocating for their people as well as for their gender. Chicana writers have pursued this bipartite task through their art. According to Castillo, "much of our writing was directed at our own people, the texts intended to contribute to the discourse of our ongoing struggle for self-definition as well as offering a sense of place in society" (*MOD* 187). This quest for self-definition has demanded innovation: Traditional literary forms do not suffice because

---

4. "Mexic Amerindian" or, interchangeably, *mestiza* is Castillo's term for the indigenous ethnic, racial, and spiritual heritage of Chicanas (*MOD* 10).

Chicanas cannot lay claim to any "traditional" American experience. In the attempt to convey the unique Chicana subjectivity, these writers experiment with forms and techniques, including code-switching (shifting freely between languages), absurdism, nonlinear narrative, and magical realism, among others.[5] The use of bilingualism is crucial to articulating Chicana subjectivity, for, as Castillo elaborates, language "is a way of seeing the world," and with "these two languages as part of our daily dynamic, we have a unique comprehension of society" (*MOD* 227). Incorporating multiple languages yields multidimensional work, as the different linguistic dynamics interact with one another in fruitfully creative ways.

Castillo's unique mélange of ironic pastiche and literary innovation serves both to challenge the traditional assignation of ontological status and to forge ways to convey a new subjectivity. Her work depicts supernatural intervention unironically, while also appropriating elements of the telenovela, such as episodic structure, the sacrifice of plausibility for effect, and a plot driven by coincidence (Mermann-Jozwiak 106–7). Elisabeth Mermann-Jozwiak suggests a dual purpose behind Castillo's appropriation of telenovela conventions: First, Castillo insinuates that life for a Chicana trying to live within the dominant cultural system *is* as preposterous as a melodramatic telenovela; second, Castillo seeks to "parody [the telenovela's] underlying assumptions and the normative behaviors it projects" (107). Castillo makes constructive use of telenovela conventions while challenging generic norms such as patriarchal gender roles and expectations regarding marriage, sex, and reproduction.

Castillo's use of the supernatural has led some to categorize her work as magical realism, a label she resists. Critics like Roland Walter have insisted that magical realism is one of the elements that gives Castillo's work political clout, linking the material and spiritual in a way that demands concrete action (87). Yet Castillo herself has stated that the supernatural elements in *So Far from God* stem from her use of hagiography and saints' lives rather than magical realism (Caminero-Santangelo 83). Other critics have noted ways that Castillo parodies or revises the conventions of magical realism for political purposes. Aldama argues that Castillo "reinvent[s] the magicorealist narrator as partially fallible" and employs "magicorealism" self-reflexively as a way to subvert "spectacularist" capitalist culture from within, avoiding "the dangers of slipping into a formulaic use of magicorealism to package and sell the Latina as consumable exotic Other" (86). Caminero-Santangelo complicates any easy link between magical realism and political import in Castillo's work, demonstrating that several of the most political episodes in *So Far from*

---

5. For a detailed survey of Chicana literary techniques, see Madsen 22–37.

God—ones linked to environmental activism—use no magical realism at all, and, furthermore, that Castillo depicts as magical many of the threats to active social engagement (82). Castillo parodies magical realism to show that real change comes not from magic or miracles but from human activism (which remains rooted in spirituality) (Caminero-Santangelo 85).

Castillo, like other Chicana writers, employs fragmentary narrative to mirror Chicanas' lived experience, the lack of "authority to create a unified vision of their lives" (Madsen 37). Marginalized by dominant social structures, Chicanas are unable to integrate themselves into their environment and attain a stable identity. As scholars have recognized, Castillo adopted this strategy in her first novel, *The Mixquiahuala Letters*.[6] This epistolary novel comprises a series of forty letters, with a preface in which the author prescribes various reading schemas for different personality types: "The Cynic," "The Conformist," and "The Quixotic." By registering a lack of coherent identity, Castillo's fragmentary structure calls attention to the process by which identity is constructed. As Lesley Larkin observes, Castillo highlights that reading is both a reflexive activity—in that the reader both contributes and receives meaning and coherence—and a social activity, as the "reading subject [is shown to be] a plural, rather than singular, self" (144). The different suggested reading approaches yield different interpretations. Castillo interrogates the construction of meaning without denying its possibility.

The use of fragmentary narrative and lack of closure recalls the techniques of iconic postmodern writers. But critics have justifiably insisted on exercising caution in labeling Chicana literature postmodern. While Chicana writers accentuate the production of meaning, they defy the assertion of many postmodern writers that the individual quest for meaning is futile. According to Holly Blackford, Chicana "novels use self-reflexive storytelling to underscore the theme that within stories the individual *constructs* meaning . . . [and] individual characters achieve a spiritual consciousness that leads them to serve the spiritual and social needs of the ethnic community" (224). In categorizing Chicana literature as postmodern, critics have at times failed to distinguish between "postmodern fragmentation" and the "lived experience of hybridity," a failure that mutes the literature's sociopolitical implications.[7] The very

---

6. See Larkin 142–43; Madsen 93; Quintana 73–74, 83; Bennett 462–64; Szeghi 433; and Carson 115–16.

7. Benjamin Carson posits a dissonance between Castillo's search for a viable Chicana identity and the "postmodern take on identity" that Castillo offers in her fiction (110). B. J. Manríquez adopts Castillo's critique of oppressive cultural norms to ground the spurious argument that Castillo is a nihilist who believes that "human beings exist in a silent, alien universe that possesses no inherent truth or meaning" (39).

dignity of the marginalized is at stake in this distinction: "Although postmodern techniques have given voice to marginalized experiences and identities, the dissolution of the author (an extension of the dissolution of the self) also threatens the validity of identities that have already been invalidated by racism and sexism" (Larkin 143). The goal of Chicana writers is to forge a via media between perpetuating oppressive normative identities and assenting to the futility of the quest for meaning, both of which "foreclose the possibility for social transformation" (Blackford 247). Chicana writers hold to the ostensibly paradoxical possibility of a constructed and fluid yet stable identity.[8]

Castillo envisions a construction of identity for those who live within but do not assimilate into dominant American social structures, and Chicana spirituality is the focus of her vision: "Beneath the definition established by the cultural enthusiasm of Chicanismo was and remains a significant component of the mestiza's identity—her spirituality. This undercurrent is the unspoken key to her endurance as a female throughout the ages: spirituality versus religion as well as spirituality versus a material dogma" (*MOD* 100–101). Chicana identity cannot be divorced from religion and spirituality. Castillo zealously arraigns the Catholic Church for sexism, but for her there is no question of jettisoning religion.[9] Rather, she seeks more vital and affirming, woman-centered, forms of spirituality.

In Castillo's view, spirituality may encompass and inform institutionalized religion, but the two are not synonymous. She remonstrates against aspects of institutional religion but insists that spirituality is the foundation of identity, "an acutely personalized experience inherent in our daily lives" (*MOD* 11). Her conception of spirituality is complex and fluid, granting primacy to subjectivity while refusing privatization. Chicana spirituality remains intrinsically social, directing one's engagement with polarizing matters like gender and race that have long been sites of marginalization for women of color. Castillo's hybrid approach to spirituality, which draws from multiple religious traditions, subverts the "binary relationships with these topics" that incline toward marginalization and carves out new territory for "women of color [to] par-

---

8. Mermann-Jozwiak argues that Chicana writing has actually helped revise the ahistoricism of theoretical postmodernism: "While postmodernism with its emphasis on the local, the margins and difference has created spaces for Chicanas to speak from, Chicana writing, together with that of other women and people of color, has contributed to creating a multicultural, political version of postmodernism" (113).

9. Castillo often uses *religion* disparagingly, usually referring to a patriarchal and hierarchical cultural Catholicism, and she uses *spirituality* to get away from this sense of religion. However, she uses *spirituality* to signify what I am calling *religion*. She does not, in her own writing, recuperate the word *religion*, but her work as a whole redefines religion in terms of practice and spiritual discipline.

ticipate and create" (Lanza, "New" 658). Scholars have affiliated Castillo with liberation theology because she encourages active resistance to oppression rather than passive acceptance of suffering.[10] However, while her "revisionist Catholicism" parallels the work of Latin theologians in striving to empower women to interpret the sacred as their own contexts demand, Castillo departs from those theologians in her quest to unearth and implement the subversive "'forgotten' memories of another worldview, the suppressed countervalues of women and Native peoples" (Pérez 58–59). Without rejecting her Catholic heritage outright, Castillo turns to non-Western traditions to formulate a woman-centered spirituality. Castillo draws from diverse expressions of spirituality and insists that spirituality is subjective, but clear criteria save her from uncritical relativism: She looks to spiritual disciplines that share "an emphasis on liberation, in the sense of aiming toward 'justice, equality, human rights, true democracy, and a greater quality of life for all.' Moreover, they emphasize concrete experiences and daily life as 'the point of departure' for all analysis and praxis" (Michael 114).

The home, traditionally the domain of women, plays a central role in Chicana spirituality. The home is a subversive and liberating site where non-Western practices may thrive, especially *curanderismo*, traditional holistic medicine. Castillo depicts the mundane rituals of home life in an affirming, even heroic light, reclaiming practices often considered subservient as indicative of strength and love. Traditional domestic activities like cooking and homeopathic medicine are thus "an assertion of cultural identity and resistance to assimilation" (Madsen 99). The home becomes a space for woman-centered, woman-led community.[11] With its walls impermeable to the politics of the dominant society, the home fosters the development of radical political consciousness and inspires local activism that extends beyond its walls.

Scholars like Theresa Delgadillo have highlighted Castillo's attention to the liberating possibilities of a mestiza spirituality but have paid little attention to her depiction of American ideology as a primary obstacle to spiritual liberation. American exceptionalism constitutes such a monolithic obstacle because it functions as a competing religion. Castillo depicts the notion of the American self (that mythical individual who has realized the American dream) as a powerfully alluring ideal that alienates Chicanxs who attempt to embody it. She offers an alternative set of spiritual disciplines as a means of living in America without suffering the constant pull of assimilation.

---

10. See, for example, Caminero-Santangelo 86 and Delgadillo, "Forms" 889–90.

11. For explications of the politics of the home in Castillo's work, see Pearce-Gonzales 6 and Johnson 40–41.

THE AMERICAN DREAM AS AMERICAN NIGHTMARE

In Castillo's novel *The Guardians,* a sign in an immigrant advocacy agency reads "The search for the American Dream could be your worst nightmare" (115). This proves to be the case for many of Castillo's Chicanx characters, as those who pursue the American dream nearly all end up on a trajectory of failure and rejection. The characters who manage some success or upward mobility largely reinforce its arbitrary nature.

Peel My Love Like an Onion

In *Peel My Love Like an Onion,* Carmen "la coja" (the cripple) attains unexpected stardom as a singer after years of disappointment in other pursuits. In spite of a lame leg resulting from childhood polio, Carmen aspires to dance flamenco professionally. Surmounting a battery of obstacles, Carmen becomes a dancer of some renown, dancing professionally for over twenty years. Her career ends prematurely as she is forcibly sidelined by the return of her polio.

Carmen's unlikely success functions as an exception that proves the rule. As hard as she works, Carmen barely manages to make ends meet during her dancing years. Though celebrated by a core of devoted flamenco fans, Carmen never gains a large audience. Her "big break" finally comes by sheer luck. Now physically unable to dance, Carmen is asked by an old dancing partner to serenade him as he dances. Carmen's singing enchants her friend and their audience, and he invites her to sing on a record he's producing. Carmen joins a musical group that achieves an impressive level of success for a flamenco group. The irony, as Jane Rose notes, is that all of Carmen's tears and hard work as a dancer garnered her little measurable success, while a lucky break has made her relatively well-off (404). Carmen's plight, prior to her breakthrough, was no fault of her own, but she is no proof that hard work brings success. Quite the contrary: Carmen the cripple reveals the lameness of the American dream. As further farce, the music that makes her successful is commodified and tokenized. The record is crafted and marketed as "international music," meaning that various styles are combined into a mélange that has no authentic musical identity. Though not exactly Muzak, the record hardly exhibits the soul of flamenco that Carmen so zealously defended during her dancing years. A listener tells Carmen that her song airs on "the new gospel program . . . right after the Howard Stern Show" (*PML* 192). A radio station that runs a gospel program after a shock jock clearly values ratings and listener base above all, and a nonreligious album that fits into a gospel hour is surely lacking in soul.

Carmen's inadvertent realization of the American dream nonetheless fails to secure her status as American. Carmen's music is appreciated, but she remains other. At the start of the novel, Carmen relates the confusion of nationality she experiences while walking the Chicago streets: "You say your city the way some Americans say this is their country. You never feel right saying that—*my country*. For some reason looking Mexican means you can't be American. And my cousins tell me . . . that over there they're definitely not Mexican. Because you were born on this side pocha is what you're called there" (*PML* 3). By the novel's end, in spite of her pluck and success, her country claims her only as an exotic, a singer of "international" music.

Sapogonia

Carmen becomes an American success story without seeking to, but such success eludes Castillo's Chicanx characters who actively pursue it. *Sapogonia* follows the emigration of artist Máximo Madrigal from his war-torn homeland of Sapogonia to the US. Máximo, determined to make a name for himself, feels his homeland too small for his ever-expanding ego. His sedulity is commensurate to his towering artistic ambition, and he believes he'll have no trouble establishing himself in America, the land of opportunity. Máximo (or Max) ultimately seeks what Sacvan Bercovitch calls representative selfhood, a mutually reinforcing process in which an individual attempts self-actualization and recognition through embodying a culturally recognized ideal, the self that everyone desires to become (*Rites* 32). Castillo's novel renders this process through its technique of alternating between first- and third-person accounts of Max's life. This narrative strategy conveys the impression of Max creating himself as the hero of own story: "Max succeeds in being both the hero and thus the central origin and source within the legend, and the narrator of that legend" (Socolovsky 80). This is precisely the logic of representative selfhood, which, in its American context, is tied to an ideological individualism: The group is unified by collectively embracing the ideal of the self-made, cavaliering individual. Rugged individualism becomes the hallmark of American identity, and America as a mythical entity is esteemed as the place where the individual may thrive.

Máximo initially gains financial success and modest fame as an artist, but at great psychological and spiritual cost. Max understands the American dream in terms of conquest and domination, self-assertion at the expense of others (Lynch 132). But his ruthless exploitation precludes his development of a stable identity. As Roland Walter notes, "Maximo internalizes the value system of the dominant culture—the frenzy for commodities, money, fame and individual recognition based on a highly competitive spirit—and thereby accentuates . . . the 'spiritual split in his collective psyche'" (86). Max's pursuit of the American dream ends not in self-integration but in self-erasure. Miguel De La Torre describes the irony of this ensnaring process: "For Hispanics to live within the borders of the US is to consent to the principle of their own subjugation while hoping that the empire, manifested as the American dream of upward mobility, will radically provide salvation from their present estranged existence" (100). Chicanxs who buy into this dream catalyze their own marginalization. Máximo's attempt to live the American dream requires preliminarily renouncing (or attempting to) his Sapogonian heritage (Lynch 131). Even as Max repudiates Sapogonian values in his bid for celebrity, his American associates continue to regard him as ethnic other and market his art as ethnic and exotic. One of his art shows is part of a monthly program showcasing artists from around the world as "a strategic move as part of the board's endless effort to practice cultural diplomacy" (*SP* 142). (The board makes no distinction between Canadian, Bolivian, and Sapogonian art.) Máximo believes he can heroically epitomize the American dream, but American society will not embrace *him* as representative on account of his ethnic identity. His success in fact depends on his ethnic identity. It is the purportedly indiscriminate offer of freedom and opportunity that makes the American dream so estimable to citizens and immigrants alike. For the ethnic other, however, the pursuit precludes self-integration from the start by forcing her to disown her heritage while she continues to retain ethnic status in the eyes of others, often in the form of tokenism (Lynch 132).

Assimilation is impossible for Máximo not only because Americans persist in viewing him as ethnic other, but also because he can never fully relinquish his Sapogonian roots, however vigorously he may try. Max is caught in the cross-pressures of being an exile and a tourist; he can neither fully leave one land nor fully assimilate into the other. His infatuation with a musician named Pastora, another Sapogonian exile, confirms the constancy of his cultural ties. Pastora evokes in Max a homesickness, but he cannot let go of his need to be the American hero. The nature of Max's homesickness likewise reveals his solipsism: The aspects of Sapogonian life he misses are hunting, bareback horse riding, and being treated well by women. These pursuits are all individualistic acts of domination or self-assertion, and none is unique to his homeland. Max views his homeland, like America, as a place to impose himself. Castillo portrays the addictive allure of the American dream: Max continues to pursue it even as it bars him from creating the sense of home that is only possible for Chicanxs like him through adopting a mestiza/borderlands consciousness. In the novel's dreamlike final scene, rendered ambiguously so it's unclear whether it is reality or fantasy, Max murders Pastora, driven by a rage that results from his inability to integrate himself into his environment.

So Far from God

Máximo's tale reveals the violence that often attends the abortive pursuit of the American dream. Likewise, in *So Far from God*, Castillo's Chicana characters find the pursuit of the American dream literally deadly. The most overt example is Fe, (whose name translates as "faith"), the representative "assimilationist" (Gillman and Floyd-Thomas 163). Fe believes truly that any dedicated person can succeed in America. She commits herself unflaggingly to sloughing off her ethnic heritage and embracing the trappings of suburban life. Fe, who "was not nearly as white as she thought she was" (*SFG* 157–58), takes her social cues from Oprah and is an exemplary consumer, spending all her money on "the long-dreamed-of automatic dishwasher, microwave, Cuisinart, and the VCR" (*SFG* 171). After years of working in a bank where she "maintained her image above all—from the organized desk at work to weekly manicured fingernails and a neat coiffure" (*SFG* 28), Fe gets a job cleaning parts for government weapons at Acme International. She believes this is "very important work," even though she is slowly being poisoned by the chemicals she uses (*SFG* 181). Ultimately, Fe's job, which she takes because the higher pay will translate into more consumer goods, consumes her.

Fe's death reveals the spiritual cost of her faith in the American dream. Belying her name, Fe is skeptical of anything miraculous, as we see in her attempts to rationalize her younger sister's resurrection from death. As critics have noted, Fe is the only one of her sisters who dies and remains dead.[12] In other words, she alone dies spiritually. The darker side of the American dream manifests itself in Fe most noticeably in physical symptoms, such as hair loss, infertility, and cancer. But the physical and spiritual are always entwined for Castillo, and Fe's ailment is spiritual as well. The novel's narrator explains that "after Fe died, she did not resurrect as La Loca did. . . . She did not return ectoplasmically like her tenacious earth-bound sister Esperanza. . . . Fe just died" (*SFG* 186). Fe's death crystallizes Castillo's assertion that this pursuit of the American dream is a form of spiritual discipline—a mortal one. As Fe's

---

12. See Sauer 82; Pearce-Gonzales 9; Michael 131; and Lanza, "Hearing" 72.

vision of the good life contracts to the silhouette of suburban banality, she abdicates all political consciousness and quashes any spiritual impulse. Her sisters return from beyond the grave after their deaths, manifesting their presence in different ways, on account of injustices suffered and unfulfilled spiritual aspirations. With nothing undone but the purchase of additional home appliances, Fe remains in the grave.

Lest we be tempted to dismiss Fe's story as heavy-handed satire, Castillo reveals Fe's real-life counterparts in Watsonville, California, a town with a Latinx majority. While leading a writing workshop there, Castillo interviewed women after a local labor strike in 1986.

> The concept of the American Dream—an illusion long fostered by the system to maintain its workforce—was an overwhelming factor that played with the hearts and minds of the Watsonville residents, the women informed me. People in Watsonville truly believed they could improve their material conditions through hard work. In fact, in comparison to the conditions they lived in [in] México, the material lives of mexicanas *had* improved. Simultaneously, in order to achieve the goals of the American Dream, the Mexican tradition of an extended family, including community, was deemed a hindrance and relinquished within the time span of a single generation. In a nation that strongly motivated people toward competition, individual achievement, and above all, material acquisitions, collective aspirations were deemed anachronistic. That is, grandparents and otherwise unemployed relatives outside of the nuclear family would become a burden on the way to material goals. (*MOD* 43–44)

Here we see a further instantiation of the representative self, which has resulted in Chicanxs rejecting cultural traditions and even their own families. Yet even after giving up so much, the work conditions for Latinxs in Watsonville were deplorable enough to warrant labor strikes. There's a paradox here. The strike is a corrective to the American dream, an attempt to justify imbalances, rather than a rejection of it. The strikers recognize injustice, but the fundamental nature of the dream, and of the way of life it requires, goes unquestioned because its values have been internalized. The dream is actualized just enough to sustain one's faith in it: Material conditions *do* improve for the workers, and yet the spiritual and social cost is severe.

In *So Far from God,* Esperanza does not suffer spiritual death like her sister Fe, but her faith in American exceptionalism results nonetheless in her untimely and ultimately meaningless death. Spiritual vagrancy drives Esperanza to ship off to Saudi Arabia as a military journalist. She has been a religious seeker throughout her life, converting from a Marxist Catholic to a cynical atheist to "pray[ing] to Grandmother Earth and Grandfather Sky" and combining sweat lodges with self-help books (*SFG* 38–39). Through attending Native American Church sweat lodges, Esperanza gains courage and spiritual affirmation that "no kind of white woman's self-help book" can give her (*SFG* 47), but she also finds the lodges patriarchal and sexist. Ruminating on her marginalization in the sweat lodge meetings, Esperanza feels a need "to bring it all together, to consolidate the spiritual with the practical side of things" (*SFG* 37). But she founders: Unable to bring herself to actively resist sexist practices, she fails to discover a spiritual discipline that both affirms her as a woman and squares with her sociopolitical perspective. She persists in a state of dislocation until, ultimately, "she abandons her own culture to go off and fight a war that is not her own. Her death is directly linked, symbolically, to her confusion about to whom and to what causes she is accountable" (Gillman and Floyd-Thomas 165). When her father begs assurance that she will not be placed in harm's way, Esperanza replies that facing "real danger" is "the whole point of being a journalist" (*SFG* 48). Her words reveal a need to brave danger on behalf of a cause. Having found no satisfactory spiritual mooring, Esperanza accepts America as transcendent, buying into the idea that the US must intervene to forestall "the imminent global crisis" (*SFG* 47).

Ironically, Esperanza dies "an American hero," according to the official letter sent to her mother by the army, and is posthumously awarded (*SFG* 159). Esperanza's spirit meanwhile appears to her sister to speak about "the president's misguided policies, about how the public was being fooled about a lot of things that were going on behind that whole war business, how people could get some results by taking such measures as refusing to pay taxes" (*SFG* 163). Significantly, Esperanza's body cannot be located and returned for burial, according to military officials. Her mother Sofia visits the Capitol several times to no avail, questioning how officials can be certain that Esperanza is dead yet cannot locate her body. Esperanza has effectively been disappeared, allowing the army elite to make her a martyr of their own fashioning. Through Esperanza, Castillo again conveys that a Chicana cannot exist in the dominant social structure *as* Chicana. Markus Heide argues that Esperanza connects her community to the larger world through her politics, inspiring her mother Sofia to political activism (175). But the America that claims Esperanza as its sacrificial hero is not Sofia's America. There's a disconnect between Esperanza's political action and the activism needed by the Chicanx community in her hometown of Tome.

A third sister, Caridad, is also victimized by American ideology, represented by a mythical force, *la malogra*. The *malogra* attacks and mutilates

Caridad, treats her like property, and renders her silent: Her "nipples had been bitten off. She had also been scourged with something, branded like a cattle. Worst of all, a tracheotomy was performed because she had also been stabbed in the throat" (*SFG* 33). Critics have rightly interpreted *la malogra* as a symbol of conquest.[13] Its description evokes Manifest Destiny:

> A thing, both tangible and amorphous. A thing that might be described as made of sharp metal and splintered wood, of limestone, gold, and brittle parchment. It held the weight of a continent and was indelible as ink, centuries old and yet as strong as a young wolf. It had no shape and was darker than the dark night, and mostly, as Caridad would never ever forget, it was pure force. (*SFG* 77)

Castillo suggests that the drive to mastery of the land endures today as the marginalizing, even rapacious, ideology of American exceptionalism.

The grisly deaths of the three girls, whose names invoke the great Christian virtues of faith, hope, and love, signify that these virtues are untenable in their patriarchal, exclusionary society (Sirias and McGarry 87). Placing faith and hope in the American dream is a deadly venture for Chicanas, one that can destroy even the capacity for love. Castillo exhorts Chicanas to a religious life in which such virtues may find more fulfilling expression. The deaths of Fe, Esperanza, and Caridad compel their mother Sofia to forge a new way of life. Gail Pérez posits that the girls are martyrs whose deaths "inspire the reevaluation of the 'backward culture' of Tomé" by galvanizing its citizens to ask, "If the American Dream can't save us, what can?" (65). Sofia, influenced by her daughters, constructs a new religious identity, one that is gynocentric and draws from "multiple forms and systems of knowledge" (Delgadillo, "Forms" 891–92). Castillo asserts that an authentic Chicana spirituality is hybrid and contextual, as well as inherently political and environmental, encompassing and dictating one's relation to her community and to the land.

AN ETHICS *PARA JODER*

Through characters like Sofia, Castillo redefines sainthood, portraying "holy *joderones*" or "bandit saints." According to De La Torre, *joderones* are concerned with the good of the marginalized rather than the prevailing main-

---

13. Pérez argues that as a depiction of conquest, it "plac[es] Caridad in the place of the raped earth and indigenous woman" (69), while Alarcón sees it a symbolic of "the Spanish conquest of the Americas and its aftermath" (146).

stream, and their role is "to challenge external oppression and uncover its internalized manifestation" (113). A brief overview of De La Torre's theology is a necessary prelude to examining the spiritual transformation of Sofia and other "bandit saints," as his liberation theology illuminates and helps to place Castillo's work.

Castillo herself has explicitly endorsed, with qualification, aspects of liberation theology. Discussing women's liberation theology (or *mujerista* theology), Castillo affirms its value "insofar as it attempts to reflect woman's reality to enable her to overcome material obstacles and to participate in a communal process with other women, her family, and community toward economic betterment within the ascriptions of her faith" (*MOD* 108). Liberation theology has been around since the 1960s, and the basic premise, most relevant here, is that "all theological and ethical 'truths' are contextual," as theology is intimately tied to one's sociopolitical context (De La Torre 4). Castillo expresses skepticism about the potential of Christian liberation theology to comprehensively address the Chicana's context, enumerating two primary reservations. First, she argues that Christianity has encouraged a body-spirit dualism that has degraded the body: "Christianity is based on the belief in a remote God (generally still accepted as a male: father), far removed from our mortal, material selves. He is an inimitable model since he is spirit and we are flesh; and yet Christianity is based on the struggle that requires man to imitate God" (*MOD* 108). Castillo acknowledges the Christian belief that divine spirit and human flesh are united in Jesus Christ, but she maintains that Catholic tradition has cast Christ's humanity in exclusively male terms and failed to account for women's experience. The expectation that humans are to imitate an "inimitable model" results inevitably in failure, which leads to Castillo's second objection: She objects to the "dualistic principle and polarization of good and evil," contending that Christianity "depends on our desire to disobey: to rebel against the repression of the human spirit and the desire to create a balance out of the celebration of flesh and spirit—to experience a life of ecstasy" (*MOD* 109).

In his *Latina/o Social Ethics*, De La Torre develops his own liberation theology, which addresses Castillo's objections. He insists that an authentic Latinx theology will adopt the "cultural symbols" of the people, including female incarnations of the divine.[14] He agrees with Castillo that the rationalism of "Western moral thought . . . that clearly demarcates good from bad" offers

---

14. When discussing De La Torre's work, I follow his terminology and use *Latina/o*. While *Latinx* is a broader term than *Chicanx*, De La Torre's work applies to the Chicanx context Castillo has in view.

no means to "incorporate the both/and ambiguity common in messiness of life" (106). De La Torre argues that a truly liberating theology will account for "the ambiguity of a Latina/o moral agency that recognizes the need at times to dispense with personal piety for the sake of the greater good of survival—survival of not just the individual Hispanic, but more importantly, *la comunidad*" (106). De La Torre's theology is relevant for analyzing Castillo's work not simply because of its basic liberationist premise, but also for the specific ethics he derives from it. While many liberation theologians come from South and Latin American contexts, De La Torre's work specifically focuses on the situation of Latinxs residing bodily in America and psychologically in the borderlands between two cultures. Castillo's work is constructive as well as descriptive; she attempts not only to diagnose the plight of Chicanxs but to pave a way forward. De La Torre's work shares her ambition, insisting upon a theology rooted in personal experience that thus "collapses the dichotomy between theory and praxis" (70). The Latinx focus of De La Torre's theological work and its corresponding contextual terminology illuminates Castillo's work by offering a grammar with which to articulate the ethical and theological convictions Castillo conveys through her fiction.

De La Torre identifies several attributes of a Latinx (including Chicanx) ethics. First, a Latinx approach must begin with *lo cotidiano*, "the everyday along with all of its particularities" (De La Torre 70). This concept "incorporates the hermeneutics of the self": Context and personal experience, rather than any Kantian transcendental, become the starting point for ethical analysis and action. Second, ethical analysis always begins *de nepantla*, from the borderlands. Because *nepantla* is a place of conflict and suspension, Latinxs live continually *en la lucha*, or "in the struggle." Disenfranchisement and the psychological experience of homelessness drive this struggle. Thus, "this daily *lucha* for survival causes any ethical Latina/o reflection to stress and emphasize identity—an identity shaped by a history of cultural, political, and economic conquest and subjugation. This self-definition is never individualistic, but a communal endeavor, a self-understanding of a people" (De La Torre 75). Though rooted in the particular and personal, this struggle to establish identity is always engaged *en conjunto*, together. The *lucha* is not simply for individual flourishing but for the advancement of the entire community. These qualities coalesce in what De La Torre calls an "ethics *para joder.*" The mildly vulgar Spanish verb *joder* roughly translates as "to screw with" (De La Torre 92). The paragon of this ethics is the trickster, a figure common to many mythological and religious traditions, including Christianity. The trickster "screws" with dominant power structures in order to destabilize them, operating in a realm beyond conventional morality. The trickster's action remains ethically grounded, "although the means used . . . to achieve liberative ends may not be considered moral by the dominant culture" (De La Torre 114).

De La Torre defends his practice of *jodiendo* by affirming a *certain form* of hopelessness: disbelief that the current system can deliver on its promises. Castillo shares De La Torre's conviction of *conditional* hopelessness. But for both, this hopelessness generates not despondency but activism. Castillo eschews religion that reinforces a body-spirit dualism, and she warns Chicanas that seeking self-definition through otherworldly spirituality tacitly sanctions the status quo. A defensible religion results in social activism. De La Torre's work demonstrates how ethical reflection must guide spiritual *mestizaje* (mixing), a conviction Castillo emphatically conveys through characters who meet with disaster. Hybridity is never an end in itself; it must always serve the ends of liberation and fulfillment.

CASTILLO'S HOLY *JODERONES*

An examination of spirituality in Castillo's work reveals clear reflections of De La Torre's method of ethical analysis. De La Torre's theoretical account of a trickster ethics thus helps us understand how to interpret the social and spiritual significance of the actions of Castillo's characters. First, spiritual development always begins *en lo cotidiano*, in the particular. American exceptionalism enthrones individualism but ultimately fosters consensus. Its dual emphasis, on the individual and on the ideal collective, ends up ignoring the local and particular. The pursuit of the American dream comes at great cost to local communities and to individuals; Castillo echoes the feminist assertion that "agency is always 'coproduced'" and insists that Chicana identity must be constructed in community, "retain[ing] a notion of the individual while moving past a narrow version of American individualism" (Michael 13). Castillo's fiction reifies De La Torre's assertion that "our liberation will be discovered only when we begin to construct our own ethical and moral foundation rooted within our social location and using our cultural symbols" (63). The hybrid spirituality that Castillo advocates functions as a gateway to greater agency for both individuals and communities, offering new forms of subjectivity and sources of knowledge. A condition of Chicana agency is the capacity to embrace plurality (multiple subjectivities) and "to accept such culturally and sociohistorically specific ambiguities and contradictions in positive, constructive terms" (Michael 115). Yet this foundation is never static; it is constantly reassessed and revised according to individual and communal experience and testimony. The remainder of this chapter focuses on Castillo's depictions of a uniquely Chicana order of bandit saints characterized by spiritual hybridity and the mode of ethical reflection envisioned by De La Torre.

Jodiendo en Conjunto: The Particular and the Communal in *So Far from God*

So Far from God follows the individual enlightenment of Sofia, only to insist that authentic spiritual development is inherently communal. Sofia's spiritual journey reflects every element of De La Torre's ethics *para joder,* beginning with an emphasis on *lo cotidiano* (daily experience). In the opening chapter, conflict erupts as the Catholic priest, Father Jerome, makes demands of the newly bereaved Sofia that convey greater concern for tradition than for human beings. During the funeral procession for her youngest daughter, Sofia's manic wailing prompts the priest to insinuate that her lack of funeral decorum discloses a lack of faith. The priest refuses to validate Sofia's questioning of divine purpose in her daughter's death. When the deceased miraculously resurrects from her coffin, the priest subtly accuses her of demon possession. As the resurrected girl, thereafter known as La Loca, tells the priest that *she* has come back to pray for *him,* we begin to see Castillo's insistence that "it is not the priest or the Catholic hierarchy who determine what faith is nor how it is practiced" (Delgadillo, "Forms" 894). As the narrative progresses, Sofia reassess her religious commitments based on her personal experience. She remains Catholic but gradually rejects patriarchy and hierarchy, looking to indigenous traditions for alternative spiritual resources.

Castillo's characters pursue what Delgadillo calls "spiritual *mestizaje.*" Delgadillo defines this as "the transformative renewal of one's relationship to the sacred through a radical and sustained multimodal and self-reflexive critique of oppression in all its manifestations and a creative and engaged participation in shaping life that honors the sacred" (*Mestizaje* 1). *Lo cotidiano,* the personal and particular, must govern the appropriation of indigenous traditions as well as culturally dominant traditions. While the contours of authentic spirituality may vary among individuals, difference does not issue from capriciousness or the will to power. Religious practice must be grounded in and shaped by personal experience—for Castillo, life as a female and a Chicana—and by life in community.

Castillo emphasizes the necessity of a communal hermeneutic through characters like Francisco who embrace a hybrid spirituality that's corrosive rather than liberating. Francisco is a *Penitente,* yet, as Daniel Alarcón recognizes, this "blend of folk Catholicism and pious, ascetic behavior provides him neither comfort nor salvation. Instead, he becomes a violent, guilt-ridden, obsessed stalker of Caridad" (151). After returning from the war in Vietnam, Francisco becomes an apprentice *santero*, a saint-maker who carves figures of wood. He crafts wooden likenesses that are fixed, ideal figures, and he transfers this mind-set to his view of human beings, namely Caridad. Caridad becomes a goddess to Francisco, so much so that he dehumanizes her. Francisco returns from Vietnam with PTSD, but he does not find the solace he seeks in the spiritual discipline he embraces. Instead, he becomes increasingly fanatical and obsessive, and he is ultimately responsible for Caridad's death. Francisco's life ends in suicide.[15]

In contrast, Sofia exemplifies Castillo's notion of authentic Chicana spirituality. The legacy of her daughters—victims of the American dream and the excesses of patriarchy—leads her toward a religion that is woman-centered and incorporates her ethnic heritage. Sofia's spiritual development is holistic, and it is only possible *en conjunto*, in community. She becomes the unofficial mayor of Tome, her community, citing her faith as her motivation. At her mayoral initiative, the community embarks on a course of revitalization. Sofia and her *vecinos* start a community cooperative, raising sheep and selling wool. She also musters the mettle to remove herself from a self-destructive marital arrangement, finally banishing and divorcing her feckless gambler husband. The Way of the Cross Procession on Holy Friday, described at the end of the novel, epitomizes Castillo's hybrid spirituality. Instead of hymns, there are protest songs; instead of bearing crosses, participants carry "photographs of their loved ones who died due to toxic exposure hung around the necks like scapulars" (SFG 242); at each station, they pray about the forces decimating their land and killing its people. They recite their account of Christ's *via dolorosa*, in which the afflictions of Christ are the sins of corporations and the government against the land and the people. Sofia takes the stand to speak about the American military's meaningless war (the Persian Gulf War) and their cover-up of her daughter's death. Indigenous Indian influence is present also, as the paraders frame environmentalist values in terms of "the responsibility we have to 'Our Mother'" (SFG 242). The subversive adaptation of traditional ritual by the people of Tome reflects the elements of De La Torre's ethical analysis. The procession registers a religious expression rooted in the particular (*lo cotidiano*). The protest demonstrates that spirituality is inextricably

---

15. Castillo does not suggest that the Penitente sect is essentially pernicious. There are positive references to the group's social activism in the novel. The problem is *how* Francisco practices the discipline. We should also consider the psychic wounds Francisco received from his combat experience: being forced to kill or be killed, and the racism of his platoon in Vietnam.

connected to the environment and, furthermore, that religious traditions are to be interpreted communally (*en conjunto*). Finally, the protests and laments reflect life *en la lucha,* in the struggle. The community of Tome fights for its very existence. In advocating a communal hermeneutic, Castillo subverts the hierarchical notion of clerical authority that traditionally characterizes the Catholic Church. Women assume leading liturgical roles in the procession, giving speeches and singing songs. As Delgadillo observes, Father Jerome (the priest Sofia and La Loca have been in conflict with) is conspicuously absent from the proceedings ("Forms" 894). Throughout her work, Castillo develops "holy [female] *joderones*" like La Loca and Sofia, whose spirituality, tied to the land and their community, compels them to challenge authority.

Visionary Archaeology: Going Native in *The Mixquiahuala Letters* and *Sapogonia*

Castillo exhorts Chicanas to embrace spiritual hybridity and reconsider their Mexic Amerindian roots, but she cautions against doing so uncritically, warning that "an attempt at obtaining such [religious] direction from our past simply by imitating or inventing ritual is not necessarily the clearest path or, rather, does not guarantee an evolved spirituality" (*MOD* 168). Early indigenous practices were no less susceptible to patriarchal influence than recent ones. The synthesis of religious forms, whether indigenous or conventional, must answer to "goals that aim to restore the feminine as a prominent component" (*MOD* 168). The concept of *lo cotidiano* superintends spiritual formation, conforming it to the contours of the Chicana context. Castillo explores the pitfalls of callow attempts to recapture the past in her first novel, *The Mixquiahuala Letters*. In the novel, a Chicana character named Teresa makes a pilgrimage to Mexico, intent upon reclaiming her ethnic roots. Teresa has failed to locate herself spiritually or culturally in the US, finding herself inalterably "othered" as Mexican. Mexico, however, proves no more hospitable to her. There, she experiences similar feelings of homelessness as Mexicans view her as a *gringa*. Teresa shares the culpability here, as she glamorizes and tokenizes Mexico's indigenous population. As Tereza Szeghi claims, "It is her location of indigenous Mexicanidad in a nostalgic past . . . that impedes Teresa's desired recovery and impairs her ability to represent indigenous peoples in a more nuanced manner" (433). Teresa idealizes the ancient Indian culture and measures the Mexico she encounters against her ideal. Her romanticism engenders unfulfillable expectations and perpetuates both her individual alienation and the "historically located indigeneity that has been used by Mexico and the

United States to justify and sustain indigenous dispossession" (Szeghi 448). Teresa's sense of selfhood is fractured, and her inability to critically engage totalizing structures leaves her depressed. She fails to engage in the "interpretive ethnography" that Alvina Quintana argues is necessary for developing Chicana identity: the process of "negotiating between two cultural systems, constructing a cultural and feminist identity as she works to deconstruct the predominantly male cultural paradigms that have worked to suppress a female perspective" (74–75). Teresa hopes to land upon a ready-made cultural identity that will offer her an immediate sense of self-realization. But by shirking from the task of cultural negotiation, she sentences herself to unremitting dissatisfaction.

Castillo looks to pre-Columbian indigenous culture to recover not a comprehensive blueprint for living but a vision: a "feminine connection" that must be refitted for the present in order to activate its liberating potential (*MOD* 10). In the afterword to *Massacre of the Dreamers*, Castillo discusses how seeing the Virgen de Guadalupe as divine as well as human is crucial for recognizing the true humanity and strength of Chicanas:

> If we do not view the female figure as divine, we surely do not see the worthiness of the female human. Imago Dei was the Latin term for men being made in the image of God. Where was I, a member of half of the human race whose monthly menses announced how the human race continued? . . . I searched for woman to speak to me through the surviving teachings of my indigenous ancestors. From Maya to Mexíca, there is no shortage of female divine figures.
>
> A goddess is not a token title. To be a goddess implies that the deity has a realm of power. (171)

Castillo finds in goddess worship a way to recuperate the qualities of the "feminine principle." The feminine principle, which Castillo emphasizes is present in all genders, is characterized by "noncategorical compassion and acceptance of all" (*MOD* 94). This recovery of the feminine, made possible in part by looking to indigenous traditions, not only counters the fear, powerlessness, and rejection many women have experienced at the hands of patriarchal religion, but also sponsors an empowered reclamation of traditionally female roles and practices.[16] Again, *lo cotidiano* is the watchword, for even goddess worship can be corrupted into a source of denigration rather than

---

16. These include uniquely female roles like childbirth and motherhood, as well as roles and practices like cooking, nursing, and keeping house that traditionally have been gendered as feminine.

liberation. Castillo asserts that Xicanistas (her neologism for Chicana feminists) "must simultaneously be archaeologists and visionaries of our culture" (*MOD* 226). Archaeology—drawing from traditional sources—must be informed by an acute awareness of one's present context as well as a vision for the future.

Castillo incarnates her ideal visionary archaeologist in Pastora Aké Velásquez, a character in *Sapogonia*. Pastora's incorporation of goddess worship instills in her the compassion and acceptance that characterizes the "feminine principle" and heightens her awareness of the ensnaring nature of the American dream. Pastora is a musical artist whose songs are driven by her social conscience. She is also a great beauty, and her looks and musical talent often find a greater audience than her social message. Men like Máximo hardly consider her lyrics, being too enamored of her aura. Pitfalls as well as opportunities attend Pastora's artistic success. A moral stalwart throughout most of the novel, Pastora allows herself to be seduced by a businessman who "had the looks of the all-American hero, the contemporary Hollywood movie star, Aryan, well built," and who "regarded her with sentimentality flourished in romance, his first true love" (*SP* 189). It is Pastora's religious practice and spiritual awakening that reinvigorate her social and moral commitments, as she recognizes that she "had forsaken those guides who watched out for her welfare for the sake of tentative things" (*SP* 185).

Pastora demonstrates the moral resources and female empowerment that Castillo links to goddess worship. Pastora practices a hybrid religion that combines elements of Catholicism and indigenous religion. She seeks guidance from Santa Clara as well as Indian "spirit guides" (*SP* 185). Santa Clara (St. Clare of Assisi) founded a Franciscan order for women and was the first woman to write a monastic rule. Pastora addresses her as one who embodies both female empowerment and the rejection of "tentative things" for more durable ones. In the Franciscan tradition, Clara is known for exhorting joy in poverty. Welfare, Pastora knows when she is spiritually attuned, is neither an individual state nor a primarily financial one. It is only through disciplined practice of prayer and meditation that she discerns the extent to which she has become self-centered and besotted with material comfort and social mobility:

> Dominant society was closing again. The youth was interested in individual achievement, financial success. No one wanted to hear about their neighbor's starvation, rape and pillage in American cities. No one joined hands and together raised them up like chains of fists.
> And she was no different, susceptible to the same illusive temptations invented by those few who had power. She allowed herself to be persuaded

by the finer things in life.... In actuality, however, this new lifestyle held less stability than when she struggled to pay the rent. (*SP* 186)

Pastora's spiritual reflection grants her insight into the shallow nature of the American dream. Unlike Máximo, Pastora perceives the importance of spiritual discipline to wholeness and stability. Max's vitriolic reaction to Pastora's "pantheon" of spirit guides is revealing: "Don't you understand? All of that is what holds one back. Worshipping idols! It doesn't matter the name you put on it, what religion it is, it's nothing but a method employed to make common people understand their place" (*SP* 180). Max's decaffeinated socialist rhetoric is rooted not in political conviction but in elitism. He cares nothing about the common people, only that he not be a common person, which would deny the world the great gift of himself. Max sees religion as a flaw because he considers commonness a flaw. "For a woman as sophisticated as you," he tells Pastora, "it is very disappointing to see your flaw is the weakness of common people" (*SP* 180). Max's solipsism manifests in his rejection of religion: He is so self-centered he fails to consider any possible connection between spiritual discipline and self-realization, which is further evident in his conflation of all religions into one article. Pastora defends her religious practice as vital to a fulfilling sense of self and subtly indicts Max for elitism:

> No one is a common person.... All persons are complex. What I have been doing over the years is separating parts of myself, the so-called energies that my soul has carried into this life, and given them names, manifested them into clay figurines, not unlike the Mayas or the Greeks. Yes, this is my pantheon, and when I need courage, I call upon the figure that symbolizes courage, and when I need strength or patience, I do likewise. (*SP* 180)

Pastora proudly defends her indigenous religious heritage and attests that spirituality is integral to wholeness. Max's puerile retort, "Why don't you just kneel before a mirror and pray to yourself?," confirms both his rejection and his ignorance of their shared indigenous religious heritage. When Pastora mocks his ignorance, Max backpedals petulantly: "I was raised Catholic but I've talked at length with the Indians of my country about the beliefs they've preserved despite the imposition of the national religion.... My grandmother is Mayan" (*SP* 180). Max's grandmother is Mayan, but he has willfully ignored all that she's tried to teach him, dismissing it as the claptrap of commoners.

Pastora derides Max further for his facile Marxist rhetoric, calling him the "Pinochet of the art world" (*SP* 180). Max repudiates the comparison, but Pastora's indictment is well founded. Max views everyone, even his wives and paramours, as exploitable, rungs on the ladder of self-advancement, but conceals his ruthlessness with decorum: "It never hurt to be courteous to people who in the future could then be called on by you for a small favor, a recommendation, a piece of advice, or a contact, because no matter what vehicle one needed to meet his objective, there was always someone there to serve as a stepping stone" (*SP* 333). He marries Laura and later Maritza for their influence in the art world and ability "to make sure it was [his] work that remained on top of the stack" (*SP* 317). Max's attitude is even reflected paratextually, as his wife Laura is reduced to a pronoun for entire chapters.[17] The biting irony is that Max's own homeland is being terrorized by a dictator and his family murdered, while Max trades on his ethnic heritage in a crazed pursuit of self-gratification.

It is palpably ironic that Max accuses Pastora of idol worship, since he is the one who makes idols of women. Castillo renders Máximo as an instructive negative example, a charge to responsible retrieval when it comes to cultural archaeology. Max's use of indigenous myth, casting Pastora as an avatar of the Aztec goddess Coatlicue, robs Pastora of her humanity and results in violence rather than appreciation (Lynch 134). For Max, to deify Pastora is to equate her with an ideal, which has nothing to do with acknowledging female strength and everything to do with the luster of an object of conquest. Max's self-absorption is evident in the way his view of Pastora changes after she bears a child:

> Pastora ceased to be the exalted celestial being. Pastora now labored and toiled like every woman. . . . Máximo was enraged. Had he wanted her wings weighed down; it would've been with him, riding on her spirit, energy, and compassion—because now he knew she was capable of self-sacrifice. He would've used her for his own purposes, wrung her. (*SP* 302)

Pastora views childbirth as a link to the deity Earth Mother and thus empowering. For Máximo, an idol has been shattered. Pastora's receptivity and empathy contrast starkly with Max's exploitative agenda. Cultural archaeology "does not guarantee an evolved spirituality" (*MOD* 168), but Pastora's politically attuned religious hybridity, which filters her cultural past through the alembic of her present experience, proves spiritually salubrious. Pastora's relation to her pantheon and her saints empowers her as woman while fostering greater solicitude for her world. Here we see the consonance of religion and lived experience, of humanity and divinity:

---

17. See, for example, chapter 30 (183–84).

> She was the personification of the deity Earth Mother, tied to the land by vastness, umbilical cords, penises. She had given birth to a man. From her body had come forth a being with testicles and brain, with heart and hands. Yes, that might still qualify her as a goddess, but not the objective one of before, not of the heart of granite detached from mundane mortality. For she had given birth to a male child and from then on she could no longer see into the eyes of a man and look upon a stranger. (SP 301)

Pastora's spiritual discipline has shaped her view of childbirth as an expression of power. Through childbirth, Pastora self-identifies with the goddess Earth Mother, but this association reinforces rather than severs her ties to the earth and to her fellow human beings.

Early in *Sapogonia*, a brief chapter is devoted to a narratorial excursus on the soul. Adopting the style of a fabulist, the narrator establishes a dichotomy between the "pure spirit" and the "intellectually advanced soul." Set apart from the other chapters by italics, this short discourse frames the entire novel, especially the relationship between Pastora and Máximo. Advanced souls, the narrator explains, "could be observed by the purity with which they regarded their lives as they interacted with others. It was not a matter of humility or a sense of servility that marked the pure spirit. It was the inborn awareness of equality with other living things on earth" (*SP* 15). In contrast, there are *intellectually* advanced souls who "could have led twisted, dark lives" (*SP* 15). Of the two Sapogonians, only Pastora proves herself a pure spirit.

Pastora proves herself an "advanced soul" as her spiritual discipline not only engenders in her a social and moral awareness but also galvanizes her to action. Equality is not a passive belief but a catalytic conviction. For Pastora, *jodiendo* means resisting both patriarchy and cruel immigration policies. In the novel, prayer and reflection immediately precede Pastora's participation in an underground railroad for illegal Sapogonian immigrants fleeing their war-torn country. Compelled to back up the social message of her songs with concrete action, Pastora makes clandestine overnight trips to various Midwestern locales to ferry recently arrived illegals from Sapogonia to Chicago. This activity eventually earns Pastora over a year in prison, which she abides with equanimity while refusing to succumb to cynicism.

At the end of *Sapogonia*, the narrator's indictment of Máximo for his objectification of Pastora (and all women) shifts to a direct address that includes the (male) reader: "She was an invention to make your world tolerable" (254). Pastora stands in for all the images and roles in which women have been trapped and essentialized. The multivalence of her character figures the situation of all women: We see her as she sees herself, we see her as a woman with agency, and we see her through the objectifying gaze of the men and women in her life. She is the goddess of men's imaginations, she is a "witch," and she is a *femme fatale*. She is also mother, wife, lover, musician, social activist, prisoner, and parolee. In the way she handles all of these roles, she remains perhaps Castillo's purest example of a "Xicanista" as outlined in *Massacre of the Dreamers*.

Bandit Hagiography: Saint-Making in *The Guardians*

In *So Far from God*, Castillo adopts the role of *santera*, an artisan who creates images of saints. Pérez cogently argues that "Castillo resemanticizes the existing logic of martyrs and saints, not as ways to dignify female powerlessness through Christian suffering, but to reveal the goddesses beneath such images who are capable of exerting agency" (67). I want to extend Pérez's point by further considering the kind of agency Castillo's saints exert. Castillo reprises her role as *santera* with *The Guardians*, producing a more developed hagiography of *joderones*, or bandit saints.

Each chapter of *The Guardians* is narrated in the first person by one of four speakers: Regina, Gabo, Miguel, and El Abuelo Milton. Excepting Milton, whose near-blindness invokes renegade Protestant John Milton, the narrators and several other characters are named for saints and angels. Gabo (Gabriel) and Miguel (Michael), along with minor characters Uriel and Rafa (Rafael), bear the names of archangels. Regina, whose middle name is Ana, is linked with both Saint Regina, the queen of heaven, and Saint Anne, the "patroness of late-in-life mothers" (*G* 152). The saintly characters in *The Guardians* expand the scope of spiritual *mestizaje* in Castillo's work. Of the narrators, only Gabo is an orthodox Catholic. Castillo adopts these celebrated names to invoke the protectoral role of angels and saints, while revising the requirements of sainthood and emphasizing the saintly activity of living human beings over canonized saints. Sainthood in this novel is characterized by compassion for others and care of the earth, and the saints are formed from varying religious backgrounds, including orthodox Catholicism. While *Sapogonia* reincorporates aspects of indigenous Indian religion, in *The Guardians* Miguel alone observes Indian religious rituals, attending a sweat lodge and praying to the Great Spirit. Gabo and Regina both follow, to different degrees, the Catholic tradition. Yet like Sofía in *So Far from God*, their Catholicism takes a nonhierarchical, earth-centered form.

In spite of her symbolic associations, Regina's character is not a flat stand-in or type. Regina is no saint, by conventional standards; she exhibits her own contradictions and problems. While she dedicates herself to environmental efforts like her organic community gardening project and social activism on behalf of illegal immigrants, she also persists in the crudest kind of American dreaming: "I've never been very good at get-rich-quick schemes anyway. But it don't stop me from trying" (*G* 7). She has tried her hand peddling products like Mary Kay and even hosted Tupperware parties. It is her spiritual maturity that separates her from characters like Máximo and Fe and curbs the temptation to sacrifice her integrity or exploit others for material gain. She tells her nephew Gabo, "What we'd never do with our dollars . . . because we got our priorities straight, . . . is nothing that would be harmful to our bodies or our souls" (*G* 8). Notably, the novel equates Regina's doomed "small business ventures" with her involvement in American politics. Regina routinely pens complaint letters to the US president and goes to the polls to "vote like everyone else" (*G* 7). She knows her letters likely go unread and make no appreciable difference, but, like hosting Tupperware parties, they make her feel American "like everyone else." Castillo suggests that these pursuits are equally hopeless for a marginalized woman like Regina. The novel's events only strengthen Regina's inchoate sense that efficacious actions issue not from elected officials but from saints and guardians like her and Gabo.

As Castillo's version of a saint, Regina exhibits many of the female virtues and qualities esteemed in traditional Catholic Latinx culture while also serving as the focal point for interrogating them. Though once married and widowed shortly thereafter, Regina remains a virgin. Her virginity marks her as a Marian figure while challenging the exaltation of female chastity as the hallmark of virtue, and it occasions a family backstory that highlights the shambolic state of immigration. Regina's virginity is one of several Marian identifiers. Details link Regina to Our Lady of Guadalupe (La Lupe or La Virgen de Guadalupe). Her nephew Gabo, who believes his aunt is "blessed," references the "small plaque of la Virgen de Guadalupe" hanging over her bed (*G* 21). Guadalupe is a Mestizo incarnation of the Blessed Virgin Mary who figures centrally in Mexican and Mexican American Catholicism. She is customarily referred to by a geographically defining title to preserve her indigenous identity. The "Mexican Madonna" is especially important for Chicanas because she appeared as dark-skinned, speaking the native language. Castillo explains Guadalupe's significance as an embodiment of "the feminine principle":

> The feminine principle to which I refer would be concerned with preservation, protection—especially of the young and less fortunate—and affiliations of communities for the common good. This feminine principle, which lies within both man and woman, is exemplified for Chicanos especially in the model of la Virgen de Guadalupe. Since the Conquest Mexicans have also worshipped Jesus Christ, the incarnated God and revolutionary, while the

Omnipotent Father, whom we fear, reminds us to stand guard against men and sin. By calling forth la Virgen de Guadalupe—the feminine principle within ourselves—we have hope. It comes from her noncategorical compassion and acceptance of all her children versus the fear of inadequacy people may feel in "the eyes of God." As we, who have been rendered powerless by the church, state, and men's movements except to serve their cause, receive ánimo from her, we are able to give to ourselves, those around us, and to the world. (*MOD* 94)

Regina embodies the vigilance and ministrations traditionally ascribed to Guadalupe, and her guardianship, extending well beyond her care of Gabo, is one resonance of the novel's title. The feminine principle transcends borders, and Regina's identification with Guadalupe highlights her care for illegal immigrants and those across the border. Through Regina's virginal widowhood, Castillo inveighs against the American citizenship-granting process, which is often marked by bureaucratic imbroglio and arbitrariness. Regina wed her late husband, a childhood friend named Junior, the day before his deployment to Vietnam, where he died in combat. Junior's military service garnered Regina American citizenship and a small pension. Regina is granted citizenship because she was married for one day to a teenager who then served briefly in the military; only by sheer chance is Regina a legally recognized American, which is "all every immigrant in the world wants, to get her papers in order. To officially become a person" (*G* 116). Meanwhile, she has lost many family members, mostly migrant workers, to the hazards of crossing the US-Mexico border illegally for work. Regina becomes actively involved in bringing to justice those who prey upon desperate illegal immigrants.

Castillo's *joderones* are activists, bandit saints who disrupt social order on behalf of the marginalized. *Joderones* are people's saints, "individuals who emerge from struggling communities and whose intercession is sought by the people, even though the official church does not recognize them" (De La Torre 117). Castillo transfers the responsibility of guardianship to living saints. Without dissolving the role of the divine in earthly affairs or the importance of traditional hyperdulia (veneration of saints), Castillo eschews expressions of religion that disenfranchise women and encourage quietism. Castillo conveys this attitude by contrasting Regina's view of saints with her mother's. Regina recounts her mother's habit of importuning Saint Anthony of Padua every time she misplaced something:

No sooner was something missing, she'd cross herself and say a prayer to el santito. San Antonio, saint of the poor, kept busy by people like my mother—

who was even capable of asking him to help her find a parking space—was a great man in his life. He made Milagros happen even while he was still alive, appearing in two places at the same time in order to heal a very sick person.

I believe in the saints as people. I can't speak for them once they've passed. (G 171)

The desired outcome distinguishes her mother's invocation of San Antonio from the way Regina and especially Gabo approach the saints. Her mother's prayers (if "answered") yield strictly material results, whereas for Regina and Gabo the saints' lives shape their values and guide their actions. Regina's recollections of her mother suggest a woman resigned to demanding little of life, a woman who, for example, taught her daughter not to "expect too much from life" by throwing away all the letters Regina had received from her late husband (G 207). In contrast, Gabo prays to the saints to strengthen and guide him so he may influence the world around him. The chapters narrated by Gabo consist of private addresses to "Su Reverencia, el Santo Franciscano, Padre Pío," asking for strength to remain holy and care for the souls of those around him and for guidance as he searches for his father. Gabo's father (Regina's brother) is missing, presumably at the hands of the *coyotes* who traffic Mexicans across the border.

The contrast between Regina and *los curos* (priests or clerics) further clarifies Castillo's saintly criteria. Frustrated by her parish priest, Regina recounts her experience of clerics as being "hard to decipher": "When he wore his collar . . . a priest would look like trustworthiness incarnated. You could surrender yourself entirely to him. . . . He would understand you. He would help you. . . . But not Father Juan Bosco and not the ones I knew growing up. They were men. Just men. And a couple of them had been good and a few had been bad" (G 99). Regina's statement indicates a clear conception of the priestly office, which, significantly, has yet to be satisfied by any actual cleric she has known. She should not have to struggle as she does to "decipher" the character of her priest. In contrast, Padre Juan Bosco and Gabo have no trouble "deciphering" Regina. Regina is a nominal Catholic: She attends Mass irregularly but refers to Padre Juan Bosco as her confessor of over twenty years and alludes to lifelong experience with clergy. She also claims that she is "doomed to doubt everything" (G 147). And yet, the padre and Gabo know unquestioningly that Regina, the self-described skeptic, is in fact a saint, citing as proof her compassion and unwillingness to abandon anyone. In a comic but symbolically rich scene, Gabo publicly serenades Regina on her birthday, singing a rendition of "Salve, Regina" so moving that it silences the rowdy crowd at the local rodeo. One of the most well-known Marian hymns of the Catholic Church,

"Salve, Regina" ("Hail, Holy Queen") addresses the Holy Queen as a merciful advocate for the exiled and forgotten—precisely what makes Regina a saint.

It is her solicitude that makes Regina a "holy *joderone*," one who's willing to provoke and challenge the powers that be. Her association with Guadalupe reinforces her "bandit sainthood." De La Torre argues that while Guadalupe is not a traditional trickster figure, "she still disrupts and turns the traditional church hierarchy on its head" (113). According to tradition, Guadalupe appeared in 1531 to an impoverished Indian peasant named Juan Diego and spoke to him in his native Aztec tongue, Nahuatl. Guadalupe appeared not to a cleric or to a person of power or wealth, but to the oppressed, and she came speaking a pagan language; thus, "salvation, rather than coming from the official colonized church to the presumed infidels, came from these so-called nonbelievers to the church" (De La Torre 113). One method of Regina's subversion is her defiance of patriarchal religious figures. While her nephew reveres the parish priest, Regina upbraids the cleric for shortcomings both religious and personal. Unintimidated by the clerical collar, Regina excoriates Padre Juan Bosco for dallying with a female parishioner and especially for disappointing her nephew Gabo. She makes a scene outside the padre's house, and she enumerates his shortcomings directly to him when he visits her home. However, unlike Father Jerome in *So Far from God*, Padre Juan Bosco proves receptive to reproof. Regina's upbraiding transforms the padre into a dedicated social activist: He badgers growers and foremen to ensure that migrant workers are treated well and receive proper medical care, and he risks incarceration and even his life on behalf of Regina, Gabo, and their family.

Gabo cuts a different figure of sainthood. Gabo's chapters are epistolary, consisting of written prayers to Padre Pio (Pio of Pietrelcina), who was an Italian Capuchin priest. Several details of Gabo's life mirror Padre Pio's, especially his stigmata, meager diet, and mystical visions. Gabo also evinces the ardent concern for the natural world traditionally associated with Saint Francis, the tradition to which Padre Pio also belonged (the Capuchins are a Franciscan offshoot). Regina recounts an apparently miraculous episode in which Gabo restores life to a dead hawk. Gabo even chastises his aunt for wanting to kill moths and scorpions that have invaded her home, accusing her of cruelty to insects.

Castillo devotes detailed attention to the way that Gabo's Catholicism shapes his life. We glimpse how Gabo's spiritual disciplines of prayer, fasting, and receiving the Eucharist, all orthodox Catholic practices, inform his sociopolitical consciousness. Gabo has been an acolyte of Padre Juan Bosco, until the priest briefly abandons his parish during a wayward period. During the padre's absence, Gabo enters the sacristy to pray and experiences a deep longing for the Host, having not received it for weeks. Conscious of his offense, he places a wafer on his own tongue, then dons "the humble robes of a Franciscan brother" that he finds in a closet (*G* 164). So adorned, he has an apocalyptic vision in which the vials of wrath poured out upon the earth by the seven angels in Revelation are identified with current political and environmental affairs. The following day, discalced and clad in the Franciscan robes, Gabo mounts a lunchroom table at his school and pronounces his vision to a room full of jeering peers.

Several notable aspects of this scene convey Castillo's picture of sainthood. First, while Gabo is an orthodox Catholic, he receives his spiritual vision directly, without sacerdotal mediation, following his self-administration of the Eucharist, suggesting that the official cleric has become dispensable. While the priest later returns to his parish as a humbled and sincerely compassionate leader, Gabo here recognizes the philandering priest as a "false apostle." Second, Gabo's spiritual vision engenders an environmental awareness. He proclaims to fellow students that the vials poured upon the earth translate to environmental contamination and global warming as well as widespread war, disease, and famine. Third, Gabo's spiritual disciplines magnify his political consciousness. He announces, "No darker hour could we be living in than this one, when a great nation sets upon declaring wars in the name of peace," and interprets the unclean spirits that issue from the mouth of the beast in Revelation to be the latest canards propagated by the president "to placate the public" (*G* 165). Finally, looking directly at a table of female gang members, he says, "*And I saw the dead . . . and the dead were judged, every person according to their works*," before his palms begin to bleed and he passes out (*G* 165–66). This pronouncement, however harsh, is rooted in compassion, which is verified by the stigmata. Gabo is addressing one girl in particular, whose soul he anguishes over, with "arms . . . still outstretched, waiting for her to be embraced by the light of El Espíritu Santo" (*G* 166). Gabo has enlisted the help of this girl, who goes by Tiny Tears, on account of gangland connections she might exploit for information about his missing father. Through their interactions, Gabo has learned that Tiny Tears has been sexually abused and enjoined by her gang leaders to commit murder, and he wants to liberate her from that life. He succeeds, in a way, but not before Tiny Tears becomes the instrument of his death, as he attempts a perilous mission to rescue her along with his father from human traffickers.

Gabo and Regina, with the help of Miguel and Milton, take it upon themselves to locate their missing family member Rafa, Regina's brother and Gabo's father. With local authorities both incapable and unwilling to help locate him, Regina and Miguel begin tracking the activities of the cartel likely responsible for Rafa's disappearance. Regina finds herself, a middle-aged teacher's assistant, staking out a suspect's house, a venture that could easily result in her own disappearance. After Miguel's ex-wife also goes missing, Gabo, Miguel, and Juan Bosco take matters into their own hands and break into the house where they suspect Rafa and Crucita are being held. Inside, they find Crucita and Tiny Tears, who have been imprisoned there for days, naked, starved, and forcibly drugged with heroin. Regina and the police arrive shortly after, just in time to see Tiny Tears, in a drug-addled rage, drive a jagged piece of glass through Gabo's heart. (Rafa is not there; the police find him in another cartel house days later, dead from being forced to make methamphetamine without protection from the chemicals.)

The final thrust of *The Guardians* is that human beings must be saints to and for one another. According to De La Torre, a Chicanx ethics must be an ethics *en conjunto* ("in conjunction"), meaning that *la lucha* (the struggle for survival) is never an individual quest (77). The community analyzes and interprets *lo cotidiano* (their particular reality) together and reflects together on how their religious convictions bear on this reality. This communal effort is rooted in "the relational imperative," which, as opposed to the categorical imperative, is based not on any transcendental but on the kind of "reflection that can only occur when one is in relationship with the oppressed and marginalized" (De La Torre 99). Regina and her fellow guardians act with and for others. The guardians in the novel are emphatically human. After Gabo (the novel's Christ figure) is killed, Regina finds herself reading the Gospel of Matthew "to find Gabo": "Maybe it don't make sense to no one else. But it does to me. Gabo talking to me through Matthew. 'For if ye forgive men their trespasses, your heavenly Father will also forgive you'" (*G* 210). Gabo professed his belief in Regina's saintliness; now he becomes a saint to her. His influence compels Regina to do the hardest thing possible: adopt the now-orphaned child of her nephew's murderer. Just as Gabo's interest in "la Tiny Tears" was spiritual, a concern for her soul and the spiritual damage inflicted by her gang life, Regina too summons the compassion to care for the very person who murdered her nephew. In adopting the little girl, whom she names Gabriella, Regina incarnates her patroness Saint Anne by becoming a "late-in-life" surrogate mother. *Joderones* may "screw with" the powers that be in ways that make them criminals by law, but they also galvanize each other to spiritually informed acts of compassion and charity.

Gabo and Regina are "people's saints," venerated on account of their actions and values. The two differ markedly in their attitude toward organized religion but share a concern for the earth and compassion for all, especially the disenfranchised. Castillo's Chicanx saints embrace spiritual disciplines that honor their ethnic identities and enlighten them to the chimerical nature of the American dream. Regina relates her own early border crossings into America as a migrant worker, and her starry-eyed view of a factory near her current home:

> The sleeping giant is Asarco, a smelter company, which was closed down in 1999 after more than a century of belching fumes into our skies. When I was a girl and came up to work in the fields, I'd see the humongous swirls of smoke coming up from the smelter. I'd feel like the way immigrants must've felt seeing the Statue of Liberty. Those puffing chimneys were a pair of lamps, calling the huddled masses. I didn't know no better. (G 51)

Regina "knows better" now the environmental threat of such an enterprise and the false light of those lamps that seemed to promise good jobs and working conditions. She is resigned to a certain hopelessness that America will embrace the "huddled masses" of Chicanxs *as Chicanxs* or that success will attend their hard work. But such hopelessness incites activism, not quietism, and elicits a resolve to no longer contribute to one's own disenfranchisement. According to De La Torre, "the semblance of hope becomes an obstacle when it serves as a mechanism that maintains rather than challenges the prevailing social structures" (92). Such hopelessness enjoins Chicanxs to the process of spiritual *mestizaje*, in which one realizes a relation to the transcendent that honors one's ethnic and gender identity.

CONCLUSION

With intended irony, Castillo selects a statement from Porfirio Diaz, dictator of Mexico during the Mexican Civil War, as the epigraph for *So Far from God* (which Miguel repeats in *The Guardians*): "So far from God—So near the United States." The quote has many valences, one being the contention that the more a Chicanx believes in American exceptionalism, the further she is from spiritual fulfillment. Castillo advocates what Walter calls the "politics of dislocation and relocation," in which one asserts one's "otherness" for oneself and not at another's behest, forging "an identity based on difference with the capacity to relocate" (92). Castillo believes it is possible for Chicanxs living in borderlands physical and spiritual to flourish, to forge integrated identities, by adopting an approach marked by hybridity and by exploiting the multiple subjectivities inherent in a borderlands state. Yet she is no quixotic idealist. Castillo is clear that there's no easy model, nor is there any pristine religious or cultural past to be recovered and imported seamlessly into the present. She exhorts Chicanas to a clear-eyed mining of their Mexic Amerindian heritage, subjecting all archaeological discoveries to critical assessment. She conveys the fraught nature of this enterprise, insisting that it must be grounded in concrete experience and undertaken in, and on behalf of, a community of others.

CHAPTER 3

The Depth of the Riches

Thomas Pynchon's Spiritual Hybridity

NEAR THE END of *Vineland,* a character named Prairie appears to be, in spite of herself, enthralled with power in the form of the novel's villain, Brock Vond. This despite the fact that Vond has brainwashed Prairie's mother, hunted her father, and generally stands for everything Prairie detests. In her uncontrollable fascination, Prairie imitates to a lesser degree her mother, Frenesi, who similarly succumbed to Vond's spell. This same motif—the seduction of otherwise radical, or at least sensible, characters by contemptible authority figures—appears throughout Pynchon's oeuvre, including in his latest novel, *Bleeding Edge,* in which protagonist Maxine Tarnow has a tryst with a shady government agent. Such scenes are not driven by latent sexism; rather, this quasi-masochistic fascination with power is one way Pynchon depicts a fundamental aspect of the human condition: the desire for transcendence.[1]

His apparent, though qualified, affirmation of anarchism notwithstanding, Pynchon recognizes that humans need stability.[2] In *Vineland* we're told, "Brock Vond's genius was to have seen in the activities of the sixties left not threats to order but unacknowledged desires for it. While the Tube was proclaiming youth revolution against parents of all kinds and most viewers were accepting this story, Brock saw the deep . . . need only to stay children forever,

---

1. Male characters throughout Pynchon's work find power equally alluring.

2. Pynchon depicts anarchism positively, or at least uncritically, in several novels. For an informed treatment of Pynchon's view of anarchy, see Benton.

safe inside some extended national Family" (269). Throughout his work, Pynchon evokes the human need for self-integration and shows how devastating the effects can be when this need is misplaced. This integration includes the need for family and community but extends to one's relations to the physical world and the transcendent. Pynchon suggests that even radical movements and well-intentioned reforms are easily co-opted, one reason being the prevalence of a quasi-religious American ideology that purports to offer the transcendence and order that Americans desire. The idea of a "national Family," as well as a national destiny, continues to figure significantly in Americans' self-understanding.

A notorious recluse, Pynchon has never granted an interview. Nevertheless, his fiction and periodic essays reveal an encyclopedic knowledge of American culture and history. His essays elucidate what his fiction reveals only through meticulous parsing: Despite his reputation as a paragon of postmodernism, Pynchon is a sincere moralist and formidable political critic. As scholars such as Cyrus Patell have registered, Pynchon indicts Americans of all ranks for complicity in systems of oppression and stasis (129). In *Vineland*, Pynchon suggests that even countercultural radicals were all too easily turned into accomplices.[3] In *Inherent Vice*, magnate Crocker Fenway smugly lectures hippie sleuth Doc Sportello on the willingness of average Americans to be bought off with shiny goods:

> "It's about *being in place* . . . we're in place. We've been in place forever. Look around. Real estate, water rights, oil, cheap labor—all of that's ours, it's always been ours. And you, at the end of the day what are you? one more unit in this swarm of transients who come and go without pause here in the sunny Southland, eager to be bought off with a car of a certain make, model, and year, a blonde in a bikini, thirty seconds on some excuse for a wave—a chili dog, for Christ's sake." He shrugged. "We will never run out of you people. The supply is inexhaustible." (347)

For many of Pynchon's characters, the enticements of power and money loom large in their willingness to overlook social inequalities and widespread spiritual malaise. Others get swept along by the demands of mundane life, too bogged down or ground down to think too much about "Them" (the shadowy

---

3. This is perhaps why, as Steven Weisenburger suggests, Pynchon is always subversive but rarely vindictive or rage-filled: He understands how easily the most conscientious objector becomes an unwitting abettor (43–44). After all, Pynchon began his literary career as a technical writer for Boeing, where he covered developments in aviation and weaponry and found himself subtly complicit in the American military machine.

entities calling the shots); such individuals are victimized by the system even if they obliquely contribute to it. But why—especially to those who won't be bought off with a measly chili dog—does the American dream continue to be so compelling in Pynchon's view? One answer is found in the aforementioned new car and chili dog. As simple material goods, these aren't irresistibly enticing, but as respective symbols of luxury and leisure, as emblems of the American dream, they tell a stirring story. The *idea* of the opportunity to buy a new car is exceedingly more powerful than possession of the car itself. The *idea* of eating a chili dog in the bleachers of Dodger Stadium on a sunny afternoon is what is compelling. The underlying ideology is that *this* nation—America—is the land of opportunity where one can make something of oneself. Pynchon posits a substantial congregation of true believers in American exceptionalism, all of whom collude unwittingly in a dubious regnant order.

This notion of exceptionalism is not only tied to the idea of freedom and opportunity; it also addresses a spiritual need by promising a kind of transcendence. Pynchon holds that we are religious beings. In his essay "Is It O. K. to Be a Luddite?" Pynchon surveys a few ways Americans have persisted in expressing faith in a higher reality:

> As religion was being more and more secularized into Deism and nonbelief, the abiding human hunger for evidence of God and afterlife, for salvation—bodily resurrection, if possible—remained. The Methodist movement and the American Great Awakening were only two sectors on a broad front of resistance to the Age of Reason, a front which included Radicalism and Freemasonry as well as Luddites and the Gothic novel. Each in its way expressed the same profound unwillingness to give up elements of faith, however "irrational," to an emerging technopolitical order that might or might not know what it was doing.

For Pynchon, a vigorous spiritual life is foundational to enlightened political action and thus to human flourishing. He claims later in the "Luddite" essay, "To insist on the miraculous is to deny to the machine at least some of its claims on us, to assert the limited wish that living things, earthly and otherwise, may on occasion become Bad and Big enough to take part in transcendent doings." Even in his earliest novel, *V.*, considered by some anticlerical, atheism is treated as harshly as an anemic and patriarchal Catholicism.[4] Spirituality is vital to human life, but not all forms of religion are salutary. American exceptionalism (or the myth of election) appears often in Pynchon's

---

4. For a perceptive treatment of religion in *V.*, see Freer 25–28.

work, with characters manifesting a religious commitment to it. America, as an ideal, assumes its own divine imperative and many ruinously turn to this ideological construct for spiritual mooring. Embracing the notion that America is destined to be the pinnacle of history results in the tendency to ignore history—to dismiss complex causes and unintended, sometimes devastating, effects.

Critics have long recognized Pynchon's insistence that autocratic systems result in dehumanization or "inanimateness." But further consideration is due to Pynchon's depiction of *how* such control is achieved. For all his excoriation of nefarious governmental machinations, Pynchon doesn't spare average citizens or would-be revolutionaries from blame, either. How, then, do such totalizing systems prevail? For Pynchon, one reason (though there are others) is that American political ideology functions as a compelling religion. Pynchon shows such ideology to inspire a toxic form of spiritual discipline, one that engenders a sanctimonious, hubristic single-mindedness that rationalizes violence in the name of national destiny. Furthermore, it blinkers its adherents to their own spiritual poverty. Pynchon exposes this ideology as a spurious religion by juxtaposing it with other religious practices in which he locates valid resources for political awareness and personal fulfillment. John McClure has astutely noted Pynchon's persuasion that "only something as powerfully transformative as a spiritual discipline can enable individuals to reclaim some mental autonomy and resist the psychological and physical coercions of the market" (*Partial* 56). But we cannot assume that spiritual disciplines are confined to the realm of traditional religion or that all disciplines are inherently salutary. Americans have more than the market to fear, and ostensibly secular ideologies such as American exceptionalism may promote their own spiritual disciplines. Pynchon depicts religious practices that shape individuals both positively and negatively, inviting readers to evaluate these practices by the caliber of individuals they produce.

"DID GOD INTEND IT ONLY FOR US?": THE MYTH OF AMERICAN ELECTION

The myth of American election surfaces in virtually all Pynchon's works. In *Gravity's Rainbow*, Tyrone Slothrop connects the Calvinist doctrine of election to America's founding by recalling the "Slothropite heresy" of his Puritan ancestor, William Slothrop. William questioned the doctrine of election in his tract, *On Preterition*, where he "argued holiness for these 'second Sheep,' without whom there'd be no elect" (*GR* 565). William ventured that Judas should be loved like Jesus because without Judas, Jesus could not have fulfilled his destiny. Unsurprisingly, these views got William expelled from the Massachusetts Bay Colony. But centuries later, Tyrone's reflection on his ancestor's ideas prompts him to consider how the notion of election has shaped American history and whether things could have been different: "Could [William] have been the fork in the road America never took, the singular point she jumped the wrong way from? Suppose the Slothropite heresy had had the time to consolidate and prosper? Might there have been fewer crimes in the name of Jesus, and more mercy in the name of Judas Iscariot?" (*GR* 565). As Tyrone stumbles through the morass of post-WWII Germany, the Slothropite heresy inspires him to contemplate the ramifications of nationalistic campaigns for global supremacy. He wonders if there's a way to start over: "Maybe for a little while all the fences are down, one road as good as another, the whole space of the Zone cleared, depolarized, and somewhere inside the waste of it a single set of coordinates from which to proceed, without elect, without preterite, without even nationality to fuck it up" (*GR* 565–66). By the end of *Gravity's Rainbow*, however, we see that this is impossible for a nation. For Pynchon, utopian ambitions too easily devolve into an excuse for tyranny. Utopian visions can exist only, as Paul Maltby states, as a "territory of the spirit" (182), though for Pynchon this is no mean thing.

The myth of American election also appears in *Inherent Vice* in Doc's dream about a boat called *Preserved*. This dream turns out to be one of Pynchon's forays into the subjunctive, a comment on how the American dream proved ever to be only a dream:

> Yet there is no avoiding time, the sea of time, the sea of memory and forgetfulness, the years of promise, gone and unrecoverable, of the land almost allowed to claim its better destiny, only to have the claim jumped by evildoers known all too well, and taken instead and held hostage to the future we must live in now forever. May we trust that this blessed ship is bound for some better shore, some undrowned Lemuria, risen and redeemed, where the American fate, mercifully, failed to transpire. (*IV* 341)

The passage implies that while the potential of the New World to be a place of freedom and flourishing was real enough, this sparkling opportunity was quickly hijacked and wielded as a pretense for subjugation. The "claim jumpers" held a nation hostage to its own election, hoodwinking people into sacrificing their own goods and freedoms for the sake of a promised national destiny. The crucial phrase "held hostage to the future we must live in now forever" superbly captures the dialectical dynamic of America's purported destiny, which is a forged facsimile of the Christian kingdom of God that is always arriving, both already here and not yet. This interpretation is confirmed in the novel's subsequent scene. The American dream apparently lingers in Doc's mind later that day as he studies a mural portraying the arrival of the 1769 Portolá expedition to the West Coast (near what is now Los Angeles). One explorer is depicted as an American Adam on whose face "there was an expression of wonder, like, What's this, what unsuspected paradise? Did God with his finger trace out and bless this perfect little valley, intending it only for us?" (*IV* 343–44). Tellingly, this mural is housed inside the palatial clubhouse of mogul Crocker Fenway's exclusive club, the Portola. The club's members are exactly those who believe America is "only for us": not the American populace but the one-percenters. It's also significant that the mural's style "reminded Doc of labels on fruit and vegetable crates when he was a kid. Lots of color, atmosphere, attention to detail. . . . Everybody in the scene looked like a movie star" (*IV* 343). This compelling vision of providentially granted possibility is pure fabricated nostalgia, a stylized scene used to market an ideology like food venders market their produce. When Doc comments admiringly about the picture, Fenway mutters that he's never paid it any attention. Doc, in his bumbling innocence, is naïve enough to be beguiled by the manufactured nostalgia. Doc admires the ideal, while Fenway—who epitomizes the WASP tycoon—gives it no consideration because this enthralling vision is the means by which men like himself fleece the rank and file. The passage indicts the likes of Fenway by rhetorically asking if God intended the new world *only* "for us." This sense of "election," Pynchon insinuates, became the root of all the new world's evils.

In *Mason & Dixon*, Pynchon's most focused treatment of American mythology, he renders the American dream as corrupted from the beginning. *Mason & Dixon* opens in a Philadelphia parlor during Advent of 1786, with a rambunctious pair of twins asking their uncle for a "Tale about America" involving conflict with Indians and with the French (7). As Pedro García-Caro points out, it's 1786 and these American youths are "already craving the ultimate American epic: the frontier tale" (111). Pynchon places the exceptionalist mind-set as part of America's earliest history, ingrained in the first post-Revolution generation. (The name of the twins' sister, Tenebrae, suggests darkly that something is already amiss in this first American generation.) As the aforementioned uncle, Reverend Cherrycoke, commences his American tale, he professes his credence in the Puritan vision of the New World as New Jerusalem. America bespeaks the opportunity to avoid the iniquities of the Old World: "I was back in America once more, finding, despite all, that I could not stay away from it, this object of hope that Miracles might yet occur, that

God might yet return to Human affairs, that all the wistful Fictions necessary to the childhood of a species might yet come true, . . . a third Testament" (*MD* 353). Cherrycoke never witnesses such miracles, however. Miracles aren't out of the question for Pynchon, but they are seldom witnessed in the inhospitable environment that America becomes. Pynchon's "realm of the Sacred" is a realm of plurality and openness, and as America is mapped and parceled, it becomes the sort of stodgy, oppressive place that Pynchon laments in his "Luddite" essay. The process of mapping confines America "into the Net-Work of Points already known, that slowly triangulates its Way into the Continent, changing all from subjunctive to declarative, reducing Possibilities to Simplicities that serve the ends of Governments,—winning away from the realm of the Sacred, its Borderlands one by one, and assuming them unto the bare mortal World that is our home, and our Despair" (*MD* 345). Any possibility that America is a realm of the Sacred is quickly undercut in the novel as Mason and Dixon visit the sight of the massacre of Conestoga Indians at Lancaster. Dixon pronounces the heinous act worse than anything he witnessed in colonial South Africa (where he was previously) and grows skeptical of the popular American claims to democratic equality (*MD* 347).

America's canonization as "third Testament" (to use Cherrycoke's term) is forever confined to the subjunctive realm, but the notion of America as the City upon a Hill continues to shape Americans' values and identities. The enduring version of election discards any obligation to be a light unto the nations in favor of a fervid, divinely sanctioned "America first." This ideology translates to a religion for many characters, as we see with Pynchon's "Christers." Pynchon typically employs "Christer" pejoratively. He applies the epithet to such loathsome villains as Brock Vond and Scarsdale Vibe as well as more ambiguous characters like Foley Walker. In *Against the Day,* Kit Traverse classifies as "Christers" those "whose allegiance, loudly and often as they might invoke Jesus Christ and his kingdom, was to that real [world] axis and nothing beyond it" (675). Pynchon's (typically male) Christer sees God as a personal genie and has little concern with Jesus's teachings. He is often connected to a hyper-evangelical variety of Christianity that is integrally linked to right-wing American politics. But his ultimate allegiance, which is absolute and at times exercised violently, is to America. For example, in *Against the Day,* ruthless robber baron Scarsdale Vibe correlates the kingdom of God with American supremacy. Vibe, whom other characters consider a religious man, sees the preservation of (*his*) America, at any cost, as his Christian duty: "What a burden it is to be told to love them, while knowing that they are the Anti-christ itself, and that our only salvation is to deal with them as we ought. . . . When the Lord's people are in danger, you know what he requires. . . . Smite often and early" (*ATD* 332–33). God and country are inseparable for Vibe, who is hell-bent on extirpating communists, socialists, and anyone else who threatens the republic. He sanctions brutality in the name of Christ the securer of individual reward and God the cosmic military general. And yet, repugnant as characters like Vibe are, they act in earnest: They are not conscious charlatans who adopt religious rhetoric for the sole purpose of manipulation. In such characters, we see Pynchon's insinuation that the heart of religion lies in the ways that one attempts to make the transcendent present. Vibe's belief in Christ isn't questioned, but his efforts to usher in Christ's reign include acts of violence and disenfranchisement that shape him into an increasingly paranoid and mercurial man.

While Vibe and his ilk conflate American politics with the kingdom of God, other characters embody an ideology in which America remains the "City upon a Hill" but God, even as rhetorical placeholder, has mostly faded from the picture. Pynchon's corpus registers the gradual process, detailed by Sacvan Bercovitch, in which the original Puritan theological underpinnings of American election are slowly effaced and America, as an ideal, becomes its own Alpha and Omega.[5] In *Vineland,* this shift is embodied by Brock Vond, a Reaganite federal agent. Reaganism surfaces frequently in *Vineland*; as Patell demonstrates, Reagan took the idea of America as a City upon a Hill seriously, alluding to it regularly in speeches, but transformed Winthrop's communal ethic into an individualistic one (x–xi). Vond professes no religion but "exemplifies a Puritan outlook" with his ideals of temperance, hard work, and "especially the distinction between the regenerate saved—a select remnant—and the vast body of the unchosen" (Cowart, *Pynchon* 102–3). This vestigial sense of election underlies Vond's cavalier political action. In one scene, a federal grand jury assembles to look into Hollywood drug usage, a nod to the historical blacklisting of actors as a means of inflaming patriotic impulses (Thoreen 221). Drug-enforcement agent Hector Zuñiga tries to make sense of the situation:

> [Hector] assumed parallels were being drawn to back in '51, when HUAC [the historically factual House Un-American Activities Committee] came to town.... But why right now? What did it have to do with Brock Vond running around Vineland like he was? and all these other weird vibrations in the air lately, like even some non-born-agains showing up at work with these little crosses, these red Christer pins, in their lapels. (*VL* 338–39)

---

5. See Bercovitch, *Puritan,* especially chapters 4 and 5.

David Thoreen has insightfully pointed out that these "red Chrlster pins" allude to FEMA and Rex-84, an emergency plan prepared by the government that entailed suspending the constitution and declaring martial law. In 1951—the year Hector recalls—Reagan, now US president in *Vineland*'s present, was president of the Screen Actors Guild. Thoreen argues compellingly that these red cross pins are both a reference to fascism, in recalling the swastika pins of German officers, and a "parody of the puritan belief in predestination, for what are they but the outward and visible signs of election? Secure in the innermost inner circle of FEMA, these men . . . can count themselves among the saved" (222). Though tasked with providing relief to victims of disaster, the resources at their disposal ensure that these men never have to suffer any trauma themselves. The force of Pynchon's parody lies in the fact that these FEMA "elect" are not elected, but rather appointed by those already in power (Thoreen 222).

One character refers to Vond and his cronies as crusaders of "the True Faith," explained as a vaguely Protestant, capitalist ideology that gets handed down "generation to generation" by the elect "living inside their power, convinced they're immune to all the history the rest of us have to suffer" (*VL* 232). This idea of immunity to history stems from entitlement rooted in a sense of destiny. While these "crusaders of the True Faith" may be unbelievers themselves, such ideology indeed functions as a religious faith, in which America assumes the aura of divinity. Anything "un-American" is equivalent to ungodliness and must be snuffed out. This faith inculcates a false transcendence by beguiling Americans into a discipline of enduring economic hardship and subtle denials of freedom in the name of national greatness. The watchword of this "True Faith" is *individualism*, making it all the more insidious. Individualism, extolled as the hallmark of the American spirit, is such a compelling ideology precisely because "the official narrative that surrounds it renders it invisible" (Patell 14). Assured they live in the land of the free, Americans are convinced that ideology only exists elsewhere, yet the dissemination of this individualism ultimately fosters conformity. In *Vineland*, Brock Vond embodies the "representative self," Bercovitch's term for a rugged, hardworking, and successful individual who functions symbolically to validate the ideology of individualism that, in turn, serves as a social unifier. The figure of the representative self anchors a mutually reinforcing relation between the ideology of individualism and the ideology of American exceptionalism that vaunts America as the land of opportunity where individuals may realize their dreams.

Pynchon's reference in *Vineland* to the "True Faith," while tinged with sarcasm, is not merely metaphorical. Pynchon recurrently portrays American exceptionalism as a religion. In *Bleeding Edge*, 9/11 infantilizes and petrifies the American people, exposing the tenuousness of this nationalistic faith. The World Trade Center attack occurs in the middle of the novel, and Pynchon describes New Yorkers watching the aftermath on television as "a viewing population brought back to its default state, dumb-struck, undefended, scared shitless" (*BE* 321). Pynchon portrays an American people who, otherwise lacking in spiritual direction, depend on a nationalistic ideology. One character observes, "The Trade Center towers were religious. . . . They stood for what this country worships above everything else, the market, always the holy fuckin market," proceeding to accuse America of "holy wars against competing religions" (*BE* 338). The market, an emblem of global capitalism, also constitutes the means by which America preserves its pride of place as world power. To worship the market, in this context, is to worship America itself. It is a frangible faith, and the flock startle and scatter easily. Pynchon depicts a vicious cycle in which national leaders prey upon the public helplessness provoked by the attack in the attempt to restore the public's faith. This is evident in the narrator's description of the propagation of the phrase "Ground Zero":

> Forces in whose interests it compellingly lies to seize control of the narrative as quickly as possible come into play and dependable history shrinks to a dismal perimeter centered on "Ground Zero," a Cold War term taken from the scenarios of nuclear war so popular in the early sixties. This was nowhere near a Soviet nuclear strike on downtown Manhattan, yet those who repeat "Ground Zero" over and over do so without shame or concern for etymology. The purpose is to get people cranked up in a certain way. Cranked up, scared, and helpless. (*BE* 327–28)

The novel indicts American leaders for shamelessly appropriating the term "Ground Zero." Their willful ignorance of its etymology (it originated with the Trinity test and the bombing of Hiroshima and Nagasaki) evinces a thoroughly cavalier approach to history. "Ground Zero" here is both a nod to and a disregard for history. It retains just enough historical baggage to imbue itself with sensationalistic and incendiary force. The result is that a vulnerable population runs for security into the muscled arms of a mighty government and willingly overlooks their loss of liberty. Self-sacrifice, in the form of forfeited liberties, becomes a demonstration of devotion. In *Bleeding Edge*, law enforcement becomes increasingly entrenched in and around New York until the city becomes a virtual police state. Even more alarming is the discrimination perpetrated under the Patriot Act. Islamophobia and other prejudices are tractably accepted by the public as part of the War on Terror. Condoning bigotry becomes a practice of commitment, couched as patriotism. Irony and fiction are said to be war casualties (*BE* 335). The very tenuousness of this faith in America has engendered an environment of fear and impotency, and the terror drives people right back to the brittle comforts and stability that this faith offers.

Pynchon portrays a similarly desperate response to terror in *Against the Day*, in which we encounter a form of organized religion diluted to a series of rituals developed solely for physical security. In an unnamed metropolis (clearly New York City) where a monstrous Visitor has wreaked havoc, the "Cathedral of the Prefiguration" has become a despairing, promiscuous attempt at physical and psychological self-defense:

> Now, in arc-light, at the church's highest point, authorities had begun to project a three-dimensional image in full color, not exactly of Christ but with the same beard, robes, ability to emit light—as if, should the worst happen, they could deny all-out Christian allegiance and so make that much easier whatever turnings of heart might become necessary in striking a deal with the invader.... "No one would venture at night into a neighborhood of known vampires without carrying along a cross," as the Archbishop had declared, "would they now? no, and so with this Our Protector," who remained, guardedly, unnamed. (*ATD* 153)

The attack of "the Visitor" (precipitated by American conquest and greed) also evokes 9/11, and Pynchon crafts this desperate pandering so as to resemble the bland civil religion that experienced a resurgence after the attacks. A supposedly Christian church skirts any direct Christian allegiance because it is only the aura of divinity that is sought. In a dually tenuous motion, the church clings for comfort to an indistinct symbol of divinity while maintaining sufficient doctrinal elasticity to propitiate an unknown yet apparently hostile "Visitor." The archbishop and his flock are perfectly willing to sell their souls, or at least amend their religious profession at first convenience, to save their skins.

Times of crisis highlight the superficiality of a religion that worships America, but spiritual anemia is the constant unrecognized reality of its adherents. Pynchon paints many of his zealously nationalistic characters as spiritually feeble. Characters like Brock Vond and Scarsdale Vibe are racked by insecurity as they cling tenuously to power and leave destruction and anguish in their wake. Vibe's mining operations pillage the land and crush laborers. Vond provokes an atmosphere of fear and distrust in the name of American security. Even the venerable Reverend Cherrycoke, who wants to believe that America will be the New Jerusalem, finds any ideology as absolutizing as American exceptionalism to be finally incompatible with openness and charity.

These negative examples have in common a want of discernible moral or spiritual illumination. Pynchon excoriates vague mysticism, along with Gnosticism that disdains the material, for its tendency to reject the world and, concomitantly, human history. The forms of religion mentioned above serve to buttress, if not actively promote, political and national ambitions. In contrast, the spiritual disciplines and religious traditions that Pynchon presents positively have in common an enlightened awareness of politics and human history as well as a moral vision that enjoins one to social action.

THE DEPTH OF THE RICHES: PYNCHON'S RELIGIOUS ALTERNATIVES

What distinguishes Pynchon's religious vision is that it holds together what are often considered polarities: the need for integration and stability, and the need to acknowledge that truth and reality are plural. According to Louis Dupré, religion was traditionally structured according to an ontotheological synthesis, which consists of a tripartite relation between the self, the transcendent, and the cosmos (or natural world). This synthesis (explicated in my introduction) dissolved with the advent of modernity (Dupré, *Passage* 248). The human interpreter now plays a central creative role in defining the relation of the self to the other two components; we now understand human subjectivity to be fundamental. Both Dupré and Pynchon view this shift as potentially liberating. By their lights, the decadence of postmodernism has been to erroneously assume that "the real as it is in itself" *wholly* depends upon "the real as it exists for itself" or as it exists for the subject (Dupré, *Passage* 252).[6] A richer vision of the world affirms subjectivity without being comprehensively anthropocentric. The human interpreter occupies a primary role in the construction of reality, but the mind maintains a *creative* (rather than determinative) relation "to that physical reality on which it in other respects depends" (252). Because of this creative capacity, spirituality plays a key role in one's understanding of the real: "Reality does not remain indifferent to modes of thinking and feeling. . . . The nature of the real is determined by the nature of the relations among its components. . . . Any change in these relations affects the status of the whole. Spiritual revolutions transform reality as much as physical changes do" (251–52). For Pynchon, the American revolution was, in this sense, a spiritual revolution as well as a political one. As a spiritual revolution,

---

6. For examinations of Pynchon's subversion of postmodernism, see Cowart, *Pynchon* 111–12 and Lensing 126–27.

American ideology has had ruinous consequences and only another spiritual revolution can grant the true liberty and fulfillment that America claims to offer.

Pynchon challenges systems of meaning that offer an absolute picture of the world and that provide clear, easy mooring yet produce spiritual indigents. Pynchon exposes American exceptionalism as an ersatz religion that offers readily available transcendence and an uncomplicated, though nonetheless exacting, mode of existence. He juxtaposes it with alternative forms of religiosity that present their own rewards as well as, in several cases, their own problems. McClure accurately claims that Pynchon undertakes Mircea Eliade's aim of "reenchantment without reenclosure" (*Partial* 31). Pynchon clearly affirms the virtue of being open to the supernatural and miraculous. But he also insists that (re)enchantment is not itself an unqualified good. Pynchon dramatizes Taylor's contention that what distinguishes our current "secular" age is not the absence of religion but the proliferation of religious expression. Furthermore, he's clear that religious practices shape one indelibly, for good or for ill.

Pynchon's work conveys the notion that the self's relation to the transcendent entails a form of pluralism that recognizes the subjective character of reality and spirituality. His fiction portrays alternate worlds existing alongside and impinging upon our own, as well as miraculous events and divine interventions. His characters observe a host of spiritual practices, from Christianity to Buddhism to Native American religions to Bogomilism. As Dupré defines it, "transcendence is not merely what lies beyond the world, but first and foremost what supports its givenness" (*Passage* 251). Pynchon's approach to transcendence is to affirm a form of spirituality that is not syncretic but hybrid. Syncretism "attempt[s] to fuse divergent spiritual and religious practices into a unified whole," while hybridity "emphasizes differing traditions and practices coexisting in the same world as aspects of the multiple subjectivities" (Delgadillo, "Forms" 890). But the spiritual disciplines presented in Pynchon's work are not all equal or synonymous, nor do they shape characters' lives in the same ways.

Theologian S. Mark Heim's approach to religious pluralism offers, to my mind, the most illuminating approach to examining religion in Pynchon's work. Heim enjoins us to acknowledge that all religious paths lead to certain desired ends and that those ends are not identical (6–7). In Pynchon's fiction, various religious practices develop individuals in different ways, not all of them positive. Pynchon acknowledges something like what Heim maintains: While there is of course overlap, religions are not just different expressions of the same truth, nor do they simply see the same world in different ways; different religions may assume disparate realities, resulting in *essentially* different value systems. In other words, salvation or spiritual fulfillment have content only in the context of a specific religion. For example, Nirvana is reached only via the Buddhist path to Enlightenment, not by Christian faith, for Nirvana is a different thing from Christian salvation.[7] This is not to say, however, that religions must remain static or that there's no commonality or grounds for peaceable interfaith dialogue. In *The Depth of the Riches,* whose title is taken from Romans 11:33, Heim highlights the various "riches" that result from the plurality of beliefs and practices. Heim stresses that every religious tradition has something to learn from every other. His view departs from pluralists who affirm the basic uniformity of all religions, focusing instead on the very real differences. In short, Heim contends that all religious systems have distinctive ends and practices, but each tradition may be made more robust and its practitioners spiritually richer by learning from others. I propose that Pynchon's work suggests a similar view, affirming especially that Westerners have much to learn from Eastern traditions. If Pynchon finds anything worthy of his contempt, it's the Enlightenment notion of progress, and the assumption that eradicating religion is a logical imperative of human advancement.[8]

Pynchon's religious characters come in all shapes and sizes: villains, heroes, tramps, humanoids, housewives. Their religious practices may lack any supernatural or divine element yet pursue transcendence in some way; quaternionists (mathematicians who study quaternions) and anarchists are depicted as religious, while there are "Christer" villains. In short, *religious* is unequivocally neither a positive nor negative category. Rather, in Pynchon's fiction, spiritual disciplines and formative systems of belief shape characters in different ways, and the spiritual *ends*—the various visions of salvation and

---

7. Here, I use the term *salvation* in its Christian context, linked to the Kingdom of God of which Christ spoke. In the remainder of this chapter, I typically use the term *salvation* according to Pynchon's broader usage to mean deliverance or preservation, or transition to a higher plane of existence. Various religions may offer salvation in this latter sense.

8. Many critics agree that Pynchon targets Enlightenment rationalism with its notion of progress as a hubristic claim to mastery. Pynchon depicts this Enlightenment mentality as a driving force of American history. Donald J. Greiner argues that Pynchon offers an ironic version of the American Adam, excoriating the Enlightenment drive for mastery embodied in Manifest Destiny (78–79). Joseph Dewey finds that Pynchon links Enlightenment philosophy with a certain "muscular" brand of Christianity that Pynchon takes to task in *Mason & Dixon* ("Sound" 113). Jeff Baker, analyzing the actions of engineer Franz Pökler in *Gravity's Rainbow,* writes that they "reveal that the 'problem' with such abstracting, idealizing systems is not only that they are unable to subsume the entire range of living experience, but that they also directly affect and shape the human beings who employ such systems in order to manipulate and control their world" (181). Other critics who take this view include Cowart, *Pynchon* 138–48 and Saltzman 64–65.

ways characters develop morally—are imbued with authorial opprobrium or approbation.

Pynchon does not affirm any religious tradition above all others. (Nor does he offer an *orthodox* picture of any tradition.) However, he offers us glimpses into religious practices that may offer viable alternatives to a religion of American exceptionalism, and the habits and values engendered through these practices are clear enough. The religious hybridity that Pynchon sanctions allows individuals to draw upon and integrate multiple ways of knowing the world. Such hybridity is not a capricious spiritual hodgepodge but serves a clear purpose: to challenge Western, Enlightenment-based notions of history and progress. The common denominator of these spiritual disciplines (the ones that escape irony or criticism), is that in their unique ways they offer alternatives (or at least correctives) to Western religious traditions. As Joseph Dewey has argued, Pynchon traces American imperialism and exceptionalism to certain Christian teleological and eschatological expectations ("Sound" 120-21). Pynchon supports spiritual hybridity as a countermeasure to such iniquities. Dewey has suggested that Pynchon seeks to temper "muscular" Christianity with elements of Eastern wisdom, but Pynchon presents other spiritual disciplines as well.

McClure contends that spiritual conversions in Pynchon's novels lead, if not to salvation, then at least to better questions: "Pynchon . . . suggests that even the most whimsical and aestheticized turning can produce unintended effects, when those who turn encounter, within the orbit of spirituality, not childhood's soothing stories but the complex and yet profound articulation of adult questions and intuitions" (*Partial* 62). These conversions do lead to profound questions, but not all conversions lead to the same questions. (And not all Pynchon's religious characters undergo conversion within the text.) To glimpse what spiritual fulfillment looks like for Pynchon, it's important to consider what these "adult questions" are and what the answers, however provisional, might be.

Having considered Pynchon's depiction of American exceptionalism, I proceed to a few of the more prevalent and developed spiritual disciplines, focusing on how these disciplines affect characters' moral and spiritual lives as well as their political and social views.[9] I aim to demonstrate that Pynchon depicts certain spiritual disciplines as necessary for achieving (1) an aware-

---

9. Amy Elias, Kathryn Hume, and Christopher Coffman have written excellent essays focusing on religious or spiritual elements in *Against the Day*. McClure's work looks briefly at *Gravity's Rainbow* and *Vineland*. My argument not only extends their work but also looks at Pynchon's other texts in order to give a more comprehensive picture of Pynchon's religious vision.

ness of the oppressive nature of ideology and totalizing systems, (2) a greater capacity for constructive political action, and (3) a more peaceable and intentional mode of life in community with others and in harmony with the natural world. Religion is redemptive, for Pynchon, insofar as it leads toward these ends. Kathryn Hume is right that religion functions as a resistance politics for Pynchon (182), but religion is not reducible to politics: Such a view would be utter hypocrisy to Pynchon, who shows clearly how susceptible religion is to co-optation. Where religion functions as a politics of resistance, it is the result of fundamental ontological questions.

"A Productive Sort of Delirium": Penance

The discipline of penance is prevalent in *Against the Day*.[10] Near the beginning of the novel, Lew Basnight suddenly finds himself scorned by everyone he knows for sins he has no recollection of committing. He is turned out by his wife and fired from his job. Lew's rejection by Chicago society proves salutary, however, as his emotional turmoil induces a "waking swoon" through which he inhabits an alternate Chicago. Stumbling through this oneiric state, Lew encounters a band of "adepts" to whom he confesses the need to atone for his alleged sins in order to regain his life. Lew's understanding of penance is radically altered as the adepts' leader, Drave, tells him, "Remorse without an object is a doorway to deliverance" (*ATD* 39). Lew then enters an outlandish novitiate, an experience he later refers to as being "disciplined in the ways of the East" (*ATD* 48). Like a Buddhist novice, he is asked to perform impossible tasks, then "struck . . . repeatedly with a 'remembrance stick'" upon failing (*ATD* 40). Drave denies "a mathematical correlation between sin, penance, and redemption," telling Lew, "There is no connection. . . . You are redeemed not through doing penance but because it happens. Or doesn't happen" (*ATD* 41). Penance, per Drave, is a discipline, not a measured response to transgression. As a Catholic sacrament, penance includes the act of confession and often the performance of duties demonstrative of one's inner attitude—and Lew's "novitiate" includes these elements—but Drave's instruction introduces a Buddhist element. This becomes clearer later on, as Lew thinks,

---

10. Hume interprets the prevalence of penance, along with references to pilgrimage and grace, as signaling Pynchon's most cogent and most Christian (specifically Catholic) religious vision (171). I agree with Cowart that Hume's case is perhaps overstated and that penance is sometimes more Buddhist than Christian, but Hume is right to point to penance as a major motif. (Hume does acknowledge the presence of other religious traditions in the novel.)

Could be all those Catholics he'd run into in this line of work . . . had it right all along, and there was nothing in the day's echoing cycle but penance, even if you'd never committed a sin, to live in the world was to do penance—actually, as his teacher Drave had pointed out back during that winter in Chicago, another argument for reincarnation—"Being unable to remember sins from a previous life won't excuse you from doing penance in this one. To believe in the reality of penance is almost to have proof of rebirth." (*ATD* 689)

In other words, rather than a guilt-ridden life of anxiety, a life of penance is a life of faith; penance in this framework is an affirmation of the openness of the future, a prophetic reclamation of possibility.

Lew's novitiate changes him profoundly. First, as a continuous and meritless discipline, penance endows him with a sense of moral topography, an understanding of the world's fallen nature and the systemic nature of its problems. There are no innocents in Pynchon's world. Even his moral and political heroes—like the Counterforce and other revolutionary groups—are ineluctably constrained to compromise somehow. Second, Lew's penitence leads to greater apprehension of his own life and destiny. Drave calls Lew's disciplinary period a "productive sort of delirium." Delirium—which, as Drave explains, "literally means going out of a furrow you've been plowing"—attains a positive valence in Pynchon's work. It allows one to transcend the snarl of furrows and track their trajectories. The metaphor of furrow-plowing is linked back to a mathematical correlation between penance and redemption. Unlike the huddled masses, who plow on, "dutiful and dumb as oxen," Lew learns "to step to the side of the day," a predictably valuable quality in a novel titled *Against the Day* (41, 44). By stepping aside the day, Lew discerns his own trajectory as paralleling that of the cattle in Chicago's stockyards, and this prompts a consideration of what he needs to change. Lew achieves a satori-like state "which he later came to think of as grace," in which he "found himself surrounded by a luminosity new to him" and "understood that things were exactly what they were . . . [which] seemed more than he could bear" (*ATD* 42). Lew becomes keenly mindful of the miraculous complexion of mundane life, astounded that, "despite the sorry history of . . . this city, the corporate neglect . . . the weekday-morning overture blared along as usual" (*ATD* 42). Lew, "transfigured and all," has become acutely aware of the smallest details of the world around him, a faculty that leads him into detective work and later enables him to perceive the morally compromising nature of his work for the US government and transfer his sympathies to the strikers and anarchists.

"Relaxing into Fate": Renunciation

In Lew Basnight we glimpse a precept normative for all Pynchon's pilgrims: Authentic enlightenment is accompanied by deeper immersion into everyday life. Yet the practice of renunciation, or vanquishing of desire, remains an important discipline in Pynchon's moral vision. For his characters, achieving a fulfilling relation to the transcendent often demands some form of extramundane sight. I don't mean Pynchon espouses a Gnosticism that subordinates the material to the spiritual; rather, he affirms the capacity to recognize supernatural or spiritual forces active in the world. Renunciation, as Pynchon presents it, serves the greater good as well as the individual. While many traditions endorse the discipline of renunciation, the practice as Pynchon depicts it is most integral to Tibetan Buddhism, where it's coupled with compassion.

Pynchon generally renders Buddhism positively and unironically, which is unsurprising given his averred affinity for the Beats and all things countercultural.[11] Scholars have mostly been content to identify Pynchon's Buddhist references and themes without further considering how these elements shape Pynchon's characters.[12] Buddhism, Hume points out, is quite suited to the ambiguities of postmodernism and thus suitable to Pynchon's moral vision (182). I would add that Pynchon sees (rightly or wrongly) in the Eastern world view a spirituality that, being less eschatological, is not as easily co-opted by power-hungry forces. Pynchon nominates the Buddhist, and more generally Eastern, mind-set as a counterbalance to Christianity and Islam. In *Against the Day* alone, several characters explicitly reference the way some religions (namely, Christianity, Islam, and vaguely Gnostic occult sects) have historically tended to become aligned with those in power.[13]

Renunciation takes several forms in Pynchon's work, one being the abnegation of personal vendettas or revenge. This practice is called Christian forbearance by "Christian anarchist" Reverend Moss Gatlin. During the mining strikes preceding the Colorado Coalfield Wars, Gatlin exhorts strikers to spare

---

11. For a compelling treatment of Pynchon and the Beats, see Freer.

12. Exceptions include Kohn's analysis of Buddhist themes in *The Crying of Lot 49* and McClure's observation that in *Vineland*, DL Chastain melds tenets of Buddhism with martial arts. Relatedly, Dewey illuminates how *Mason & Dixon* draws from the broader Eastern intellectual tradition to temper strains of "muscular Christianity." See Kohn 74; McClure, *Partial* 51–55; and Dewey, "Sound" 113–17.

13. Positive depictions of Christianity and Islam elsewhere suggest that Pynchon aims to temper imperialist tendencies exhibited in eschatological religions, rather than reject them outright. Pynchon doesn't seem to endorse the (generally fallacious) line of thought that rejects a religion simply because its organized form has been co-opted. As evidence, Dwight Prance, one character who gives voice to this line of thinking, offers it as a defense for his own employment by the powerbrokers of Britain's Whitehall Lane.

the "scabs" (strikebreakers), "if by [forbearance] we may thus further the dumb scab's education" (*ATD* 1009). The reverend's "Christian forbearance" exhibits a Buddhist slant, being rooted in a conviction of cosmic balance that resembles the notion of karma: "It is a law universal as the law of Gravity and as unforgiving that today's scab is tomorrow's striker. Nothin mystical. Just what happens" (*ATD* 467). Pynchon doesn't disdain violence categorically—anarchists may resort to it—but it must further a greater end than personal vengeance. Violence that is personal—motivated by honor, revenge, or vendetta—exacts the heavy toll of reducing the perpetrator to an object for consumption. When, later in *Against the Day,* the Chums of Chance prevent Heino Vanderjuice from assassinating (with compelling cause) a heartless robber baron, they save his life from becoming a "cheaply-sold and dishonored thing" (1079). Had Heino carried out the killing, his life would have been reduced to a contract handed on to some other killer. Frank and Kit Traverse evince the same life-depleting effect of violence after they resolve to avenge their father's murder. The debt of vengeance utterly dictates the trajectory of their lives, until each comes to his own renunciation of violence.

Cyprian Latewood embodies another form of renunciation: the transcendence or sublimation of sexual desire. Hume considers Cyprian "the most fully developed religious character in any of Pynchon's novels" (179–80). While she's probably correct, we shouldn't be quick to assume that he is Pynchon's ideal. We first encounter Cyprian as a campus "sod" at Cambridge, where he's embraced a life of decadence and "unreflective obedience, day into night, to the leash-pulls of desire" (*ATD* 699). Cyprian revels in sadomasochistic submission; rejection and scorn excite him. Yet he proves himself a sod with a soul, revealing a sensitive, searching spiritual side: "Most who met him found it difficult to reconcile his appetite for sexual abasement—its specific carnality—with what had to be termed a religious surrender of the self" (*ATD* 877). Cyprian's spiritual hunger outstrips his skepticism:

> Cyprian, while rejecting his family's High Church faith, strangely had begun . . . to glimpse that, precisely because of its impossibilities, the disarray of self-important careerists and hierarchy-obsessed functionaries, the yawning and fidgeting town-lad choristers and narcotic sermonizing—it was possible to hope, not so much despite as paradoxically because of this very snarled web of human flaw, for the emergence of the incommensurable mystery, the dense, unknowable Christ, bearing the secret of how once on a hilltop that was not Zion, he had conquered death. Cyprian stood in the evenings, at the Compline hour, just outside the light cast from the chapel windows, and wondered what was happening to his skepticism. (*ATD* 497–98)

Hume's gloss, that Cyprian has "found Christ through the very ordinariness of the people at a Church of England service" (180), is too simplistic. Rather, this is the first instance of the negative theology that Cyprian later develops more fully: Cyprian finds *not*-Christ and embarks on a spiritual journey, far from the ordinary people, seeking the "unknowable Christ."

Cyprian's initially psychosexual enjoyment of self-abasement is eventually sublimated into humble religious obedience, culminating with his entrance into a convent. Cyprian's spiritual quest is interrupted, however, as "the Crown," exploiting his submissive nature and acquaintance with the more disreputable urban quarters, conscripts him to foreign service. His service to the Crown is largely involuntary, rather like the prostitution he has at times resorted to. But while shuttled among various continental locales, he begins to transmute his desire "to lose oneself" and "surrender . . . the ego" from a physical to a communal desire (*ATD* 708). In Vienna, he seeks out not the seamy quarters of the city but the working-class grids, moving among the workers "not so much seeking exotic flirtation as to be absorbed somehow into a mobility, a bath of language he did not speak, as he had once sought in carnal submission an escape route from what it seemed of the world he was being asked to bear" (*ATD* 715).

Yashmeen Halfcourt, a fellow Cambridge student, first recognizes Cyprian's capacity for self-surrender as "religious" rather than masochistic. The pair take solace in discovering in each other one who seeks to transcend "a world every day more stultified, which expected salvation in codes and governments, ever more willing to settle for suburban narratives and diminished payoffs" (*ATD* 877). Galvanized by Yashmeen's estimation of him, Cyprian refuses to countenance any longer his physical and emotional abuse by his monomaniacal superior officer. It is at this point that Cyprian commences cultivating a set of spiritual practices. Cyprian discovers "a perverse fascination in Patience, not so much as a virtue but more as a hobby requiring discipline, like chess or mountain-climbing" (*ATD* 813). This discipline of patience reflects a new approach to surrendering his ego, transforming Cyprian's treatment of others and mitigating his proclivity for sarcastic retort.

During a "fool's errand" mission, assigned by a malicious superior officer bent on his demise, Cyprian experiences an epiphany, a subjunctive glimpse of life in a truly indifferent universe:

> When he tripped and fell, Cyprian for the first time was delivered into an embrace that did not desire him, as he became only another part of the mechanical realm, the ensouled body he had believed in until now suddenly of far less account than mass and velocity and cold gravity, here before him, after him, despite him. As the storm roared all around, he slowly struggled

... to his feet. Danilo had vanished.... He stood in rain just at the edge of sleet and considered praying. (*ATD* 837)

This exposure to a cosmic void is Cyprian's dark moment of the soul. The desire to pray is not uncommon in moments of peril, but subsequent events show this experience to have a lasting legacy. This brief sense of mechanical emptiness compels Cyprian to greater investment in others and in his daily tasks. The practice of compassion, especially, acquires a new priority. Cyprian finds his vanished partner Danilo, whose leg is broken, and undergoes a spiritual transformation while caring for him. As Danilo's stand-in "mother," Cyprian is "surprised to find emerging in his character previously unsuspected gifts, notably one for soup, as well as an often-absurd willingness to sacrifice all comfort until he was satisfied that Danilo would be safe for another spell, however brief" (*ATD* 839). Cyprian realizes that "questions of [sexual] desire" have never arisen during this period and experiences great joy at his "first encounter with release from desire":

> He was ... tending to Danilo's sleep, as if he must be prepared in an instant to intervene if needed, to walk the other man's painscapes of dream or delirium.... [H]e found that for some undefined time now he had not even been imagining desire, its arousal, its fulfillment, any occasion for it. The imbalance he was used to experiencing as a numb space in the sensorium of the day, as if time were provided with sexual nerves, a patch of which had been waiting unaddressed, was, somewhat mysteriously, no longer there—it was occupied by something else, a clarity, a general freshening of temperature. (*ATD* 839)

The willingness "to walk the other man's painscapes" is the very essence of compassion, and Cyprian's compassion yields further advancements. He achieves unprecedented clarity and wholeness, no longer being subject to vertiginous sexual longing. Though temporary, this enlightened state becomes his benchmark: "He found himself always unexpectedly trying to locate it again, as if it were something at least as desirable as desire" (*ATD* 840). With continued practice, Cyprian finds he can recapture this lucidity. His spiritual transformation also magnifies his appreciation of communal life. When Danilo is reunited with his family after years of exile, Cyprian shares in his joy, whereas "once, in another life, Cyprian would have replied in his most withering tones, 'Of course, charmed I'm sure'" (*ATD* 842).

Cyprian's disciplined detachment not only augments his capacity for love. He is also no longer concerned with self-preservation, especially if it demands moral compromise, which has political ramifications. Now unafraid of reprisal, he refuses any further orders from his despotic boss, Derrick Theign, effectively demitting his role as a stooge of British intelligence. Cyprian further manifests his detachment by electing not to be present at Theign's demise. Name notwithstanding, Theign is no loyal soldier; he's a tyrant, and his maltreatment of numerous parties provokes what Pynchon would call karmic retribution. Cyprian provides information crucial to Theign's undoing, but he's motivated by justice for the aggrieved rather than vengeance and refuses to participate directly in the killing. Cyprian's choice to defy Theign and abdicate his military duties galvanizes other servants of Whitehall Lane. Later on, Ratty McHugh, now emitting "the radiance of an awakened spirit," tells Cyprian, "The way you dealt with Theign was an inspiration to so many of us—sudden personnel vacuums all over Whitehall, amounting in some shops to mass desertion" (*ATD* 932). Cyprian's example empowered Ratty to abandon his Whitehall desk and become an anarchist activist.

Cyprian's detachment transforms rather than curtails his political engagement, which is now dictated by his moral compass rather than government orders. After the narrowest of escapes from death while on assignment in the Balkans, Cyprian had vowed never to return. He registers his own spiritual progress when he discovers himself willing to return in order to destroy a poison gas pipeline. Performing a risk-reward analysis, Cyprian considers the sparkling trio of money, sex, and fame and is "puzzled to find there was nothing the world could plausibly offer that he wanted enough" (*ATD* 939). The single sufficient inducement is the preservation of innocent human lives, especially those of Yashmeen and her unborn child. Cyprian no longer considers his life his own. By "relaxing into fate" and abandoning his frantic quest for pleasure, Cyprian paradoxically experiences much greater fulfillment. One example is the joy and karmic connection he experiences when he first holds Ljubica, Yashmeen's newborn daughter. Cradling the child, Cyprian feels a wash of "familiarity, as if this had already happened countless times before," which prompts him to confess to Yashmeen, "I knew her once—previously—perhaps in that other life it was she who took care of me—and now here is the balance being restored" (*ATD* 950). Cyprian's view of individual identity and purpose has radically altered: "Once he would have been reckoning up, anxiously, how much remained to him of youth, looks, desirability, and whether it would get him at least to the next station of the pilgrimage, but that—he knew now, knew as if with some inner certitude—was no longer quite the point, and in any case would take care of itself" (*ATD* 939-40). Pynchon suggests here that progress—in the Western sense—is never the *point* of pilgrimage.

Cyprian's spiritual journey culminates with admission into a Bogomil convent, which he discovers adventitiously as he, Yashmeen, and Frank are making their way out of the Balkans. Upon learning about the convent, Cyprian immediately discerns it is a place where he may finally be at home. He tells Yashmeen, "They are taking me in as exactly the person I am. . . . No more of these tiresome gender questions" (*ATD* 958). Cyprian enters the convent as a "Bride of Night," adopting a performative female identity. He explains to Yashmeen,

> They have adapted the σχῆμα . . . the Orthodox initiation rite, to their own much older beliefs. In the Orphic story of the world's beginning, Night preceded the creation of the Universe, she was the daughter of Chaos, the Greeks called her Νυξ, and the old Thracians worshipped her as a deity. For a postulant in this order, Night is one's betrothed, one's beloved, one seeks to become not a bride at all really, but a kind of sacrifice, an offering, to Night. (*ATD* 959)

The order's religion has a strongly Manichaean aspect, affirming "the unyielding doubleness of everything": "Part of the discipline for a postulant was to remain acutely conscious, at every moment of the day, of the nearly unbearable conditions of cosmic struggle between darkness and light proceeding, inescapably, behind the presented world" (*ATD* 956–57). Hume posits that Cyprian's discipline of remaining conscious of such doubleness resembles Pynchon's own attitude. Acknowledging that this "sounds more Manichaean than Catholic," Hume suggests that if we "read 'dark' as forces of oppression, especially capitalist forces," then Cyprian's attitude parallels Pynchon's own (180). Yet the "night" to which Cyprian betroths himself isn't a force of evil but the notion of creative potentiality. Such is evident in the account of the "second sight" with which Cyprian observes the carved saints in the convent chapel: "Gazing into it as if into a cinema screen where pictures moved and stories unfolded which he must attend to. Shadowless faces of Zalmoxis and the saints. And depending on a kind of second sight, a knowledge beyond light of what lay within the wood itself, of what it was one's duty to set free" (*ATD* 957). A strong current of negative theology suffuses the practice of this sect. Cyprian's dedication to night is a testament to the incompletion of the "presented world" and a hopeful expectation of what may yet come to be.[14]

14. As a form of negative theology, this notion surfaces earlier when Cyprian enters the remote Anarchist spa of Yz-les-Bains. Key descriptions announce the function of this spontaneous commune. The entrance is marked by "late-ripening vines . . . that looked like garlanded crucifixes" (*ATD* 931). This description highlights the nobility of sacrifice and evokes the notion that sacrificial death, even martyrdom, may be necessary for salvation (however defined). Andrea Tancredi's death earlier exemplifies such a sacrifice (742). Another passage details a choir practicing in Yz-les-Bains's elliptical town plaza. The choir stands "near one of

In the end, it's unclear whether Cyprian's is a martyrdom that Pynchon affirms. In his zeal, Cyprian appears to adopt a new naïveté regarding the world outside the convent. When Yashmeen admonishes him to reconsider taking vows because the convent lies directly in the path of a coming war, Cyprian—who will supposedly be reflecting continuously on the struggle between light and dark—blithely denies that any war will come to pass. Though the merit of Cyprian's final decision remains unclear, the salutary effects of his renunciant path have already manifested manifoldly.

"Love in Action": Attunement

Pynchon's work includes a strong environmentalist facet: He portrays the earth as a sentient being that demands respect and nurture from humans. (Pynchon's earth is also vindictive and quite capable of wreaking havoc on abusive or neglectful human populations.) American exceptionalism has often underwritten a view of the natural world in which the land exists to indulge human desires, a relation of domination rather than mutual respect. Pynchon depicts a number of characters heedlessly pillaging the land: coal mining in *Against the Day,* deforestation in *Vineland,* and the proliferation of landfills due to unbridled consumption in *Bleeding Edge.* Pynchon implies not only that a harmonious relation to the environment is paramount for human flourishing, but also that this relation to the environment is inextricably connected to one's relation to the transcendent. For Pynchon, respect for the natural world is rooted in the acknowledgment of spiritual forces at work.

Pynchon introduces into his work non-Western practices that engender attunement. Adopting novelist C. E. Morgan's definition, I'm defining attunement as "love in action" (19). Attunement entails a degree of intimacy such that one apprehends another's nature and desires, even perceiving that other's history and future. Pynchon establishes human history as inseparable from the natural world. Attunement thus occurs at the intersection of the natural, the spiritual, and the human.

One practice that engenders attunement is the application of feng shui, a nontheistic philosophy (though not inherently incompatible with theism). Some might balk at the inclusion of feng shui among religious practices, per-

---

the foci of the ellipse . . . practicing a sort of counter-Te Deum, more desperamus than laudamus, brining news of coming dark and cold" (931). Figuratively, the fact that they do not stand in the center suggests the possibility of a balancing voice emanating from the other focus—a Te Deum—but this voice is absent. The result is a very apparent absence, the perception of which ideally prompts critical reflection as well as lament.

haps having seen the term in an ad for a trendy furniture store. But by Pynchon's robust account, feng shui fits my established definition for religion in that its aim is harmony with the Tao. This discipline is exemplified by Dr. (or Captain) Zhang in *Mason & Dixon*. Zhang, a Chinese exile and astronomer of sorts, has made his way to the "new continent," where he plies his trade of "*Feng-Shui* jobs." Zhang consults in the construction of new buildings, using his *Luo-pan* (a kind of compass) to help design structures that harmonize with the energies at play in the natural world.

Zhang's feng shui sensibilities impel him to criticize the "Visto" that Mason and Dixon's party is clearing in order to carve out their famous Line. Upon seeing their work, Zhang interjects, "Terrible *Feng-Shui* here. Worst I ever saw. You two crazy?" (*MD* 542). Their ensuing conversation reveals Zhang's feng shui–inspired objections to hewing a line across the land for the sake of boundary drawing:

> "[The Visto] acts as a Conduit for what we call *Sha*, or, as they say in Spanish California, Bad Energy.—Imagine a Wind, a truly ill wind, bringing failure, poverty, disgrace, betrayal,—every kind of bad luck there is,—all blowing through, night and day, with many times the force of the worst storm you were ever in."
>
> "No one intends to live directly upon the Visto," Mason speaking as to a Child. "The object being, that the people shall set their homes to one side or another. That it be a Boundary, nothing more."
>
> "Boundary!" The Chinaman begins to pull upon his hair and paw the earth with brocade-slipper'd feet. "Ev'rywhere else on earth, Boundaries follow Nature,—coast-lines, ridge-tops, river-banks,—so honoring the Dragon or *Shan* within, from which Land-Scape ever takes its form. To mark a right Line upon the Earth is to inflict upon the Dragon's very Flesh, a sword-slash, a long, perfect scar, impossible for any who live out here the year 'round to see other than as hateful Assault. How can it pass unanswer'd?" (*MD* 542)

Zhang's feng shui subordinates human aspirations to cooperation and supplies a standard for judging the merits and purpose of technology. Practitioners value harmony with the earth and with one another. Artificially imposed boundaries, while often necessary, ineluctably separate individuals and may engender conflict-provoking possessiveness. Zhang refers to the Line as a "Tellurick Injury" that is his destiny to resist, which brings him into further conflict with his longtime enemy, the Jesuit priest Zarpazo.

The nature of Zarpazo's hostility further elucidates Zhang's priorities, which derive from the Chinese understanding of yin and yang and cosmic balance. Zarpazo opposes the "abhorrent Magick" of feng shui because it makes the Chinese people unreceptive to Jesuit proselytization:

> Why prevent the Chinese from practicing *Feng Shui?* Because it works. . . . It carries the mark of the Adversary,—It is too easy. Not earn'd. Too little of the Load is borne by the Practitioner, too much by some Force Invisible, and the unknown Price it must exact. What do you imagine those to be, that must ever remain so unreferr'd, and unreferrable, to Jesus Christ? And, as His Soldiers, how can we ever permit that? (*MD* 523–24)

But Zarpazo's hunger for ordered control far supersedes any evangelistic impulse. He would sustain religion through coercion. A devotee of radical "ortholatry" (worship of right lines and angles), Zarpazo believes an "ortholatrical" approach is necessary in this confounding new world where "Sects [are] nearly as numerous as Settlers" and the gravity of heresy is lost on them:

> The Model . . . is Imprisonment. Walls are to be the Future. Unlike those of the antichrist Chinese, these will follow right Lines. The World grows restless,—Faith is no longer willingly bestow'd upon Authority, either religious or secular. What Pity. If we may not have Love, we will accept Consent,—if we may not obtain Consent, we will build Walls. As a Wall, projected upon the Earth's Surface, becomes a right Line, so shall we find that we may shape, with arrangements of such Lines, all we may need. (*MD* 522)

Boundaries are the surest way to secure order. In contrast, Zhang believes the earth is a "living Creature" and that violating its natural contours, showing "indifference to the true inner shape, or Dragon, of the Land" by imposing artificial lines, invites the dragon's wrath (*MD* 601–2).

The broader thrust of the feng shui philosophy is a correspondence between the external, natural world and the internal, spiritual world. Zhang pronounces that any injury to the land precipitates bad blood among people. His concern proves well founded as the ruinous effects of drawing the Line begin to accumulate. The Line interferes with long-standing travel routes of Native American tribes, particularly their Warpath, inviting their retribution and inflaming intertribal hostilities. The novel suggests that the concept of boundary marking and mapping, implicated as it is in property ownership, perverted traditional Indian views regarding land possession. The Line also sunders communities and even families, arbitrarily creating insiders and outsiders. Zhang predicts it will eventually result in civil war. Explaining that "*Sha* takes time to accumulate and accelerate," Zhang affirms Zarpazo's conviction that lines and divisions are key to ruling over others, while insisting also that such division creates strife that suppurates and explodes:

> "To rule forever," continues [Zhang], later, "it is necessary only to create, among the people one would rule, what we call . . . Bad History. Nothing will produce Bad History more directly nor brutally, than drawing a Line, in particular a Right Line, the very Shape of Contempt, through the midst of a People,—to create thus a Distinction betwixt 'em,—'tis the first stroke.—All else will follow as if predestin'd, unto War and Devastation." (*MD* 615)

The Mason and Dixon Line did, of course, contribute to "Bad History." Zhang also foreshadows the development of the American West, warning that carving up the land by lines and angles will make of it "A Prison" and that "Settlers [will be] moving West into instant Control" (*MD* 617). Zhang finally convinces Mason and Dixon, who initially dismiss him as insane, that the Line forms "a conduit for Evil" and threatens to vitiate the character of the incipient republic. The pair of surveyors consider for the first time the Line's probable application and beneficiaries. Dixon concludes that "something invisible's going on. . . . We're being us'd again" for the sake of "American Politics" (*MD* 478–79). Ultimately, Pynchon links mapping to Manifest Destiny, a doctrine rooted in American exceptionalism and marked by the willingness to kill and steal in the name of a transcendent destiny.

Zhang incites the surveyors to question not only the true nature of their task but the very nature of science. The pair slowly recognize that scientific methods may serve good or ill and that science uncoupled from teleology is open to exploitation. Assessing his own culpability, Dixon concludes that "Men of Science . . . may be but the simple Tools of others, with no more idea of what they are about, than a Hammer knows of a House," and that it thus matters immensely for whom the man of science is working (*MD* 669). A scientist cannot refuse culpability when his work is employed for evil.

Feng shui is not the only discipline that engenders an attunement with the land. In *Against the Day*, Frank Traverse "save[s] his soul" through "Native magic" (927–28).[15] A Tarahumare *brujo* (shaman) instructs Frank in the shamanistic practice of mystical journeying, which enlarges Frank's consciousness of the natural world and of human history. Frank's spiritual development begins in the Mexican desert, after he meets a trio of Tarahumare Indians who credit Frank with saving their lives. The *brujo*, El Espinero, divines that Frank is in Mexico hunting his father's killers. He tells Frank, "You have fallen into

---

15. For a thorough treatment of the novel's ecological ethics, see Coffman.

the habit of seeing dead things better than live ones. *Shabótshi* all do. You need practice in seeing" (*ATD* 392). As "practice," El Espinero gives Frank *hikuli* (peyote) to remedy his myopia. Frank, "taken out of himself, not just out of his body . . . but out of whatever else he thought he was, out of his mind, his country and family, out of his soul," finds himself flying, led by a Tarahumare guide through a series of underground caves until they reach one where it is continuously raining (*ATD* 392). Frank's guide then relates a myth, both creation story and moral parable, that imputes the existence of the desert to the original sin, greed. The cave rainfall is water that should be nourishing the desert land. This vision implants in Frank's mind a connection between natural resources, human greed, and devastation and suffering. Here, the devastation is manifested in the land, but Frank will see how greed shapes human history, too.

After his first "trip," Frank finally succeeds in tracking down and killing one of his father's murderers, which proves utterly ungratifying. Rather than justice, Frank feels, "something like a cloak of despair was settling down over his soul, useful, like a duster out on the trail" (*ATD* 471). Only gradually does Frank "understand how much harder and less inclined to mercy it was making him" (*ATD* 471), but he begins finally to grasp El Espinero's admonition about seeing the dead better than the living: The obsession with vengeance is blighting his capacity for fellowship.

When Frank embarks on his second mystical journey, he is again in Mexico, near Casas Grandes, the ruins of an Indian settlement that was suddenly abandoned in the fifteenth century. Frank enters a dreamscape where he witnesses mundane life in an ancient Aztec city, then beholds the hurried flight of the Aztecs at the onset of Spanish occupation. Frank then glimpses an alternate Tenochtitlán, one that would perhaps have existed had Cortez not invaded. During his vision, Frank briefly possesses a stereoscopic form of sight, simultaneously seeing history and alternative, subjunctive history, what was and what could have been. The result is a clear impression of the magnitude of life that was dashed by Spanish conquest. The import of Frank's mystical journey is clarified shortly after, when he visits Casas Grandes:

> The site still bore the signs of abrupt departure. . . . Seeing the spectacle of mud dilapidation, sliding toward abandonment since long before the first Spaniards showed up, Frank understood immediately that this was where the *hikuli* had taken him the other night, what El Espinero had wanted him to see—what, in his morose and case-hardened immunity to anything extraliteral, he had to begin to see, and remember he saw, if he was to have even an outside chance of saving his soul. (*ATD* 928)

Frank has an epiphany, at last catching on that El Espinero is leading him to develop the diachronic breadth of vision to see the history and the future of a place. To "save his soul," Frank must attain the capacity to envision alternate histories and discern the consequences of human greed and predation. While Frank's initial journeys are enabled by *hikuli*, the point was to learn to see the world differently, which he is now adept at doing without hallucinogenic aid. Beholding the ruins of Casas Grandes, he reconsiders American history filtered through the scene before him:

> He understood for a moment . . . that the history of all this terrible continent . . . was this same history of exile and migration, the white man moving in on the Indian, the eastern corporations moving in on the white man, and their incursions with drills and dynamite into the deep seams of the sacred mountains, the sacred land. (*ATD* 928–29)

The son of a Colorado miner, Frank sees mining afresh, as the depredation of both land and labor force by company execs interested solely in profit margins. Frank the assassin becomes Frank the revolutionary.

Arriving back in Colorado, Frank learns the mine workers' union has been on strike for months, resulting in the eviction of families from company housing and the formation of tent colonies. Martial law has been declared and violent skirmishes have broken out. Operating at the behest of corporate interests, government forces are preparing to raze the tent colonies where Frank's friends are living. Again, the legacy of conquest contextualizes Frank's reading of the situation. He perceives that greed is the inciting force in the declaration of martial law and the impending slaughter. Without hesitation, Frank joins a relief convoy headed to the mine fields, knowing that "everything's voluntary. Nobody makes a profit or gets paid, not even credit or thank-yous" (*ATD* 997). At the coal fields, Frank risks his life to secure escape for others as the National Guard moves in with armed force to raze the tent colonies and rout anyone left.

Frank's mystical journeying has disabused him of the notion that there's honor in vengeance and illuminated for him the nexus between the earth, human greed, and human suffering. While hallucinogens are the inceptive catalyst for these journeys, they are a provisional means of recalibrating Frank's vision. The discipline in focus is the ability to gauge the world in terms of human cost, to reverse the "habit of seeing dead things better than live ones." Frank's augmented vision translates into greater compassion and increased sensitivity to the health of the land.

"The Journey Itself Is a Kind of Conscious Being": Pilgrimage

Pynchon's longest novel, *Against the Day* tracks various pilgrimages, spanning the twentieth century and the globe. These intersect in the search for Shambhala, which becomes an index for all quests spiritual, financial, and political. Shambhala is a mythical city that figures in strands of Buddhist and Hindu tradition. Today, it's typically used to refer to a Buddhist pure land, a place that's most important as a spiritual domain even if it's geographically locatable. Because Shambhala is, in Pynchon's novel, both a spiritual territory and a lost desert city, its pursuers include greedy capitalists salivating with oil interest as well as spiritual seekers. But Shambhala remains inaccessible to any with commercial or imperialist ambitions. Reaching it requires a pilgrimage of the spirit.

Like many of Pynchon's pilgrims, Kit Traverse embarks initially on a political mission, more quest than pilgrimage. Kit (Frank's brother) grew up in a coal-mining community. His father, Webb, is a miner and closet anarchist whose political convictions and disenfranchisement lead him to moonlight as a bomber. When Webb is found out and assassinated at the decree of his employer, Kit turns to intellectual pursuits as his ticket out of mining country. He heads to Yale, then Göttingen to study mathematics on the dime of a generous patron, mining magnate Scarsdale Vibe, who, Kit later learns, funded his father's murder. Kit is doubly beholden, caught between the onus of familial loyalty—vengeance for his father—and his debt to Vibe for his patronage. To escape both, Kit sets out for Inner Asia to gather intelligence for the British regarding the international race to discover Shambhala.

Kit's journey holds no apparent religious significance for him. What mystical sensibility he possesses has hitherto been directed toward advanced mathematics, in a vain attempt at "transcendence . . . to escape the world governed by real numbers" (*ATD* 675). To Kit, the journey to Inner Asia "was not for God . . . nor even any longer for the cause of Vectorism—maybe nothing more than the simple preservation through flight of his increasingly worthless ass" (*ATD* 745–46). Kit is told he is bound for the "spiritual capital of Inner Asia," but he's concerned only with escaping his debts.

During Kit's increasingly inscrutable mission, British intelligence dispatches him, along with Lieutenant Prance, to establish connections with the Tungus people in "shamanic Asia." The pair are instructed to pose as Buddhist Buriats on pilgrimage to Lake Baikal and to observe the traditional conventions. Kit realizes this journey will be unanticipatedly demanding when the Doosra (a mad, Mauser-toting desert prophet) pronounces they will require a guide: "It isn't only the difficult terrain, the vipers and sandstorms and raiding parties. The *journey itself* is a kind of conscious Being, a living deity who does not wish to engage with the foolish or the weak, and hence will try to dissuade you. It insists on the furthest degree of respect" (*ATD* 765). Kit finds himself, begrudgingly, on pilgrimage. Hume accurately observes that in Pynchon's work, "some kind of pilgrimage with its associated hardships increases the likelihood of an ordinary mortal's sensing the sacred" (175). Yet beyond that, pilgrimage inspires a radical revision of one's values and allegiances.

Underway, Kit unexpectedly experiences a spiritual awakening. The journey's first leg requires the pilgrims to proceed through the reputedly unreachable Tushuk Tash or "Prophet's Gate," an area that, significantly, cannot be represented properly by cartographers. This holy site is a reality greatly exceeding its physical dimensions: While some locals see it as a natural wonder, others believe "it [is] not a feature of the landscape but something more abstract, a religious examination, a cryptographic puzzle" (*ATD* 769). With maps useless there, only the spiritually adept can negotiate the terrain. Kit and Prance's guide Hassan retreats to pray upon learning they will have to pass through the arch, and he insists upon strict observance of the pilgrim's rites. If Pynchon stresses that the pilgrim's journey is its own destination, as Amy Elias argues, he also insists that pilgrimage is more than an objectless pursuit of mystical experience.[16] The rites and rituals are crucial to individual development, even if the pilgrim begins lacking understanding or intent.

The journey constrains Kit to expand his vision beyond the ocular. The canyons and rock formations cease to be simply products of natural forces. He notices, "Kara Tagh looked like a stone city, . . . blocks and buildings windowless as if inhabited by that which was past sight, past light, past all need for distinguishing outside from in" (*ATD* 770). Passing through the Prophet's Gate, Kit is granted a vision:

> The moment he passed through the Gate, Kit was not so much deafened as blinded by a mighty release of sound . . . bringing, like a brief interruption of darkness in the daytime, a distinct view now, in this dusk, of sunlit terrain, descending in a long gradient directly ahead to a city whose name, though at the moment denied him, was known the world over, vivid in these distances, bright yellow and orange, though soon enough it would be absorbed into the same gray confusion of exitless ravines and wind-shaped rock ascensions through which they had labored to get here. (*ATD* 770–71)

---

16. Elias proposes that *Against the Day* is best categorized generically as "postmodern pilgrimage." Drawing on Victor Turner's work, Elias argues that although the novel exhibits elements of the quest genre, *pilgrimage* better describes it because the journey itself rather than possession of a grail is the object.

Kit, "blinded," mystically glimpses Shambhala, which for him proves to be not primarily a place but a state of mind: one marked by compassion.

Kit is eventually liberated from the debts he seeks to escape. After passing through the arch, Kit has a recurrent dream, in which "the Arch has been replaced by Kit himself, a struggle he feels on waking . . . to become the bridge, the arch, the crossing-over. The last time he has the dream . . . [a] voice he knew he should recognize whispered, 'You are released'" (*ATD* 771). The voice's ambiguous familiarity grants Kit release from both nagging debts: his debt to Vibe and vengeance for his father. Absolved and no longer at odds with himself, Kit's focus is directed outward. As the pilgrims follow the Silk Road, Kit glimpses the shadow of suffering cast by ruthless commerce, including "nephrite quarries where dust-covered spectres moved chained together on their own effortful pilgrimage toward a cup of water and a few hours' sleep" (*ATD* 771). He "understand[s] that this space the Gate had opened to them was less geographic than to be measured along axes of sorrow and loss" (*ATD* 771). The destination of his pilgrimage is but nominally geographic; the real journey is toward a new consciousness. Kit realizes "that forms of life were a connected set" and that he is thus personally implicated in this "sorrow and loss" (*ATD* 782). Still in the employ of the British Crown, Kit discerns the grave consequences of "the Great Game": The vying of nation-states for supplemental land and natural resources results in human subjugation and terrestrial devastation. Crossing a barren expanse, Prance explains to Kit that this area—"picked over" by Germans—was once the true historical Shambhala: "a convergence of gardens, silks, music—fertile, tolerant, and compassionate" (*ATD* 772). Its demise resulted from political conquest, first by Muslim invaders "and next [by] Genghis Khan, and after him the desert" (*ATD* 772). In essence, as in fact, a Pure Land cannot countenance conquest.

The structure of this chapter of the novel parallels Kit's spiritual development. It begins in media res with Kit's narration of reaching Lake Baikal (their pilgrimage destination), then rewinds to chronicle the preceding events of the pilgrimage before resuming the narrative. Only upon reaching Lake Baikal does Kit accept his pilgrim identity. Initially Kit had balked at the injunction to strictly observe the pilgrimage, insisting he was neither Buriat nor a pilgrim. The peremptory reply of his guide, Hassan—"for a devout Buriat the object of pilgrimage must be the great stone at the mouth of the Angara, where the river flowed out of the lake"—implies that Kit is a pilgrim, whether or not he elects to accept it (*ATD* 768). When the pilgrims reach Lake Baikal, Kit finally understands "why it had been necessary to journey here, and why, in the process of reaching it, penance, madness, and misdirection were inescapable" (*ATD* 768). This pilgrimage changes his perspective on his life to this point:

> A journey to [Lake Baikal] was not a holiday excursion. In some way he was certain of but had not quite worked through, it was another of those locations like Mount Kailash, or Tengri Khan, parts of a superterrestrial order included provisionally in this lower, broken one. He felt swept now by a violent certitude. He had after all taken the wrong path, allowed the day's trivialities to engage him—simply not worked hard enough to deserve to see this. His first thought was that he must turn and go back to Kashgar, all the way back to the great Gateway, and begin again. (*ATD* 769)

Pynchon suggests that the transformative power of pilgrimage is not tethered to belief, at least not initially. For those like Kit, who begin as skeptics, the pilgrimage incites a kind of faith. For those who begin in faith, like Hassan their guide, pilgrimage affirms and deepens it. The pilgrimage itself can utterly change an individual, regardless of her initial attitude. Kit's pilgrimage affords a vantage of his wayward past and heightens his awareness of his complicity in political machinations.

The journey attunes Kit to the insidious side of American exceptionalism and its expansionist project. Kit recognizes what he doesn't want to believe: America is no less imperialistic than Britain, just less transparent about its imperial aspirations. Prance disabuses Kit of his belief that America possesses no state religion, arguing, "Your whole history in America has been one long religious war, secret crusades, disguised under false names" (*ATD* 777). Enlightened, Kit refuses to report back to the British agency sponsoring his mission about the Tungus people he encounters.

Kit acquires a new spiritual discipline, learning how to regain through meditation the enlightened state he achieved during his pilgrimage. Kit uses this practice to help him "get back to the right piece of trail," morally and geographically, when he has taken a wrong turn (*ATD* 1074). Thus, near the end of the novel, Kit realizes his engineering work for the Italian air force has been aiding a nascent movement that is to become the fascism of Mussolini. Kit has "allowed himself to be seduced into the Futurist nosedive, with its aesthetics of blood and explosion" (*ATD* 1073). He develops aeronautical modifications that enable larger fighters to execute the newly developed "nosedive," believing that such technological advancement heralds greater human flourishing. But Kit's work proves most useful for quelling labor strikes. By returning to Shambhala through meditation, Kit sees his own complicity and comprehends that the mode of flight he's been abetting is not the gesture toward transcendence he'd supposed but rather one more tool of political coercion.

Pynchon's novels portray numerous other pilgrim characters. There's Auberon Halfcourt, a lieutenant colonel who's been overseeing British colonial interests in Asia long enough to establish his own oasis fiefdom. He also seeks

Shambhala, a site that reveals how easily conflated are religious, national, and commercial concerns. After a pilgrimage of his own, Auberon, too, realizes that the true Shambhala is a state of being: "not the discovery of a place but the act of leaving the futureless place where I was" (*ATD* 975). Auberon perceives how politics and commerce become soul-crushing bedfellows. He later confesses to his adopted daughter, Yashmeen, "I am not who I was. . . . Out there I was the servant of greed and force. . . . All the while believing myself a military professional. The only love they permitted me was indistinguishable from commerce. They were destroying me and I didn't know it" (*ATD* 974). Love that is "indistinguishable from commerce" isn't love but rather the reduction of persons to salable objects. Auberon then explains that he's faked his own death and deserted the military, placing his desire to reconnect with his adopted daughter above all else. The text asserts a direct connection between Auberon's military duties, which entailed the objectification of a colonized people, and his inability to love his adopted daughter without eroticizing her as an object of titillation.

Then there are the "sky-pilgrims," the Chums of Chance, adventurous aeronauts who patrol the skies as a force of good. They are, initially, loyal servants of "the Hierarchy," a thinly veiled governmental agency, and an unwitting instrument of American propaganda. The Chums, too, are deployed by a government with imperialistic ambitions to find Shambhala, only to realize that it is a spiritual destination, attainable only through spiritual transformation. Their maturation, both physical and spiritual, is correlated with their repudiation of their commanding office. The young pilgrims realize their "balloon-boy faith"—an easy confidence in America as the rightful recipient of "the Blessings of Progress"—has rendered them gullible and exploitable (*ATD* 555). They replace their naïve faith with a "project of the spirit" focused on inculcating compassion. WWI serves as their stations of the cross, with the trenches as the via dolorosa, teaching them that true compassion means perceiving others' suffering as one's own, regardless of nationality. The Chums become "the Compassionate Ones," individuals working of their own initiative for the good of others. Pynchon suggests an inverse correlation between blind nationalism and compassion: So long as one can without compunction justify suffering and death as necessary sacrifices for the good of the flag, one cannot do the "Work of the World."

CONCLUSION

In *Bleeding Edge*, Pynchon recurs to the image of dowsing the desert. He is keenly aware that it takes spiritual resources to dowse the spiritual desert that is our modern American environment. Pynchon has been accused of turning to religion as a kind of magical thinking to replace the failed utopianism of the 1960s counterculture.[17] But religion holds for Pynchon something more tangible than utopian thinking: practical disciplines.

For Pynchon, spiritual vitality is a pressing concern, as he stresses in his essay on acedia:

> Unless the state of our souls becomes once more a subject of serious concern, there is little question that Sloth will continue to evolve away from its origins in the long-ago age of faith and miracle, when daily life really was the Holy Ghost visibly at work and time was a story, with a beginning, middle and end. Belief was intense, engagement deep and fatal. The Christian God was near. Felt. Sloth—defiant sorrow in the face of God's good intentions—was a deadly sin. ("Sloth")

Pynchon laments that we live in a time and place when acedia is no longer a spiritual problem but a crime against progress, a politically motivated, profit-driven notion of progress that shrinks human life to a thing measurable by productivity. He rues that we can't truly be guilty of spiritual despair because we've no true spiritual self to begin with. The spiritual disciplines that Pynchon presents in his work—those depicted unironically and in earnest—translate into greater investment in the world: works of compassion, care for the earth, and opposition to all forms of domination. For Pynchon, doing the real "work of the world" is contingent upon connection to the transcendent. Pynchon, as a perspicacious student of history, may be wryly skeptical of our potential, but he is far from hopeless. Hope lies in recovering the conviction that our souls hang in the balance. In presenting a hybrid form of spirituality and exposing the limits of American ideology, Pynchon exhorts us to spiritually richer lives.

---

17. See McCann and Szalay for a version of this argument.

CHAPTER 4

Redefining Bountyland

George Saunders and the Gift of Humanity

GEORGE SAUNDERS'S story "Isabelle" opens, "The first great act of love I ever witnessed was Split Lip bathing his handicapped daughter. We were young, ignorant of mercy, and called her Boneless . . . for the way her limbs were twisted and useless" (*CWL* 27). The narrator lives in a place where mercy is rare. Even Split Lip, who cares for his daughter so lovingly, commits racist hate crimes on duty as a police officer. The narrator becomes the daytime caretaker of Boneless. He tells us, "I came to care about her. She tried so hard. I read to her and taught her to type using a stick held between her teeth. I brushed her hair until it shone and made sure her smocks were clean" (*CWL* 32). Through such care, the narrator preserves Boneless's humanity. She is given a way to express herself, and the hygienic and beautifying practices affirm her dignity. This story, like many of Saunders's, sets a trap, tempting readers with a false dichotomy. Boneless appears to be the only character whose dignity, as well as her physical needs, *requires* the intervention of others. After her father dies, Boneless goes to a deplorable state home, until the narrator brings her to live with him. The story ends: "Now we're pals. Family. It's not perfect. Sometimes it's damn hard. But I look after her and she squeals with delight when I come home, and the sum total of sadness in the world is less than it would have been. Her real name is Isabelle. A pretty, pretty name" (*CWL* 33). Through the narrator's care, Boneless becomes Isabelle. The difference is that between a thing and a person. Intersubjectivity is implied. The trap is that the reader thinks Isabelle alone needs drastic intervention to be fully human. It's true the narrator's compassion preserves Isabelle's dignity, but what elevates this story above sentimentality is its subtle insistence that *everyone*, narrator included, must receive their humanity as a gift from others.

A glance through the raft of George Saunders's interviews reveals vaunted writers like Zadie Smith and Jennifer Egan becoming tongue-tied in admiration, but Saunders has achieved a reputation as a saint that has possibly outpaced his reputation as a writer. Joshua Ferris writes, "Saunders writes like something of a saint. He seems in touch with some better being. He teaches us not only how to write but how to live. . . . He seems sent—what other way to put it?—to teach us mercy and grace" (xviii). That's a tall order for a writer. Saunders, with characteristic humility, owns up to it, but he also insists that we do not become merciful and gracious by dint of mere will. More hagiographically, the *Wall Street Journal* pronounces Saunders "Literature's patron saint of goodness" and exalts his work as a "Gospel of Compassion" (Sacks). In interviews over the years, Saunders has recurred to the terms *empathy* and *compassion*, and journalists have latched onto them. But this canonization has at times resulted in a padding of the barbed quality of Saunders's work. *GQ* named Saunders "life coach of the year" in 2013 (Duncan), tongue in cheek one hopes, given that Saunders pillories self-help gurus as purveyors of solipsism. The very fact that Saunders's empathy is so newsworthy speaks volumes about our current moral and political climate, and Joel Lovell rightly called Saunders the writer for our time, given that "our time" is marked by fears that are hard to name and the ability to remotely bomb others a world away (25). Saunders offers a moral vision that contemporary America desperately needs and desires. But perhaps not all Americans would be so accepting if they understood his contention that a truly compassionate way of life is contingent upon a world view that is antithetical to much of American culture.

Saunders's virtuous reputation reached popular audiences when his 2013 Syracuse University commencement address (later published as *Congratulations, By the Way: Some Thoughts on Kindness*) went viral. People who'd never read Saunders were suddenly praising him as a generous spirit and moral exemplar. In that speech, Saunders, admitting that "kindness, it turns out, is *hard*," encourages graduates to immerse themselves in the disciplines of a spiritual tradition ("Advice"). This same conviction is evident in his fiction: Our culture and our practices of commitment shape us decisively. Kindness and other virtuous acts and attitudes don't just happen. What becomes clearer through Saunders's writing is that the difference between kindness and niceness or decency is that one can be nice and remain solipsistic. It is hardly taxing to be "decent" to others. But kindness, as Saunders intends it, is an active form of other-regard that is rooted in compassion. We could accuse of Saunders of pandering in that speech. But I would rather focus on the erumpent profundity of his fiction than on any conventionality in a brief speech to a stand-full of proud hopefuls, because Saunders's "Gospel of Compassion" is toothier and more radical than a commencement speech can convey, more even than reviewers and critics have gleaned from his fiction.

SAUNDERS'S FIERCE COMPASSION

The moral timbre of Saunders's work has not gone unnoticed. But neither has it been fully appreciated. Saunders has spoken frequently about empathy and compassion over the years, returning often to several central tenets. First, a reflexive, mutually reinforcing relationship obtains between empathy and fiction (in both reading and writing it). This is, for Saunders, axiomatic: He insists that empathy is a basic necessity for writing well, though he confirms that his religious commitments also inform his focus on empathy. A lack of empathy precludes good stories. Saunders is quick to refuse any rigid claims about what art should do, however. In typically hyperbolic fashion, he states, "If you start saying what art should do, pretty soon you're saying what art *must* do, and then some reactionary comes along and says, 'Hey, your art isn't doing what you said it *must* do, go to the Gulag'" ("How Art," *Vox*). Art may instruct and enlighten, but it must also "reserve the right to be truly useless" ("How Art," *Vox*). In other words, there is slippage between the function of art and its creator's intentions.

Nevertheless, empathy has a political dimension, which makes reading and writing inherently political practices. Fiction can "soften the boundaries and reduce the level of projection" by reminding us that things are always more complicated and contingent than we like to think ("Sam Lipsyte," *BOMB*). Increased exposure to difference tempers our propensity to make snap judgments. Empathy leads, in short, to self-expansion and, in the process, heightens our awareness of our own fallibility and limited perspective. We are inherently capable of empathy, but we must choose to exercise it, and fiction can help: Reading and writing fiction entails the temporary inhabitation of another's consciousness, which Saunders sees as a form of conditioning for compassion. Saunders aims at a kind of fiction that is satirical but refuses to make other people into "assholes," working instead "on the assumption that They Are Us, on a Different Day" (qtd. in Wilson 222).

Compassion is a widely employed term with an imprecisely demarcated semantic territory. We use it in popular parlance to cover feelings and actions from the fleeting to the momentous. Saunders's use of the term is informed by his religious formation, both Buddhist and Catholic. Compassion, in his understanding, is neither pity nor a heady feeling; it is toothy and unafraid of conflict and resistance. It is uncondemning but not decaffeinated: "Compassion doesn't have to be wimpy . . . compassion in Eastern traditions is fierce. It's basically calling someone on their bullshit" ("Interview," *Goodreads*). This sort of cuffing is a kindness, rooted in the understanding that we are *all* suffering: "If someone is on a wrong or dull path, and someone else startles them into awareness of that, then that's a blessing" (Woodiwiss). The ultimate aim is to help others see themselves, and reality, better.

The bulk of the limited scholarly treatment of Saunders's work also centers on compassion and empathy. Some scholars corroborate through close reading what Saunders himself has discussed in interviews: his unconditionally empathetic treatment of his characters. Saunders renders *every* character with loving attention, from murderer to prom queen to doting grandfather. He "honor[s] their struggles," even if the characters acquit themselves poorly (Del George 128). Other scholars focus on the narrative techniques and strategies whereby Saunders positions readers to empathize with his characters. Analyzing Saunders's "Al," a story about a petty, perhaps delusional and certainly unpalatable character named Al, Richard Lee argues that "this is the gift that Saunders gives to us: since we are all 'Al,' we get a gentle piercing of our own narcissistic bubbles even as we are allowed the defensive, delusional, comforting safety that is story" (89). But Saunders doesn't always leave the reader such "comforting safety." Michael Basseler offers a compelling account of how empathy structures Saunders's stories formally, as well as thematically, highlighting Saunders's reliance on autodiegetic narrators and eschewal of omniscient narration. This strategy of "narrative empathy" denies "the reader an epistemologically and ethically secure position from which to judge the narrative events" (Basseler 162). The reader is transposed to a register where her ingrained convictions have no purchase and she must suffer uncertainty and conflict with the character. Saunders creates an innovative form of political art by combining empathy with a habitual refusal to resolve moral dilemmas. This combination establishes "a kind of equality in its production and reception," and the political potential lies in the "third thing" that is produced when active audience participation meets a work of art that is liberated in some way from authorial intention (Morris 123). According to Laura Morris, "the difference between the reader and the writer is blurred in Saunders' fiction, prompting the reader's own investigation of our complex reality through and with Saunders' texts" (124).

While these critics have offered some excellent insights into Saunders's use of empathy, they remain incomplete, partially disengaged from the entirety of Saunders's moral vision. Critics largely agree that Saunders attempts to venture beyond the detached irony of postmodernism and sincerely engage ethical questions without "reducing a complex and ambiguous reality to a simple and univocal moral position" (Morris 121). But when one assumes, as Layne Neeper does, that "in many ways, George Saunders is a quintessential postmodernist"—especially in the distrust of metanarratives—there's only so much one can say about the role and necessity of compassion, in terms of its practical, tangible ramifications. It's difficult to avoid landing on liberal platitudes about treating each other well and respecting difference. Neeper elegantly articulates Saunders's notion of empathy as "the primal faculty of recognizing the mindedness of Others; it is the human capacity to 'feel into' another consciousness; it is an act predicated on receptivity to and acceptance of the Other, even when—especially when—the Other is stupid or deluded or degenerate, in other words, when the pathetic Other expressly does not deserve our benevolent receptivity" (287). Neeper is on the mark here, as Saunders's work is populated largely by the have-nots and washouts who are corrupted at worst and shortsighted at best. By directing us to identify ourselves in this uncouth lot, Neeper concludes, Saunders encourages us to "therefore recognize and pardon ourselves and all others for our sad and existential brokenness, our shared inheritance" (287). But Neeper's wonderful definition of empathy isn't fully connected to Saunders's "toothy" notion of compassion.

Empathy that is constricted to a common identification of suffering is lacking in imaginative awareness and in hope. Narrative empathy of Saunders's mold has sociopolitical significance in that it impacts the mode in which we engage others. Basseler contends that Saunders's cultivation of narrative empathy is a "politically minded" choice to emphasize "the role of storytelling in imagining other people" (154). Empathy is for Saunders an ethical imperative, "a choice we make, even if it is a natural capacity" (Basseler 167). And nurturing this natural capacity is, as Michael Trussler argues, a requisite for political justice because empathy is correlated with our ability to face and engage pain, especially others' pain (206). Saunders makes interconnectedness the bridge from empathy to compassion. Acceptance of the other is predicated not only on our shared inheritance but also on our interdependence, which necessitates a benevolent but resolute corrective dimension as well. Empathy is no mean feat, and it's sorely needed in American society, but it can end in ethical dilemmas if it stagnates at the point of accepting understanding (Basseler 167). Robert Cameron Wilson has shown that Saunders's narrative use of "close third-person" creates an "atmosphere . . . where [characters'] voices never exist outside of contact with other voices" (224). Wilson's insightful analysis of "microdialogues" posits intersubjectivity as the core of human relations, moving beyond the axiom that humans are social animals to the suggestion that we do not fully exist as people apart from our social relations. Our lives are helplessly interconnected, which is a source of suffering as well as a source of creativity and human fullness.

Empathy and compassion are axiomatically understood to be goods that are universally installed, fundamental to a functioning society. And virtually every major religion emphasizes their importance. Americans are, in general, inured to individualism but put off enough by selfishness and solipsism to know the value and appeal of compassion. But without a shift in our thinking about personhood, empathy remains a temporary bridge between islands and compassion is reinscribed into a system antithetical to it. Saunders's work decries the individualism at the root of the American mythos. *If* compassion is touted as a good within that system, it exists in a parasitic, ironic relation. I posit that Saunders is exhorting us not just to empathy and compassion but also to a radical shift in thinking, a revised *anthropology*, that makes compassionate living possible. The meaning of compassion is often limited by the common conception of humanity as a fundamental threshold rooted in dignity and individual rights. Saunders insists that humanity is not simply an ontological fact but something we must give to one another.

Saunders is clear that compassion does not just happen. It requires discipline and a vision of human dignity that is not characterized by a potentially violent, forcible establishment of "rights" that are rooted in a vulgar sense of entitlement. In what follows, I examine Saunders's view that American exceptionalism exists as a set of spiritual disciplines that inure individuals to violence and cultivate the solipsistic conception of human worth that sustains America's thriving self-help culture. Saunders's work depicts a political and spiritual wasteland resulting from America's individualistic consumer culture. A better America begins, according to Saunders, with a revision of human dignity and a more compassionate mode of life.

STARS 'N STRIPES FOREVER: AMERICAN EXCEPTIONALISM AS SPIRITUAL DISCIPLINE

American exceptionalism appears in Saunders's work in various guises, often demonstrating how "different historical ideologies converge to comprise the complex web of contemporary exceptionalist discourse" (Moore 64). Many characters embrace a crassly materialist version of the American dream, expecting as birthright the life of luxury that America allegedly affords its citizens. In "Brad Carrigan, American," characters accept as their due the "bumper crop" in which corn grows bountifully not only in the fields but also in their living room. Elsewhere, characters evince an outsized Puritanism, seeking to prove their exceptionality through hard work, suffering, and moral perfection. In "Bounty," the narrator describes the Church of Appropriate Humility, whose members, called Guilters, hold the great "human frailties [to be] arrogance and mediocrity" (*CWL* 123). Guilters measure their progress toward salvation by "quantifying pain" in units called Victors. In *The Brief and Frightening Reign of Phil*, Phil inverts the logic of the Guilters. Phil, a conniving autocratic politico, says, "I've been thinking about our beautiful country! Who gave it to us? I've been thinking about how God the Almighty gave us this beautiful and sprawling land as a reward for how wonderful we are" (9). As Hayes-Brady notes, "This passage invites shivers of familiarity, evoking the political discourse of the millennial turn: 'There's power, wonder-working power, in the goodness and idealism and faith of the American people'" (26). Of course, this is not just the "discourse of the millennial turn" but ideological rhetoric with a long history.

These different versions of exceptionalism are united in that all "still subscribe to the rhetoric of America as providing exceptional and accessible opportunities, meting out some kind of success to those who work hard enough" (Moore 64). Ubiquitous (though invariably undercut) in Saunders's work is the entrenched myth of the self-made individual, according to which, one achieves success through hard work and ingenuity. In "Bounty," the American dream is typified by Blay, founder of GlamorDivans. Blay "built mud huts for minimum wage for five grueling years," surviving on bread crusts, forgoing alcohol and recreation to work overtime. With his savings, he "built the most ass-kicking clean-air geodesic dome you've ever seen" to grow ash trees and produce high-end furniture called GlamorDivans (*CWL* 127). But Blay is more the exception than the rule (not to mention, only those profiting unjustly from gross inequalities can afford his products). The "bootstrap mentality" emerges more often as a conviction of the have-nots. Freddie, for example, fervently believes anyone can do anything, though he himself has managed to do virtually nothing. Freddie is a pollster who earns ten dollars per poll calling divorcees and asking how frequently they have sex with their ex-husbands. He nonetheless offers this unsolicited advice to his girlfriend's ne'er-do-well children:

> Let me tell you something ... about this country. Anybody can do anything. But first they gotta try. And you guys ain't. Two don't work and one strips

naked? I don't consider that trying. You kids make squat. And therefore you live in a dangerous craphole. And what happens in a dangerous craphole? Bad tragic shit. It's the freaking American way—you start out in a dangerous craphole and work hard so you can someday move up to a somewhat less dangerous craphole. And finally maybe you get a mansion. But at this rate you ain't even gonna make it to the somewhat less dangerous craphole. (*P* 106)

The discrepancy between being able to "do anything" and "someday mov[ing] up to a somewhat less dangerous craphole" is lost on Freddie, who's hardly the paragon of hard work, but he speaks earnestly. We see a similar conviction in Marty. In a letter to his son, the first in the family to attend boarding school, Marty appeals to familial sacrifice to exhort his son to succeed: "Think of . . . Paw-Paw and Mee-Maw, and Great Paw-Paw, who came over here from wherever . . . in some kind of boat, and fixed shoes all his life in a shack or whatever? . . . Why'd he do that? So you could eventually be born!" (*P* 13). This is the classic immigrant success story, without the success. Generations on, continually denied upward mobility, Marty remains convinced that the timeless American virtues will yield fruit. He instructs his son, "Do your best and don't take no shit from nobody, unless taking shit from them is part of your master plan to get the best of them by tricking them into being your friend. Just always remember who you are" (*P* 13). Marty conflates the values of authenticity (i.e., not taking shit) and ambition, but they are incompatible here. Anyone willing to do literally anything to get ahead cannot also possess integrity and a strong sense of identity. What emerges from these examples is a fervent but blinkered belief in self-sufficiency. In Saunders's work, it's the characters who haven't found success who believe most fervently in its attainability.

Through a character in "Bounty," we begin to see how Saunders renders American exceptionalism a powerfully formative ideology that, self-referentially coupled with a vague belief in a higher power, functions as a religion. After meeting Blay (mentioned above), the narrator of "Bounty" encounters a beleaguered father of nine, whose "nineteen [work] hours a day minimum" have aged him severely. This harried man nonetheless feels compelled to exude contentment and clings to a patently delusional model of self-sufficiency. "If you want something nice, you've got to get it for yourself," he says, adding, "Nobody said it was going to be easy. And this is definitely not easy. Wow. . . . But hey. You've got to get up and keep on going. You snooze, you lose. Ouch. Yikes. Concentrate, concentrate" (*CWL* 133–34). These platitudes are paradoxically coupled with a nebulous belief in a higher power. The father calls a halt (his wife and all children old enough to speak are working manically, too) for a "silent prayer moment," after which he remarks, misty-eyed, "With love there's always hope. With hope there's always healing. Yes. Yes" (*CWL* 134). This notably silent prayer somehow sanctions his conviction of self-reliance and affords him the psychological stamina to subject himself to further suffering. Unendurable suffering is not only borne but glamorized. The man punctuates descriptions of his impossibly difficult life with the qualification, "But I love it!" This, after all, is Bountyland's official slogan: "Where merit is king—and so are you!" (*CWL* 136).

As a religion, American exceptionalism proves spiritually formative in pernicious ways, generating a set of disciplines that ultimately inure individuals to suffering and encourage solipsism. I want to highlight three of these disciplines that recur in Saunders's work, before returning to his vision of compassion. The three disciplines are corruptions of traditional Christian disciplines: gratitude, sanctification, and suffering or self-denial. Saunders's account of American exceptionalism is constructed inductively by inferring from characters' ingrained, internalized attitudes and values and beliefs.

Self-Improvement

One discipline connected to American exceptionalism is the "classic American project of self-improvement." In assuming a moral dimension as well as a material one, this "project" dimly mirrors the traditional Christian notion of sanctification. Implicit here is the purportedly Christian axiom that neither Christ, Paul, nor even James ever uttered: God helps those who help themselves. This conviction, moreover, encourages an absurdly inflated confidence in willpower. In "My Amendment," Saunders excoriates a fetishization of the human will that positions even secondary sex characteristics within the will's sphere of influence. Saunders frames the story as a letter to the editor in which reader Ken Byron responds to an implied editorial opposing same-sex marriage. Ken ardently endorses the proposed amendment to ban same-sex marriage and argues for a "supplementary" amendment to properly define masculinity. Ken, "in the interest of moral rigor," proposes the "Manly Scale of Absolute Gender" to determine "Samish-Sex Marriage," which occurs when one or both partners fail to express their "true" gender characteristics (*IPN* 67). Thus, not only is a man who, say, has long hair or knows nothing about cars functionally female; his wife is functionally gay. In Ken's androcentric scale, men receive a manliness rating of 0 to 10, while women only receive a score of negative manliness. As Ken's misogyny suggests, self-improvement easily devolves into self-centeredness, with others seen with a cold utilitarian eye.

Ken submits that those who do not score satisfactorily on the scale should undertake the "classic American project of self-improvement" and make themselves more "Manly" or "Fem" accordingly (*IPN* 69). In addition to the sexism and homophobia implicit in his scale, Ken's exaltation of the individual will produces disregard for insurmountable obstacles. "Self-improvement" includes everything from voice modulation and hand gestures to gait and neck size to willing oneself to be attracted to a certain type of individual (*IPN* 70). Ken insists on defying prodigious limitations and natural endowments, like the size of one's Adam's apple, only to subject the apparently limitless self once more to an unrealistic, not to say undesirable, gender ideal. Ken offers himself as proof that such change is possible, but his testimonial belies his ideology. The reader gradually perceives that Ken continues ineffectively to battle the inclinations he has labored to curb. For example, after years of working on speaking slowly and without gesturing, Ken's epistolary style succumbs to breathless, verbose flights of reverie—especially about the long flowing locks he had as an adolescent. Ken's logic is likewise internally inconsistent in its selective acknowledgment of external constraints upon individual expression. His inordinate estimation of the human capacity for self-transformation presupposes that humans are virtually plastic, yet his Manly Scale implies that gender is anything but fluid. While positing a rigid standard for each gender, Ken insists that individuals are capable of extreme modulation of their given traits in order to comply with those standards. Ken's own descriptions demonstrate the enormously varied and subjective character of gender expression, undercutting any rigid, essentialist set of gender norms. Yet, while Saunders is far from reinscribing normative gender standards, he interrogates a belief in self-sufficiency that refuses to admit that "factors outside of the self (such as biology or circumstance)" influence human lives profoundly (Boddy 8).

Ken roots his proposed amendment in a political ideology that is equally inconsistent. In his concluding exhortation, Ken appeals to American exceptionalism to justify his scale, arguing that Americans must restrict freedom to certain permissible expressions in order to protect the freedom that makes this country great: "I, for one, am sick and tired of this creeping national tendency to let certain types of people take advantage of our national good nature by marrying individuals who are essentially of their own gender. If this trend continues, before long our towns and cities will be full of people . . . 'asserting their rights' by dating, falling in love with, marrying, and spending the rest of their lives with whomever they please" (*IPN* 70–71). Ironically, to preserve the unique character of America ("national good nature"), which is supposedly characterized by freedom and democratic equality, Ken proposes a denial of freedom. Ken fears the possibility of "a nation ruled by the anarchy of unconstrained desire," and he adopts a belief in one form of unconstrained self-assertion in order prevent another (*IPN* 71). The possibility of individuals changing in order to conform to Ken's standards depends upon just such a range of individual expression. In this derivation of Puritan covenantal theology, suffering and self-sacrifice are, of course, connected to self-improvement. However, any positive, unconditional correlation between suffering and improvement is confounded by systemic injustices as well as natural and biological constraints.

The bid for self-improvement, undertaken with the conviction of self-sufficiency, may produce an unjustified sense of accomplishment in some and, obversely, an unwarranted sense of guilt in others. In addition to willful ignorance of individual limitations, the exaltation of individual willpower also leads, as Rachel Greenwald Smith notes in her consideration of neoliberalism, to the "pathologization of structures of dependence [that] calls upon subjects to see themselves as entrepreneurial actors in a competitive system" (2). In "The 400-Pound CEO," Saunders exposes the delusion of self-sufficiency through two characters who undertake to improve themselves without acknowledging human interdependency. The poster child of self-improvement is Tim, founder of Humane Raccoon Alternatives, a firm that purportedly captures the pests and releases them into the wild but actually bludgeons them to death and dumps them in a pit. Tim is admired as a community success story. He is also, it quickly becomes apparent, a psychopath. Tim spent a decade in jail for manslaughter after he "purposely backed his car over a frat boy" (*CWL* 45). While incarcerated, "he earned his MBA by designing and marketing a line of light-up Halloween lapel brooches." Tim is a masochist and a sadist as well as a patriot, and he sees no hypocrisy in this:

> Tim was inducted into Rotary and we all went to the luncheon. He spoke on turning one's life around. He spoke on the bitter lessons of incarceration. He sang the praises of America and joked with balding sweetheart ophthalmologists, and after lunch hung his Rotary plaque in the torture chamber stairwell and ordered me to Windex it daily or face extremely grim consequences. (*CWL* 55)

That Tim sees no discrepancy here indicates just how solipsistic the drive to self-realization can be. He is sincerely proud of his Rotary club membership. And he is capable of perpetrating extreme violence upon others but interprets his own success and socioeconomic rise as a form of moral progress. Saunders undercuts "success stories" like Tim by presenting their success as contingent in ways the triumphant character fails or refuses to notice. He also makes it clear that contingencies may cause an individual suffering for which he or she is absurdly held responsible.

The real power of "The 400-Pound CEO" lies in the way that this same notion of self-sufficiency and expectation of self-improvement has been internalized by Jeffrey, the story's hapless narrator and eponymous 400-pound CEO. Middle-aged, morbidly obese, and hopelessly single, Jeffrey is the office pariah of Humane Raccoon Alternatives: Coworkers leave hippo magnets in Jeffrey's cubicle and compete in most grievously insulting him. (His role is generally limited to invoicing and marketing.) Jeffrey despises Tim and aspires to be a moral, caring man. He is miserable on account of his own failures, guilty because he believes it's within his power to make things otherwise. Jeffrey's "days unraveled as one long bad dream," as he laments the turpitude surrounding him and longs to do good. In the name of self-improvement, he attempts to sublimate all his misery and abuse by turning his disparagement and self-effacement into redemptive self-sacrifice. However, much of his well-intended resolve amounts to withdrawal from life rather than sublimation.

Jeffrey believes moral improvement will lead to material improvement. He stops visiting the "Consenting Adult Viewing Center," convinced it's a shameful mockery of romantic love and that he'd "rather be sexless than evil" (*CWL* 47). Jeffrey's description of his moral resolve is revealing: "I've tried to live above the fray. I've tried to minimize my physical aspects and be a selfless force for good. When mocked, which is nearly every day, I recall Christ covered with spittle. When filled with lust, I remember Gandhi purposely sleeping next to a sexy teen to test himself. After work I go home, watch a little TV, maybe say a rosary or two" (*CWL* 47). As a selfless force for good, Jeffrey becomes quite literally self-less: He nullifies every aspect of his life that would connect with others, and thereby has nothing left that might be considered a self—no identity, no passions, no loves. No one would blame him for seeking to minimize pain and suffering. But his desire to be a "force for good" conflicts with his aim of disengagement. "Thirty more years of this and I'm out of it without hurting anybody or embarrassing myself," Jeffrey thinks to himself at work (*CWL* 48). Unlike Christ and Gandhi, Jeffrey's suffering has no productive side; it redeems no one. Furthermore, his plan doesn't work. He's still miserable: "If only I could stop hoping. If only I could say to my heart: Give up. Be alone forever. . . . But no. My heart's some kind of idiotic fishing bobber" (*CWL* 53). Part of Jeffrey's problem is that he thinks he can solve his problem alone. Jeffrey rejects the materialistic measure of success of those around him but then tries to attain spiritually fulfilled selfhood in a vacuum, without community. Religion that proceeds as a theologically grounded form of self-help is no better than empty slogan-based forms of self-help.

Gratitude

The human will has limits, and, according to Saunders, what keeps the multitude of unfulfilled American dreamers faithful to American exceptionalism is the inculcation of a spirit of gratitude. Like self-improvement, gratitude is also a traditionally religious discipline. Saunders's story "The Falls" takes us into the mind of Morse, a feckless father of two who works an entry-level office job and still lives in his hometown. The story opens with Morse walking home from work along a river, contemplating his lot in life:

> The wide Taganac River . . . picked up speed and crashed over Bryce Falls a mile downstream near Morse's small rental house, his embarrassingly small rental house, actually, which nevertheless was the best he could do and for which he knew he should be grateful, although at times he wasn't a bit grateful and wondered where he went wrong, although at other times he was quite pleased with the crooked little blue shack covered with peeling lead paint and felt great pity for the poor stiffs renting hazardous shitholes even smaller than his hazardous shithole, which was how he felt now as he came down into the bright sunlight and continued his pleasant walk home along the green river lined with expensive mansions whose owners he deeply resented. (*P* 175–76)

Morse's thoughts here continually flit between twin fears of failure and ingratitude. In Saunders's work, Americans experience the dual expectation to become someone else (one's "best self") and to express gratitude for living in this peerless, providentially favored nation. Both expectations induce guilt, resulting in a double bind. If conditions foreclose an individual's potential to become her "best self," she is discouraged through social pressures from blaming the nation-state. Such grievance would convey ingratitude and concede that America is not the exceptional place it's widely reputed to be. On the other hand, a posture of gratitude and contentment tends toward complacency and failure to realize one's true potential. Even Morse's wife "blamed their poverty on his passivity within earshot of the kids" when they were fighting (*P* 183). At work, Morse "was known to punctuate his conversation with brief wild laughs and gusts of inchoate enthusiasm," which he quickly stifles out of fear his coworkers will question the sanity of an underachiever who's unaccountably content with his lot (*P* 176). He is then further embarrassed by his own obvious, public embarrassment. Morse is faced with a catch-22: It's shameful to be ashamed of his lowly status, and it's shameful to be positive and content given his shamefully low status. Throughout the story, Morse's thoughts recur repeatedly to his need to "become somebody" and to the need to be grateful that he lives in a place where he has the opportunity to become somebody. The result is mental unrest approaching schizophrenia: "His childhood dreams had been so bright, he had hoped for so much, it couldn't be true that he was a nobody, although, on the other hand, what kind of somebody spends the best years of his life swearing at a photocopier? Not that he was complaining. Not that he was unaware he had plenty to be thankful for" (*P* 182). This neurotic double-pressure is formative: It has shaped Morse's expectations of his children as well as himself. Morse's interactions with his son Robert unconsciously reproduce the same paralyzing pressures, an augur that Robert is likely destined for the same kind of middling existence as his father.

From Morse's perspective, the available options for quieting his roiling psyche are limited to two provisional practices. One is to practice self-help exercises and attempt positive thinking. Walking home, Morse "enjoy[s] a few minutes of centered breathing while reciting his mantra, which was Calm Down Calm Down," before facing his unruly children and domestic duties (*P* 178). Underlying this inane mantra is the assumption that an individual can—and should—modulate his emotional and psychological state by sheer force of will. Morse has embraced the notion that one "predestine[s] failure via negativity" and accepted the fallacious corollary that positive thinking is likewise self-fulfilling. Morse's second, more mystical and outwardly focused practice is to reflect upon the enduring power of his blessed nation. Morse counters thoughts of his individual failure with consoling reflections on American ascendency: "He gazed out at the beautiful Taganac in an effort to absorb something of its serenity but instead found himself obsessing about the faulty latch on the gate, which theoretically could allow Annie to toddle out of the yard and into the river, and he pictured himself weeping on the shore, and to eradicate this thought started manically whistling 'The Stars and Stripes Forever'" (*P* 178). Morse's reactionary impulse to the threat of danger (and his own failure as a guardian) is to sing not a traditional religious hymn but a nationalistic one. The superior power that provides vaguely conceived reassurance is not a god but a mythical nation.

It is indicting how insubstantial Morse's coping mechanisms are. The story's central conflict retrospectively ironizes the above scene. (Before he gets home, Morse espies two young girls stuck in a canoe heading for the falls.) Morse is so habituated to perceiving the world as a source of threat that he cannot enjoy natural beauty. On the other hand, the river is a threat to young girls (as well as a source of beauty), a threat pretty much immune to human foresight and will, individual or collective, and Morse's neurotic mental disaster rehearsal allows him to see this threat more accurately than he can see the threat posed to him by his own society. The story ends with Morse jumping in after the girls, believing he will probably perish, along with them, in the attempt to save them. The final irony of the story is that Morse acts heroically while viewing his own actions as unheroic, flawed, and probably doomed to failure.

The practices of gratitude and self-improvement rely on the "sophisticated architecture of denial and disavowal" on which the ideology of American exceptionalism is structured (Moore 62). Individuals must deny that their own nation victimizes some of its citizens. They must deny that there are variables beyond their control that promote or impede success. Saunders suggests that the result is a population of deluded, manipulable, selfish people. Demanding gratitude is a way of curbing expectations without crushing dreams. It engenders false humility, fabricated contentment, and a spurious rejection of greed that parades as virtue. The practice of gratitude takes a different, more ominous, form in "My Flamboyant Grandson." This story is both a celebration of the freedom of choice (a loving grandfather allows his grandson to be his "flamboyant" self, without regard for public opinion) and a scathing reminder that we can imprison ourselves by ostensibly reveling in freedom of choice.

In the world of this story, gratitude operates more overtly as a means of coercion and propaganda; it is leverage for a surveillance state. The story's not-so-alternate America is virtually technocratic. The quintessential American value of freedom, here narrowed to freedom of choice, has become a fulcrum for manipulation. Americans are legally required to complete monthly "Everly Preference Worksheets" detailing their consumer proclivities and to equip their shoes with synchronized "Everly Strips." When in motion, "Everly Strips" are read by ubiquitous embedded sensors that cue a literal invasion of advertisements consonant with one's "Personal Preferences." These ads appear on buildings and "Sudden Emergent Screens" that pop up inches from one's face, paired with an individually tailored audio feed beamed directly into one's ear. Marketing companies, now openly dictating public policy, have access not only to browsing and purchasing histories but also to consumers' personal histories. Watching, or, rather, withstanding, such invasive ads is called "Celebrating your preferences" (*IPN* 17). Celebration of one's preferences is, of course, compulsory.

Walking around New York City with his grandson, Leonard Petrillo's feet began to bleed, a result of an old Korean War injury. He removes his shoes for relief, only to be immediately confronted by a Citizen Helper asking why he has "caused [his] Everly Strips to be rendered Inoperative . . . sacrificing a terrific opportunity to Celebrate [His] Preferences?" (*IPN* 17). When Leonard insists he's seen more than enough personalized messages, the Citizen Helper states imperiously that Leonard has neither the authority nor proficiency to decide when he has "received enough useful information from our Artistic Partners" (*IPN* 19). Leonard bolts, shoes in hand, so that he and his grandson can make a musical on time. For his crime, Leonard is required to view a video, *Robust Economy, Super Moral Climate!* and "under the supervision of that Citizen Helper, retrace [his] steps, shoes on, thus reclaiming a significant opportunity to Celebrate [His] Preferences" (*IPN* 21). Behind the unctuous diction—*opportunity, helper, celebrate*—lies the ideology of exceptionalism, here veneered as avuncular benefactor, while under the surface lurks the threatening expectation of adherence. Noncompliance is interpreted as ingratitude. It's simply unfathomable that anyone would elect, like Leonard, not to enjoy the bounty on offer. Ingratitude is not only unpatriotic, but, as the video's title suggests, immoral. Here, probity remains a central tenet of American exceptionalism, and the covenantal logic of Winthrop's famous "City upon a Hill" address is retained. However, the original correlation between godliness and a robust sense of human flourishing has been pared down to a linkage of the nation's moral and economic health. The causal logic is reversed, too: The video title and the nature of Leonard's prescribed penance both imply that economic health, rather than the moral climate, is the conditioning term. Gone, too, is Winthrop's Christianity: The citizen's covenant here is not with God but with Uncle Sam.

Subtly, the expectation of gratitude, the (forced) common acknowledgment of national exceptionalism, morphs to a noxious paternalism. As Leonard demonstrates his "change of heart" by completing his supervised makeup trek, the Citizen Helper, Rob, delivers the story's most disquieting passage: "Isn't that amazing, Mr. Petrillo, that we can do that, that we can know you so well, that we can help you identify the things you want and need?" (*IPN* 21). We're no longer dealing with appeals but with dictates; we've transitioned from the register of rhetoric to that of fascism. Gratitude is a powerful discipline. Saunders suggests that over time, gratitude easily slips into allegiance, then into obligation, then, finally, into bondage.

The Valorization of Suffering

Suffering caused by an individual's quest for self-improvement is rationalized through either valorization or trivialization. "If you want something nice, you've got to get it for yourself," says the overworked father in "Bounty" who can hardly make ends meet, let alone get ahead (*CWL* 133). Never mind that the grueling toil entailed in the "getting" destines the man for an early grave. His suffering is taken as evidence that what is sought is worthwhile, and the ability to endure hardship is a sign of moral fortitude. Saunders's mordant stories perspicuously reveal the extent to which American exceptionalism and corporate culture have become enmeshed in an environment where neoliberalism is the order of the day. As Adam Kelly states, one thing that "defines neoliberalism as a specific project of governmentality" is that it "operates . . . by having the subject sign up 'freely' to the terms of his or her own subjugation" (47). The unremitting pressure "to evaluate oneself and one's colleagues" fosters a sense of "suffering agency," so that suffering is experienced as a mark of progress (Kelly 47).

Saunders pillories a culture in which individuals are "sainted by pain" even though their suffering is inefficacious. In "Sea Oak," Aunt Bernie is a paragon of patient endurance. A possessive father deprived Bernie of romance and a family of her own, then omitted her from his will. She has supported herself by working in a drugstore, living paycheck to paycheck with her nieces and nephew in an unsafe subsidized apartment complex. Bernie embodies and affirms the quintessential American values of hard work and positivity, refusing to succumb to bitterness even though she's been allotted none of the esteemed perquisites of American life: At sixty, she owns no car or home and has never been promoted in spite of years of hard work. Her sanguine outlook differs markedly from the cynicism of her nieces, Min and Jade, who marvel at Bernie's unflappable equanimity. By contrasting Bernie's optimism with her nieces' cynicism, Saunders insinuates that "she 'corrects' negative visions of their working-class life through her lens of patience and pleasantness" (Rando 442). We may decline to judge Min and Jade too harshly—they've endured their share of gratuitous adversity—but their lackluster attitude serves as the foil for Bernie's positivity, which we're invited to admire. Bernie seems to transfigure her wretched existence by abiding her suffering (however clumsily) with grace.

Saunders positions readers to perceive the characters according to prevailing forms of cultural discourse, only to subvert those discourses. Min and Jade are depicted as hapless bimbos, victims of misfortune that they exacerbate by their own stupidity. They cannot work because the only babysitter they could afford kept getting drunk while watching their children. Yet, while studying for their GEDs, they define regicide as a virus and insist Churchill was an opera star. We feel sorry for them yet find it difficult not to laugh at them. But, as David Rando demonstrates, Saunders sets us up to become "consumer[s] of working-class realist satire" (449). By laughing at Bernie's nieces, we consume their story in the same manner that they absorb a fictional TV program called *How My Child Died Violently*, in which the host is "always giving the parents shoulder rubs and telling them they've been sainted by pain" (*P* 93). The host's "insincere compassion serves as the pretense for sensationalistic thrills at the suffering guests' expense" (Rando 449). Readers who adjudge Min and Jade's choice of entertainment objectionable but find pleasure at their expense commit the same offense.

Saunders sets another trap in his rendering of Bernie. The reader is tempted to valorize Bernie for her stalwart optimism in the face of futility. But doing so allows her suffering to be redeemed, which is just as blameworthy as overlooking suffering for the sake of entertainment. By emulating Min and Jade's validation of Bernie's positivity, we are reconciled to Bernie's situation like she apparently is, based on the juxtaposition of her attitude with that of her nieces. Saunders leads us (before radically redirecting the story arc) to become inured to both Bernie's suffering—because it doesn't seem to set her back, much—and that of her nieces because it seems that they could improve their situation with just a bit more positivity. If we fall into Saunders's trap, we are not only culpably entertained (as with Jade and Min), but also further indoctrinated in the ideology to which Bernie subscribes.

Bernie's world view is the remarkable product of two ideologies: the suffering saint and the American dream. The first, traditionally Christian, is eschatological, predicated on belief in a kingdom not of this world and a heavenly reward. The second ideology promises success in this life, through hard work. Both ideologies commend suffering: It is, respectively, a sign of holiness and the hallmark of those destined to get ahead. In Bernie's case, the two ideologies merge so that long-suffering endurance is reconstituted as living the American dream. Rando is right to read this story as a religious parody, but the religion parodied here is a vestigially Christian form of American exceptionalism. Bernie's ostensibly virtuous patience isn't the product of a heavenly citizen ethos, in which Bernie sees herself as just passing through. Rather than future blessedness getting her through, it's a belief in the blessedness of the American way of life. "I mean, complain if you want," she says. "But I think we're doing pretty darn good for ourselves" (*P* 98). The implied warrant for Bernie's positivity is the superlative quality of American life, where hard work and optimism are putatively rewarded. Bernie's subsistence-level life is the conceptual backdrop by which upward mobility is understood, and suffering is thus revered as a testament of progress. But Bernie reconciles herself to crushing labor by cultivating patience and gratitude based on the delusional conviction that her reward has already been received.

Bernie has internalized a Protestant work ethic degenerated to the glorification of grinding toil as its own reward. With all the eschatological tension dissolved, the future-oriented, forbearing hopefulness is redirected to the present as vapid positivity. The ascending trajectory of upward mobility is flattened out and compressed: Bernie doesn't expect anything more of life than she has already. Her buoyant positivity can be supported only by a delusional appreciation of the life she leads. Bernie deals with suffering not by channeling it redemptively but by trivializing it: "You know what I do if something bad happens? . . . I don't think about it. Don't take it so seriously. It ain't the end of the world. That's what I do. That's what I always done. That's how I got where I am" (*P* 98). In no sense can this posture be classified as a species of hope; optimism bears no intrinsic relation to hope.[1] And lacking hope, Bernie's optimism should be confounding rather than admirable. What Bernie exhibits is not hope but the anesthetizing power of positive thinking.

Saunders uncouples Bernie's positivity from any redemptive result. The barrenness of her life is evident at her funeral, as her nephew struggles to compose a eulogy: "What's there to say? She never had a life. Never married, no kids, work work work. . . . After fifteen years as Cashier she got demoted to Greeter" (*P* 102–3). If Bernie is "sainted by pain," her suffering is explained away and its implied reward affirmed. But Bernie is not redeemed by suffering and thus cannot acknowledge it. She copes through a double illusion: that her suffering isn't as bad as it seems, and that she's materially better off than she is. Precisely because suffering is valorized as a measure of progress, suffering must be trivialized when it's not efficacious: either dismissed as unreal or endowed with the patina of privileged martyrdom. To beatify Bernie is to exalt delusion to the status of virtue and perpetuate a cultural ideology whose currency is contingent upon a "particularly selective engagement with reality" (Trussler 208). Bernie's manner of death implies that her quaint understanding of American life cannot accommodate the cutthroat reality of a system in which individuals will go to any lengths to get ahead. This reality kills her: She is literally frightened to death by intruding thieves. Then, lest anyone continue to feel that Bernie's positive attitude redeems her suffering, Saunders interrupts his realist satire with Bernie's resurrection. Bernie returns from the grave, not as one who has put on imperishability, but as undead, an animated corpse whose decomposition continues unabated. Her altered mentality also emphasizes the speciousness of her previous optimism. She returns from the grave aggrieved at the inconsequence of her life, determined to make up for lost time by satisfying unfulfilled desires.

---

1. For a fulsome explication of the relationship between these two, see Eagleton, *Hope*.

Having returned from the dead, Bernie is fully cognizant of the lack of dignity she suffered during her life. But because she is "unable to imagine modes of satisfaction that aren't defined by consumer capitalism" (Trussler 207–8), she resolves to secure personal fulfillment through means that are inimical to a robust notion of personhood. The undead Bernie is hell-bent on the pleasures she was previously denied, but what she envisions are adulterations of greater goods. Bernie never experienced romantic love, so now she wants impersonal sex "like in the movies" (*P* 113). She insists that her nephew and nieces work their way out of poverty by any means necessary, and the means she prescribes are invariably sexual and self-debasing in nature. Now, as before, no one in Bernie's family can climb the socioeconomic ladder through honest hard work alone. Bernie doesn't redeem anyone, at least not from the system that victimized her. Her nephew achieves a very modest degree of upward mobility by marketing his body. The purpose in life remains the achievement of a certain threshold of material comfort.

Bernie is owed dignity, but not because she endured relentless circumstances with composure—a logic that would affirm the very system that denied Bernie her dignity. The very fact that she was compelled to reimagine her awful existence as a rewarding, dignified life is the epitome of indignity. It's reasonable to read this story as a Marxist critique of religion, agreeing with Rando that "the theological grotesquery of 'Sea Oak' exposes the complicity of religion in containing working-class discontent [and] . . . suggests that redemption must come during one's life and cannot be deferred" (453). But Saunders complicates such a reading by negating the possibility that Bernie could find redemption in her earthly life. Saunders uses Christian tropes to suggest that nationalistic ideology has superseded Christianity as a religion by aping its logic and structure and substituting the power of positive thinking for supernatural grace. The religion that consoles the working class isn't Christianity but the American dream.

Dignity is precisely what Saunders wants to defend and redefine. Saunders posits a link between human dignity and human imagination—one's sense of the realm of the possible. Because Bernie has calibrated her vision of the good to a commodity-saturated version of the American dream, she's destined for "an afterlife in which it is impossible to think outside of the parameters of consumer capitalism" (Trussler 206). Redemption for Bernie can come only by escaping the totalizing cultural imaginary that has constrained her vision of fulfillment. The ending is not entirely hopeless. Just before Bernie dies (again), she poses a question to her nephew (the narrator) that afterwards recurs in his dreams: "Some people get everything and I got nothing . . . Why? Why did that happen?" (*P* 125). The story ends with the narrator's confession that he's yet to find an answer to Bernie's question. Victims of systemic violence and injustice, writes Trussler, "require a response that contravenes any sort of metaphysical recuperation" (214). Bernie's nephew cannot metaphysically recuperate her suffering. He cannot understand the logic of the system—why some people come out on top and others don't. Saunders offers no answer either, and the question remains open. But it is the first step toward imagining a different kind of society, one constructed along avenues of fulfillment that aren't mapped and bounded entirely by consumer capitalism.

Saunders offers no programmatic answer, but the moral thrust of his work is that the way forward lies in a radical revision of our thinking about personhood and dignity. Compassion engages suffering without metaphysically recuperating it. But Saunders's notion of compassion—rooted in the religious traditions he's practiced, Buddhism and Catholicism—is utterly incompatible with the self-sufficient individualism so central to American culture. To fully grasp Saunders's robust sense of compassion, it must be understood within his broader religious vision. Saunders often discusses religion in interviews, but it features infrequently in his fiction. Where it does appear, it's frequently in commodified form, like the "Chill'n'Pray, an overpriced cooler with a holographic image of a famous religious personality," and "O My God," a mall store that sells "vintage religious statuary" (*CWL* 56, 68). Especially in his earlier work, Saunders depicts the religious options available as tainted by regnant cultural logic. Organized religion has apparently little to offer the downtrodden souls seeking spiritual fulfillment. In "Bounty," religion is no longer even the drug of the people; narcotics are the drug of the people, and the clergy supply them.

That is not to say that Saunders's characters utterly lack religious impulse. They often turn to prayer in desperate moments. Thus, the narrator in "Offloading for Mrs. Schwartz" prays, "God, I've botched this life but good. I've failed you in all major ways. You gave me true love and I blew it. I'm nothing. But what have you got against Mrs. Ken Schwartz? Forgive me. Help me figure this out" (*CWL* 76). And the narrator in "The Semplica Diaries" prays, "Lord, give us more. Give us enough. Help us not fall behind peers. Help us not, that is, fall further behind peers. For kids' sake. Do not want them scarred by how far behind we are" (*TOD* 121). Prayer is a promising admission of self-insufficiency. But making the divine present in one's life requires an ongoing reevaluation of the nature of one's need, and the prayers of several characters remain self-centered or conditioned by consumer desires. Saunders undercuts any individualistic religious consolation. He depicts an environment where nominal belief in God remains common but religion has assumed the complexion of consumer capitalism. Here, the role of religion "is to describe authoritatively and to resolve problems" (R. Williams 16). When religion is reduced to this functionalist role, there is little to impede the transition from established religion to the religion of American exceptionalism, which is highly conducive to self-help practices.

DIGNITY AS GIFT: "WINKY"

By enjoining individuals to these disciplines of gratitude, self-improvement, and meritorious suffering, American exceptionalism paves the way for the self-help culture. Positive thinking becomes necessary to the endurance of the American dream. Such dreaming becomes an exercise in delusion rather than imagination. American exceptionalism rests on the possibility of happiness and success; positive thinking numbs individuals to their suffering, so that this possibility is preserved. The narrator of "Pastoralia," worrying about his son's health problems, talks himself into the necessity of positivity:

> Certainly, dwelling on problems doesn't solve them. Although on the other hand, thinking positively about problems also doesn't solve them. But at least then you feel positive, which is, or should be, you know, empowering. And power is good. Power is necessary at this point.... What I need to remember now is that I don't have to solve the problems of the world. It is not within my power to cure Nelson, it is only necessary for me to do what I can do ... to keep my chin up, so I can continue to do a good job. (*P* 35)

Revising Kierkegaard's phrase, we might call this a sentimental suspension of the teleological. As an individual motivational device, it's lamentable enough—fatuous perhaps but probably not vicious. But the same mental workaround becomes far more insidious when self-help is predicated upon dissolving all human engagement.

The self-help culture thrives on the notion of dignity. Self-help buzzwords—*potential, power, worth,* and the like—all come back to the dignity of the individual self. But here dignity is understood as a basic natural right and is acknowledged selectively, always with the self in focus. In Saunders's view, the most salient danger of "the power of positive thinking" is not that it's baseless and delusional, nor even that it reconciles individuals to their own disenfranchisement, but that it selectively ignores the role of others in one's own successes and failures. Positive thinking involves "increased pressure on the individual, [which] necessarily encourages a kind of sharp-elbowed individualism" (Millen 134). It predisposes one to objectify and exploit other people.

Saunders suggests that human dignity emanates from two sources. First, there's what I'll call juridical dignity: dignity as a universal right, substantiated either by natural law or by some form of theological anthropology. Such dignity is universal in principle even if not in fact. Second, there's dignity as a gift: dignity as given and received, dependent in a real and existential sense on others. Dignity on this latter account is dynamic, not a static quality or right. We must not only be attuned to what we owe others but also willing to receive humanity from them.

Without the second component, the assertion of one's dignity easily slides into an aggressive defense that objectifies others as potential roadblocks. We see this in Saunders's story "Winky," which comically portrays our self-help culture as the inevitable metastasis of individualism. "Winky" focuses on sibling roommates and fellow pariahs Winky and Neil Yaniky. The story opens with Neil attending a self-help seminar. On stage, a masked figure in a gold hat drags a series of personified character flaws including "Chronically Depressed," "Clingy," and "Helpless" to the "Pokey for Those Who Would Keep Us from Inner Peace." (That "Chronically Depressed" and "Clingy" are classed as species of the same genus is itself revealing.) The masked figure then turns to the audience and asks, "What time is it?" They respond in tandem, "Now Is the Time for Me to Win!" Dramatically, the masked man reveals himself as none other than seminar founder Tom Rodgers, who has two concepts to share with these future winners: oatmeal and crap. Holding up a bowl of oatmeal, Tom says,

> Now, if someone came up and crapped in your nice warm oatmeal, what would you say? Would you say: "Wow, super, thanks, please continue crapping in my oatmeal?" Am I being silly? I'm being a little silly. But guess what, in real life people come up and crap in your oatmeal all the time—friends, co-workers, loved ones, even your kids, especially your kids!—and that's exactly what you do. You say, "Thanks so much!" You say, "Crap away!" You say, and here my metaphor breaks down a bit, "Is there some way I can help you crap in my oatmeal?" (P 72)

Behind the frivolity lurk pernicious assumptions: Human interdependence is a thing to be conquered because inner peace, defined in strictly negative terms here, is synonymous with extrication from obligation. Tom amplifies the trope of family drama to validate his chilling verdict that because family impedes "inner peace," one must disengage oneself. His humor masks a flagrant disregard of even the most fundamental site of love, commitment, and self-sacrifice. Relationships (real ones, which entail obligation) may impact one's happiness, but only negatively. Other people are obstacles to be overcome.

Tom lends his glib address an air of gravitas by appealing to dignity as entitlement. Inner peace (a life of crap-free oatmeal) is one's right as a child of God. Tom explains that he decided to renounce caring for his disabled brother, Gene, because he'd become embittered by the self-sacrifice required for Gene's care. Tom's defense: "I for one love myself and want the best for me, because I am, after all, a child of God" (*P* 73). Tom directs the audience to impute their personal setbacks to their own, likely unidentified "Gene" figures, because "God doesn't make junk. If you're losing, somebody's doing it to you" (*P* 73–74). Since God doesn't make losers, to be fully human is to be a winner. Tom slickly redefines dignity in terms of material success and insists that being a child of God sanctions the forceful seizure of one's inner peace. The rest of the seminar is geared toward identifying and confronting that problem person ("Gene"). Tom propounds a bellicose version of self-sufficiency ironically unburdened of personal responsibility: If your oatmeal is bad, it's because someone else has befouled it, never because you made bad oatmeal.

The seminar concludes by ritualizing violence quite literally. Participants write the names of their oatmeal-spoilers on a mannequin and symbolically "confront" them by bludgeoning them with a bat. Neil has identified his sister as his problem, writing, "Winky: Crazy-looking and too religious and needs her own place." After he whacks pseudo-Winky upside the head, he's sent on his way with a reminder that a good confrontation is "Gentle, Firm, Loving" (*P* 79). The self-help culture operates on the premise that dignity is everyone's birthright but not everyone's reality. Everyone deserves it, and it must be seized or achieved.

The story then shifts to Winky as a focalizing character. Neil's description of her is apt. Winky is "crazy-looking": a pink-faced Shirley Temple, if Shirley were an obese adult whose headful of red ringlets had grayed and been tonsured. And she is zealously, mawkishly religious:

> She looked dreamily out . . . [and] the meadow . . . reminded her of the kind of field where Christ with his lap full of flowers had suffered with the little children, which was a scene she wanted them to put on the cover of the singing album she was going to make, the signing album about God, which would have a watercolor cover like *Shoulder My Burden*, which was a book though but anyways . . . the point of the book was that if you take on the worries and cares of others, Lord Jesus will take on your cares and worries, so that was why . . . she prided herself on keeping house for Neil-Neil and never asked him for help. (*P* 80–81)

Winky has a deeply held sense of justice, expressed primarily in jejune daydreams where stock characters like predatory, cane-wielding fat men and abusive older siblings threaten vulnerable children with disabilities. And in her mind, the healing power of love always wins out. The story juxtaposes the two siblings, and Winky's Pollyanna religion at first seems to mirror Neil's self-help seminar as a panacea for an ill-starred life. Yet Winky's general outlook, in contrast to Neil's, is marked by humble gratitude and compassion rather than maudlin bitterness. When a urine-soaked bum responds to Winky's unsolicited kindness by telling her she's too ugly to sleep with, she thinks, "Okay, praise God, he's only saying that because he's in pain, and [she] smiled ... because even if she was a little yugly she was still beautiful in Christ's sight, so for her it was all a party, a little party before a bigger party," before shifting her thoughts away from herself, "but what about Neil-Neil, where was his party?" (P 83–84). Her response to pain and insult is to recall that human worth is transcendentally secured—everyone is beloved of God. This conviction is not simply a means of consolation, however, but an impetus to love and compassion. (She thinks of the "pee-man" as "the least of her brothers.") Winky understands that need and suffering are universal, that humanity is given and received.

Both siblings are painfully aware of suffering and the fact that others contribute to it. Both siblings believe they are aiding the other undetected. Neil invited Winky to live with him only because her roommates voted to kick her out and called Neil in secret. Even Winky's minister called Neil secretly to request she not volunteer so much. Winky keeps house, never asking Neil to help, so that he can work. She is, however, an exceedingly inept housekeeper, and the place is a dirty wreck. Neil sees Winky as a burden and social liability; she thinks of him as "her pal to the end, the only loving soul she had yet found in this world" (P 84). Readers are set up to see this as a very lopsided relationship. The gain is all Winky's, the loss Neil's.

The story's climax occurs when Neil returns from his seminar. Winky has been ineptly readying a tea party for Neil, who has meanwhile been mentally rehearsing his confrontation speech, ready to give Winky the boot. He's been thinking about his future life, when he will drive a Jaguar and shop for "golden statues of geese" and "porcelain frogs" by "point[ing] out items with his riding crop" (P 84). Arriving home, Neil rings the bell. The door opens, Winky says, "Welcome home!," bowing grandly. As she does, a dirty sock falls off her shoulder and she bangs her head getting it. Watching this unfold, Neil falters. He can't do it. His speech "seemed now to have nothing to do with the girl who stood wet-eyed in the doorway" (P 88). It's not just pity restraining him. He realizes that he and Winky need each other, a painful realization that he accepts begrudgingly as a curse. Envisioning years ahead stuck with Winky, Neil is enraged at the cruel world. He's also angry with himself because, by Tom Rodgers's standards, he's weak: It's weakness that he can't bring himself to deprive Winky of his love, and weakness to need the love of such a hapless creature. It takes vulnerability to receive one's humanity from another, rather than assert it by force. But Saunders insists that in this vulnerability *is* dignity. The two siblings respond very differently to the fact of interdependence, evidence that simply recognizing interconnectedness does not determine how one responds to it. Neil's reaction echoes Rowan Williams's point that "deciding that you are obliged to be responsible [for others] is not something you can instantly derive from belief in an interconnected universe" (89–90). There must be some transcendent notion of human dignity that directs one toward responsibility. Neil has apparently retained Tom Rodgers's measure of dignity and fulfillment, and his resentful reaction challenges Winky's naïve conviction of the "healing power of love." But Winky has, at least, succeeded in preserving the possibility of reciprocity.

Saunders refuses to honor conventional categories and simple dichotomies, and his few "religious" characters are no exception. Characters like Winky (and Gil in "CommComm"), whom others pejoratively identify as "religious," are somehow both saccharine and sincere, hard to like but commanding of respect. They are attuned to a higher reality that impels them to see others with an imaginative awareness that preserves dignity and the possibility of reciprocity. Winky's vision of the kingdom of God is plainly puerile, but Saunders tempers any impulse toward smug criticism by insisting on the universality of ignorance. Saunders insists on a higher reality that "is so much bigger and [more] divinely inflected and unknowable than our puny ideas about it" ("Why"). "Winky" arms readers with manifold reasons to pity and dislike Winky and to fault her for her feeble, sentimental religion, only then to constrain us to justify any inclination to derision. We are forced to ask what, exactly, we should fault Winky for, and why, exactly, we should pity her. Pity becomes an inappropriate response because it issues from a place of superiority and entails a dismissal of her agency and her spiritual gratification. Winky is not simply subjected to suffering but rather willing to give of herself, to the point of suffering, for others' sake. (We learn she is engrossed by stigmatas.) There's plenty to object to in Winky's world view, but, crucially, Saunders never allows religion to be an easy consolation or a justification for suffering. Rather, it shapes how she responds to suffering. While refusing to offer any programmatic path to spiritual fulfillment, Saunders insinuates repeatedly that some form of disciplined commitment is foundational to the imaginative awareness necessary for calling dignity into reality.

DIGNIFIED SUFFERING: "TENTH OF DECEMBER"

Against the backdrop of a consumer environment wherein religion has become a set of pat answers, Saunders offers a religious vision that is hopeful but refuses easy consolation. Saunders presents no programmatic alternative to the religion of American exceptionalism. Instead, he veers away from any approach that could be considered programmatic, subverting the notion that religion is primarily a resource for solving problems. A truly religious vision, for Saunders, is neither epigrammatic nor characterized by seamless logic, nor does it rationalize or incentivize suffering. The divine is a transcendent reality that individuals move toward and conform themselves to and invite into the world through compassionate living. There is no deus ex machina in the Saunders universe. But, while he remains cautious about stipulating the character of the Ineffable, Saunders often, if obliquely, insinuates a greater reality impinging upon our finite earthly view of things.

In Saunders's "Tenth of December," a middle-aged man named Eber sits in a park in midwinter, exposing himself to the elements in the attempt to thereby commit suicide and make it look accidental. In stark contrast to Neil Yaniky's attitude that family is an obstacle to his success, Eber, ostensibly out of love, wants to remove himself as an obstacle to his family's well-being. Yet while Eber's motivation differs markedly, he reproduces Neil's logic in inverted form. At fifty-three, Eber has terminal cancer. He believes that in staging an accidental death, he is acting out of love for his family, sparing them the pain of watching his body and mind fail. Having watched his own stepfather suffer through dementia, Eber knows about "painful last images that might endure for a lifetime" (*TOD* 225). He fears being a burden and saying things he doesn't mean to those caring for him in intimate ways. He's afraid of soiling the legacy of familial love he shares with his wife and kids. Eber also understands his diagnosis as evidence of divine indifference. He perceives his suffering as proof that there is no loving God active in the world: "He'd kept waiting for some special dispensation. But no. Something/someone bigger than him kept refusing. You were told the big something/someone loved you especially but in the end you saw it was otherwise. The big something/someone was neutral. Unconcerned. When it innocently moved, it crushed people" (*TOD* 231). As the story progresses, however, the text subverts both the notion that love is measured by sparing the beloved pain and the notion that religion's function is to solve one's problems and offer metaphysical resolution.

Eber foils his own plan by rescuing a boy named Robin who falls through the ice nearby. Eber exerts every last reserve of energy and will to trudge, half-frozen already, through drifts of snow, then pull the overweight teenager to safety. Throughout the remainder of the story, Eber resolves not to end his life early but almost perishes anyhow in the effort to save Robin. As this transpires, Eber carries on an intermittent mental dialogue with God: thanking God for the strength to reach Robin; deciding he does not want to die out in the snow and pleading with God to preserve him for now; and finally concluding that the mundane joys of each living day were greater evidence of divine goodness than terminal illness was evidence of divine absence. Eber locates the divine in the will and capacity to subordinate his own desires for the sake of another. What emerges is a vision of divine grace as present in the world through the ways human beings elect to love and sacrifice for one another.

Eber realizes that what he's been fearing is a different kind of community, marked more profoundly by vulnerability. He thinks,

> If some guy, at the end, fell apart, and said or did bad things, or had to be helped . . . So what? . . . Why should he not do or say weird things or look strange or disgusting? . . . Why should those he loved not lift and bend and feed and wipe him, when he would gladly do the same for them? He'd been afraid to be lessened by the lifting and bending and feeding and wiping, and was still afraid of that, and yet, at the same time, now saw that there could still be many—many drops of goodness, is how it came to him . . . and those drops of fellowship were not—had never been—his to withheld.
> Withhold. (*TOD* 248–49)

Eber realizes that it is not his right to withhold his own presence from others, even for the sake of sparing them responsibility for his bodily needs, because doing so deprives them of their opportunity to love him. Eber's concern for his family is never in doubt, but he must learn to receive love as well, and allow others to enact his own dignity through love and compassion. For Saunders, our humanity is not just *a* given; it *is given*. It must be courageously, even sacrificially given to others, and courageously, even humiliatingly, received. Suffering does not efface dignity. If compassion is not grounded in a robust notion of dignity, suffering can be confused with what is really inconvenience or a mere denial of consumer preferences. True compassion wills suffering to end but is also willing to suffer with and for others for the sake of plenitude. Suffering is neither rationalized nor valorized. Compassion is not an individual achievement but a communal mode of life. Thus, compassionate other-regard entails attention to the self, because the lives of others are impacted (and may be augmented) not only by an individual's self-denial but also by her self-fulfillment.

All human beings occupy a slice of life that is inherently limited, making us fallible and ineluctably ignorant in many ways. Saunders affirms this as not just an accepted tenet of postmodernism but a religious truth. Given this state of affairs, suffering is an inexorable human reality. In *Lincoln in the Bardo,* two characters articulate in tandem the world view implicit in virtually all of Saunders's work: "We are all suffering, limited beings . . . Perennially outmatched by circumstance, inadequately endowed with compensatory graces" (304). Saunders's account of suffering appears more Buddhist than Catholic (as the Christian notion of sin doesn't seem to factor into it), although one needn't be Buddhist to believe that suffering is the basic human condition. Suffering is also inevitable because everything is interconnected. For Saunders, this has little to do with globalization; it is a metaphysical reality as well as an ontological one, more to do with karma than semiotics or fiber-optic cables. Saunders insinuates a foundation of need as the default state of existence. Our interconnectedness with other fallible beings is thus a principal cause of suffering *but also* a source of melioration. Saunders's Catholic impulse appears most palpably in his frequent attention to the absence of perceived grace. But this graceless state, referenced in the above-cited passage, is the starting point, not the ending point.

Redemptive moments in Saunders's fiction, such as there are, always turn upon an admission of self-insufficiency and dependence. Goodness begins with the recognition of need: one's own and that of others. Suffering is shared just as joy is shared, neither valorized nor rationalized but mitigated whenever possible. Saunders refuses to allow his characters facile religious consolation or special dispensation with regard to earthly suffering, but he does affirm a form of grace active in the world. We may mediate grace to one another through compassion. At times, such as with Eber, this grace is apparently divine, but it is also, and always, mediated through human interaction, evident when an individual's humanity is called into reality through the loving attention and actions of another. This is both empowering—as one holds great power to harm or help others—and humbling—because one's life remains radically contingent upon circumstances and the choices of others. This is not simply another way of saying that our individual choices ramify in others' lives, that our lives impact theirs. Rather, our choices, attitudes, and actions determine, to a significant extent, the choices *available* to others. Grace is an enabling entity. So, my choices impact the limits and possibilities and thus the happiness of another's life. What's in view here is something radical: the difference between believing we should treat others well and understanding that we shape the very contours of their lives.

SEEING AS SEEN: *LINCOLN IN THE BARDO*

In *Lincoln in the Bardo*, Saunders has found innovative ways to depict human interconnectedness. It's a work that defies easy classification. Ostensibly, the novel tells the (possibly apocryphal) story of Lincoln visiting the crypt of his recently deceased son Willy and cradling Willy's body in his lap. Some chapters narrate episodes in the life of Lincoln and his family, which are conveyed through a collage of excerpts from various, often contradicting, though *mostly* authentic, historical sources. These chapters create a robust, if internally inconsistent, picture of the public view of Lincoln by his contemporaries, allowing for a plurality of voices that achieves a mosaic effect. But the majority of chapters are narrated by one or more of a graveyard-full of ghosts. The basic premise is that these ghosts who inhabit the graveyard remain because of some lingering, unmet earthly desire that they refuse to forfeit. While other recently dead pass into the next realm (depicted as a final completion and peaceful terminus), these ghosts remain, harboring the vain hope of finally satisfying their unfulfilled longings. In the novel, Saunders renders human intersubjectivity quite literally by allowing the ghosts to inhabit one another as well as living beings. Such intersubjectivity involves shared suffering as much as any shared joy and collaborative creation. To differing degrees, all the ghosts bear grotesque iterations of their respective unsatisfied desires. (For example, one ghost who died before consummating his marriage has monstrously enlarged genitals.) But those ghosts whose attention is solely directed inward are undergoing erasure; they are becoming less and less themselves, less recognizably human, increasingly less selves at all. In other words, the utterly self-absorbed individual is not a self at all; there is something missing that is essential to their being fully human. The novel is, of course, a work of imagination. And, in spite of its Buddhist title, Saunders has admitted to taking great liberties with the notion of the Bardo, partially out of necessity. But its lack of conformity to Buddhist "orthodoxy" does not discredit the underlying ideas that Saunders projects upon his wonderfully worked spectral characters.

For my purposes here, the novel's most significant aspect is its depiction of Lincoln, which is a powerful indictment of contemporary American individualism. In Saunders's account, one of America's mythological heroes is subjected to suffering on several fronts—not only the battlefronts of the Civil War but also the loss of his beloved son Willy. Far from a stalwart model of self-sufficiency, Lincoln is wracked by grief to the point of near paralysis. Willy's death occurs in the middle of the war, at a point when victory for the Union is most in doubt. In his grief, Lincoln becomes keenly aware of the universality of suffering:

Though on the surface it seemed every person was different, this was not true.
    At the core of each lay suffering; our eventual end, the many losses we must experience on the way to that end.
    We must try to see one another in this way. (*LB* 304)

The loss of his son catalyzes a deeper understanding of what is at stake in war and radically revises Lincoln's decision-making going forward. He becomes more attuned to the moral ambiguity of war and the *almost* pyrrhic nature of every victory. His grief, for the moment, eclipses any geographical or ideological boundary, and the possibility of victory is emptied for him of any sense of vindication. Here again, two ghosts inhabiting Lincoln jointly narrate his internal thoughts:

His sympathy extended to all in this instant, blundering, in its strict logic, across all divides.
    He was leaving here broken, awed, humbled, diminished.
    Ready to believe anything of this world.
    Made less rigidly himself through this loss.
    Therefore quite powerful.
    Reduced, ruined, remade.
    Merciful, patient, dazzled.
    And yet.
    And yet. He was in a fight. Although those he fought were also suffering, limited beings, he must— (*LB* 304)

For a moment, all sense of division and antagonism vanishes from Lincoln's mind, and even when that awareness returns—that he is "in a fight"—the understanding of commonality is preserved. Hate, as a character says in Graham Greene's *The Power and the Glory*, is a failure of imagination. Conversely, compassion requires imaginative awareness of the other. What is required for spiritual fulfillment and human flourishing isn't just empathy; empathy may recognize suffering without moving to mitigate it and/or come from a place of elitism or privilege. Lincoln's imaginative awareness makes him compassionate rather than just empathetic. Rowan Williams describes the kind of imaginative awareness that sees others not only as they relate to oneself but also as they relate to others besides oneself: This disciplined vision is a "willingness to see things or other persons as the objects of another sensibility than my own, perhaps also another sensibility than our own, whoever 'we' are, even if the 'we' is humanity itself. The point is that what I am aware of, I am aware of as in significant dimensions not defined by my awareness" (13). In Saunders's novel, Lincoln recognizes the suffering—the pain and fear—of those he's fighting, *and* he sees them as others beside himself might see them. He recognizes that the Confederate soldiers who have fallen and might yet fall mean more to people in their lives than he could possibly imagine:

> He must (*we* must, *we* felt) do all *we* could, in light of the many soldiers lying dead and wounded, in open fields, all across the land, weeds violating their torsos, eyeballs pecked out or dissolving, lips hideously retracted, rain-soaked/blood-soaked/snow-crusted letters scattered about them, to ensure that we did not, as we trod that difficult path we were now well upon, blunder, blunder further (we had blundered so badly already) and, in so blundering, ruin more, more of these boys, each of whom was once dear to someone.
>   *Ruinmore, ruinmore,* we felt, *must endeavor not to ruinmore.*
>   Our grief must be defeated; it must not become our master, and make us ineffective, and put us even deeper into the ditch. (*LB* 306)

Lincoln, as a parent who's lost a child, now envisions every dead soldier "as a special sort of object for a subjectivity not [his] own" (R. Williams 17), as a source of untold grief to all of those whose lives he had populated.

Lincoln's resolute decision to continue to fight is made only after compassionate identification with the Confederate troops. Lincoln's compassion is also grounded in a larger vision of human dignity. The issue of ordering violence in the name of saving the Union is grounded in a meditation on what it means to be fully human: "On the surface it was a technicality (mere Union) but seen deeper, it was something more. How should men live? How could men live?" (*LB* 307). Lincoln can only continue to order his soldiers to fight in the understanding that it is human dignity in its fullest sense that's at stake, and not only *his* welfare. Compassion in its active sense is defined by two obverse intentions: mitigating suffering and preserving possibility. The latter requires an imaginative awareness that must be developed through conscious and continuous exercise. The very attempt to imagine the possibilities and circumstances of others' lives is necessary but only possible to a certain extent, at which point we must recognize our own limited understanding and assume a posture of humility. Lincoln, in the novel, is never aware of the ghosts who variously inhabit him and read his thoughts, but as he leaves the graveyard, convinced of what he must do and that the war must go forward, he leaves permanently aware of the company of ghosts: "*What that new state is, I do not know, and patiently wait to learn, even as those three thousand fallen stare foul-*

eyed at me, working dead hands anxiously, asking, What end might this thing yet attain, that will make our terrible sacrifice worthwh—" (LB 310).

Compassion requires the imaginative awareness to see others as seen. In other words, it's an acknowledgment that interdependence exceeds that of myself and another. The person I behold is beheld by others as well. And so, in addition to the fact that my subjectivity informs and, to an extent, constrains another's subjectivity, there will always be, crucially, a part of the other that is inaccessible to me. Others are ourselves on a different day, as Saunders insists, but they are also, crucially, *not* ourselves, on any day. This practice of imaginative awareness engenders a recognition of other modes of life that are as valid as or potentially superior to one's own. The ability to do this, and to live compassionately, hinges upon some sort of transcendent perspective. But it is a discipline—a habit of seeing that must be inculcated—rather than a belief. And it's a faculty that Saunders suggests is uncommon in our contemporary American culture. It is those whose prayerful acknowledgment of insufficiency impels them outward, into community with others, who approach the divine. Beginning from ignorance and incompletion, we expand our vision of the divine reality (which remains always incomplete but less so) through the ways we love and accompany others. What makes Saunders's work so compelling and so morally salient is that this hopeful outlook, the life of compassion, is, when given legs, very messy work indeed and, at best, inconstantly consoling. Spiritual fullness, Saunders stresses, is a difficult business, especially because it is never a strictly individual endeavor.

CHAPTER 5

Creeds Fall Away

Marilynne Robinson's Democratic Individuality

MARILYNNE ROBINSON occupies a unique place in the contemporary literary landscape. She's an anachronism to some, as she has no anxiety of influence or penchant for novelty and overtly engages religion. Yet she has captivated secular readers and prize panels. Like the other writers discussed in this book, Robinson refuses to separate religion and politics and is more concerned with religious practice and spiritual discipline than doctrinal exactitude. She differs in being the only one to openly identify as an orthodox Christian (Congregationalist, to be exact). In the preface to her recent volume of essays, Robinson says she is "too old to mince words" (*WDH* xiv). But Robinson, a prolific essayist, has never been one to gloss or soft-pedal her views. (She had the audacity, as an *American,* to write a critical exposé on environmental degradation in England and title it *Mother Country.*) She has embraced a role as a Christian public intellectual, and she proclaims to a sizeable readership that America needs to recuperate its abandoned Puritan heritage. Robinson has long been an enthusiastic defender of Puritanism and a searing critic of the politically ambitious, right-wing Christian resurgence in America. At stake, for her, is nothing less than Christianity on the one hand and America on the other.

Robinson is a particularly interesting case among the authors considered in this study, because she attacks a form of American exceptionalism that is explicitly religious in its rhetoric but that Robinson argues is purely ideological. This ideology *is* a religion, according to the definition I've established, in that it entails its own practices and spiritual disciplines, but Robinson vehemently denies it has any trace of true religious impulse. Robinson suggests that nationalistic ideology has become an ersatz religion because America has forsaken the religious vision that made the nation exceptional.

In her essay "Fear," Robinson challenges the ultranationalistic, embattled stance of those who believe America must defend its Christian citizens and Christianity itself by raising the drawbridges and resorting to military aggression (*GOT* 124–40). Robinson's essay style tends toward juxtaposition, and she turns characteristically to history, comparing the religious persecution of Protestants in France with current religious persecution—namely of Muslims—in the name of Christianity. The common denominator is a climate of fear, which today is rooted largely in Islamophobia and xenophobia. Robinson provocatively asserts that underneath the high-flown rhetoric and seething pride is no Christian impulse but a cultural, and racial, ideology. Her essay ostensibly affirms the separation of church and state, for the authenticity of the church and the welfare of the state. Robinson unequivocally eschews the notion of making America a "Christian 'establishment,'" which she insists it's never been.

However, for all the commendable points of the essay—and there are many, especially that strident doesn't mean right—Robinson adopts a seemingly circular logic that threatens to confute her own argument. She lambasts a certain version of America as a Christian nation, in the name of America as a (fortuitously) Christian nation. The problem, apparently, is not *that* but *how* we consider America a Christian nation. Robinson states, "When Christians abandon Christian standards of behavior in the defense of Christianity, when Americans abandon American standards of conduct in the name of America, they inflict harm that would not be in the power of any enemy" (*GOT* 134). She effectively addresses Americans as Christians and Christians as Americans. The "standards of conduct" here are indistinguishable. Her essay says, in effect, that any country that calls itself a Christian nation, *if* it were a Christian nation, would not be cowed by such fear and anxiety. (And, there's no need to call ourselves a Christian nation, because we are a nation of Christians.) Elsewhere, Robinson explicitly acknowledges and celebrates America's religious and cultural pluralism. What to do, then, with her apparent internal inconsistency?

To make sense of it, we need to further examine how Robinson understands "Christian standards of behavior" and "American standards of conduct" and who, exactly, is guilty of abandoning them. Christopher Douglas has rightly suggested that Robinson castigates the right-wing Christian resurgence as a threat to the future of America even as she's a part of the recent American Christian resurgence (104). Robinson's position is that America *is* and should be a religious nation with an important separation of church and state. She aims to demonstrate to *all* Americans the enduring necessity of a Christian vision to the future of American democratic life, while opposing the fundamentalist Christians who seek to make America a Christian nation through public policy. But her attempt to address a diverse audience unsurprisingly poses some difficulties. She uses denominationally specific Christian theology while arguing for religious pluralism and emphasizing personal experience over doctrinal belief. The result is what I consider a form of transcendentalism. Her impassioned but careful defenses of Calvinist Christianity and democracy are inseparable, and her caustic rebuke of the politically ambitious Christian right emanates from her conviction that they threaten both Christianity and democracy. Ultimately, I contend, it is a Christian aesthetics, or a theopoetics, that Robinson finds crucial to democracy, and she seeks to address all Americans, Christian or not, by making democracy itself a religious practice. This practice is remarkably similar, as we'll see, to what many call democratic individuality.

IDEOLOGY AND MONOCULTURE

Robinson's transcendentalist leanings need to be situated within her take on the current American culture wars and the centrality of ideology. Much of her treatment of religion and, especially, political ideology comes in her nonfiction, so this chapter departs somewhat in attending more directly to the author's nonfiction. The form of American exceptionalism Robinson identifies as most conspicuous, and therefore in need of address, carries an explicitly Christian backing. It's not only conservative Christians who are guilty of trading in ideology, however. Robinson laments that all sides in the culture war "have surrendered thought to ideology," from vociferous nativists to ardent multiculturalists (*WDH* xii). Ideology, Robinson says, is a discursive disease endangering democracy by making us fractious and suspicious.[1] Ideological thinking is so prevalent and beguiling because it is difficult to recognize as such. Ideologies achieve authoritative status by appearing "as exhaustive accounts of reality rather than, at best, as instruments of understanding suited to particular uses" (*WDH* 44). Ideology, "thinking that by definition is not

---

1. For Robinson, *ideology* is categorically pejorative. Her usage is at times unduly narrow in assuming that ideology is consciously and therefore culpably embraced, which isn't necessarily fair. We're all products of our environment *to an extent*, which Robinson admits.

one's own," purports to interpret experience while willfully ignoring it (*WDH* xiv). Robinson superbly articulates its operation: "What is being invoked is the notion of a precious and unnameable essence, second nature to some, in the marrow of their bones, in effect. By this view others, whether they will or no, cannot understand or value it, and therefore they are a threat" (*WDH* 23). The nebulous essence around which ideology constellates is ahistorical, though it is embedded in a spurious historicity: "Perhaps the worst thing about ideological thinking is that it implies a structure in and behind events, a history that is reiterative, with variations that cannot ultimately change the course of things and are therefore always trivial" (*WDH* xiii).

An unwelcome corollary of ideological discourse is that all parties tend to regard Americans as a monoculture. Robinson insists the term *American* should be "a remarkably difficult one to define" because American culture at its best is marked by openness and diversity; thus "attempts at self-definition that exclude what have been formative influences, or preclude new ones, need to be resisted where possible" (*WCR* 167). Speaking of America as homogenous debases America's greatest asset, its democratic culture, but ironically, everyone is doing it. This pretense of homogeneity provokes nativism and a corresponding narrative of decline that Robinson locates at the heart of current culture wars. Nativism requires (and inevitably produces) enemies adjudged responsible for national decline. Robinson finds it quite intriguing but even more dismaying "to learn that nativist rhetoric can have impact in a country where precious few can claim to be native in any ordinary sense" (*WDH* 23). But nativism isn't the sole domain of those seeking racial or religious hegemony. It is rather "an impulse or strategy to shape the culture with which it claims to have this privileged intimacy," by all who "are wildly unhappy with the country they claim to love and are bent on remaking it to suit their own preferences" (23). Nativism is ironically un-American precisely in its eschewal of dialogue. Robinson indicts all sides for their tendentious accounts of history. The conservatives exalt ideas that represent but a select part of the cultural heritage, thus regarding "context as an impertinence and change as decline . . . yielding a robust sense of loyalty to certain national values" (*WCR* 169). Meanwhile, the left embraces a "toxic heritage approach, the perverse nativism . . . [that] treats context as irrelevant and change as never more than superficial" (169). Neither side offers "a meaningful standard of change" by which we may accurately assess our current situation (*GOT* 125). How we talk about the past matters immensely, and Robinson offers her own historical corrective.

Lacking a clear benchmark for change and a rich grasp of cultural history, productive discourse is at best unlikely. A democracy must expect discord. The hope isn't to avoid conflict but to have the resources to weather it constructively and as amicably as possible. Democracy depends upon "the moderating effects of broader identification" and is thus imperiled when any party responds to conflict by retreating to "some narrower definition of identity." For a democracy to handle the conflict inherent to it, everyone must be committed to democratic practice. Retreat into sectarian identities "destroys every community—not only through outright suppression or conflict. Those who seemingly win are damaged inwardly and insidiously because they have betrayed the better nature and the highest teaching of their community in descending to exclusion, suppression, or violence" (WCR 26–27). Robinson believes that both Christianity and democracy are characterized fundamentally by a broadening of identity and that tribalism is antithetical to both. And tribalism is what she sees as the looming legacy of the right-wing Christian resurgence. Robinson highlights that American exceptionalism today is typically marked by its emphasis on imminent, precipitous national decline, eliciting a dangerously defensive posture. It's in this context that Robinson locates the dogmatism of Christian fundamentalism.

Robinson castigates the resurgent Christian right for surrendering religion to ideology and confusing religious devotion with cultural identity. She warns, a bit histrionically, that America's Christian population is headed for a "religious monoculture" (GOT 102). Far from an ecumenical triumph, this emerging Christianity is a travesty: It's "not a neutral averaging of the particularities of all the major traditions. . . . [Instead,] the whole focus is on 'personal salvation,' on 'accepting Jesus as your Lord and Savior.' Theologically speaking, the cosmos has contracted severely" (GOT 102). Ironically, denominational differences are elided in the name of particularity, and theological diminution is complemented by intensified intransigence. Robinson attributes such reductive dogmatism to the unbefitting fear that Christianity cannot survive intellectual ferment: "Christianity was induced to excuse itself from explorations . . . to tend to its own truncated magisterium . . . to stumble forever at its own threshold, fretting over the issue of belief versus disbelief, having accepted garden variety credibility or plausibility as the appropriate standard to bring to bear on these reported intrusions of higher truth upon human experience" (GOT 145–46). Robinson considers anti-intellectualism tantamount to blasphemy because it spurns the intelligence and imagination by which humans glorify their Creator. She doesn't deny the importance of religious belief but insists that it's more a mode of life, a movement out of the self toward a higher reality, than an intellectual position. Fundamentalism mistakes dogmatic belief for an artificial certainty, which amounts to an expurgation of the mystery proper to a God professed as transcendent. Probing the divine mystery is an essential human task, but attempting to demystify the divine is Promethean hubris. At the same time, religion that is afraid of intellectual exploration is already slumping into ideology.

In its perfervid dogmatism and desire to dissolve mystery, fundamentalism assumes the character of the secularism it fears and loathes. *Secularism* has become, for the Christian right, a cipher for all forces threatening the cultural status of their particular Christianity and, thereby, threatening America and its cultural heritage. They "now think in terms of a Manichaean struggle between secularism and all we hold dear" (*WDH* 314). Certainly the US has witnessed, like most of the developed West, a shift in cultural imaginary: the pluralization of modes of life and the heightened awareness in individuals of the freedom to choose among them. But the Christian right has tended to confuse, perhaps willfully, every form of secularism for the programmatic kind (an ideology that equates secularism with progress defined as the triumph of rationality and the dissipation of magical thinking).[2] And, by reducing religious belief to a series of definitive propositions that provide the architecture of a clear, navigable world view, fundamentalists vainly attempt to combat secularism by reproducing its own assumptions.

Robinson candidly confesses that as a Christian she finds little to commend in this Christian crusade. In her eyes, the rise of this new "self-declared elect," which "some have seen as a resurgence of Christianity, or at least a bold defense of American cultural tradition—even as another great awakening!" has but introduced "a harshness, a bitterness, a crudeness, and a high-handedness into the public sphere" (*GOT* 103). Revealingly, she likens the current political polarization to that which immediately preceded the Civil War. Robinson is so acerbically critical of the Christian right because she views them as a threat to both Christianity *and* democracy. The practices entailed in this religio-political coup are, in her eyes, as utterly unchristian as the endeavor to make America Christian via political policy is undemocratic. An atmosphere characterized by "distrust or resentment or rage as the manufactured outcry of a virtual populace" is not an atmosphere in which "religion is likely to retain its character as religion" (*GOT* 105). Robinson insists that the Christianity proclaimed by this group "to be under threat on that most secular continent is merely sociological and cultural, in effect racial" (*GOT* 127). It is, in short, a nationalistic form of cultural identity. Ostensibly patriotic aims are furthered by enjoining them as religious obligation. The upshot is the installation of God

---

2. Robinson sees the resurgence of the Christian right and the advent of a militant, ideological secularism, represented most vociferously by the "new atheists," as coeval and equally myopic.

as "a tribal deity, our local Baal," but one who clearly isn't powerful enough, or there wouldn't be such fear and antagonism (*WCR* 136).

What the Christian right is fighting for, Robinson maintains, has little to do with Christianity. It is an ideology of American exceptionalism ballasted with Christian rhetoric, which she calls "Christianism." Christianism, which she labels an ideology, *is* by my definition a religion: The transcendent deity is conflated with America, and the practices it inspires are pernicious. Because a majority of Americans still do identify as Christian, the term is used interchangeably for a demographic and a religious tradition. This equivocality is easily exploited, as it has been before: "A ferocious secularism can carry on its internecine wars under the names Catholic and Protestant" (*GOT* 98). In response to their threatened cultural status, the Christian right has hitched its Christian identity to a certain account of national identity and cast any threat to its own existence as a threat to American heritage. The narratives of American exceptionalism and national decline are welded together to incite fear and resentment: fear of what might become of us, and resentment of any who might hasten our downfall.

Robinson declares *this* the real threat to American heritage, as fundamentalists attack the state for "maintaining institutional distance that was meant in the first instance to protect religious freedom" (*GOT* 92–93). Confusing nonsectarian for secularist, they have subsequently sought to install themselves in positions of power within the "secular" state as a moral crusade against it. They "see an onrush of secularism intent on driving religion to the margins, maybe over the edge, and for the sake of Christianity they want to enlist society itself in its defense" (*WCR* 134–35). This only inflames the problem and increases its polarity. Robinson generalizes for the sake of polemic, but the movements she has in view are visible enough to influence public perception and discourse. Robinson responds by positioning democracy within the register of religious practice yet attempting to appeal to all Americans.

CHRISTIANITY: IDENTITY VERSUS ETHIC

In order to articulate her view of Christianity's proper relation to democracy, Robinson distinguishes between Christianity as ethic and as identity. The latter, when unfettered from the former, tends to capitulate to the ideological thinking that plagues American cultural discourse. *Christian* then becomes a tribal identity, which Robinson asserts is fundamentally unchristian. Rather reductively, Robinson suggests that a truly Christian ethic runs "steadfastly against the grain of what we consider human nature. The first will be last;

to him who asks give; turn the other cheek; judge not. Identity, on the other hand, appeals to a constellation of the worst human impulses" (*GOT* 104).

Addressing the Christian right, Robinson posits an indefensible lack of fit between their Christianity identity and their ethics. Since they claim a Christian America, she supplies a rebuke on their own terms, censuring them for unchristian politics (while affirming separation of church and state herself). Her arguments rely on appeals varying from the evangelical (how non-Christians will perceive Christianity), to the ecclesiastical, to the doctrinal. She reproves American Christians for neglecting responsibility for Christianity's global reputation, arguing that if they considered this responsibility, "some of us might think a little longer about associating the precious Lord with ignorance, intolerance, and belligerent nationalism" (*GOT* 124). Elsewhere, she asks, "How is it consistent with the belief that the church is the body of Christ, a belief I share, to think it has no intrinsic life to be relied on, and must, for the sake of its survival, be fastened to a more vigorous body, that of the nation?" (*WCR* 136). And finally, she insists, "If the claims to Christian identity we hear now are rooted in an instinctive tribalism, they are entirely inappropriate, certainly uninformed, because in its nature the religion they claim has no boundaries, no shibboleths, no genealogies or hereditary claimants" (*GOT* 104–5). (There is a certain irony in this last claim, as Robinson makes a normative, even doctrinal, claim about Christianity's doctrinal fluidity; we'll revisit the issue of Robinson's (in)coherence below.) The collective argument here is that Christian identity without Christian ethics is a farce.

Yet the semantic slippage in *Christian* also makes Robinson's own views sometimes difficult to pin down. Robinson's essays can try one's patience in many ways, one being that it's not always clear who her intended audience is. Many of her essays focus on the relation between politics and religion, and she argues *from* a position that oscillates between an explicitly religious perspective and a generally American one, while directing her argument to an audience that also appears to shift between Christians and the general public. Thus, her argument may become more or less persuasive depending on the religious commitments of the reader.[3] This approach is frustrating, but it becomes evident that Robinson wants her two primary arguments—the essence of Christianity and the essence of democracy—to be heard by two audiences: a narrower Christian audience, and a larger audience of the general American populace. She adopts a very particular theological approach to sustain this broad appeal. I suggest that a further motive for her rhetorical strat-

---

3. Her recent volume *What Are We Doing Here?* is an exception because the essays are transcribed addresses to specific audiences, often at religious institutions.

egy is to convey to non-Christian readers that orthodox Christianity needn't look like fundamentalism. Robinson's derisive use of "Christianism" to signify the conflation of Christianity and nationalism reinforces the point by denying it the status of orthodoxy and classing it as ideology.

Robinson also argues that by conflating religion and nationalism, the Christian resurgence threatens American political culture, warping proper commitment to American democracy into vulgar nationalism. Robinson takes pains to distance herself from religious exceptionalism, saying, "I am the sort of Christian whose patriotism might be called into question by some on the grounds that I do not take the United States to be more beloved of God than France, let us say, or Russia . . . or Iran" (*WCR* 136–37). Robinson distinguishes democratic exceptionalism from a nationalistic American exceptionalism. She affirms the separation of church and state but also believes American culture is Christian in its heritage and that this heritage must be preserved. The "tribalism" of the Christian resurgence amounts to a failure of the imaginative love that Robinson considers the heart of both Christianity and democracy: fundamentalists betray in the name of America what Robinson sees as dearest to America.

Robinson castigates the Christian right for unchristian ethics, but she believes the significant contribution of Christianity to American culture is aesthetic (then derivatively ethical). Thus Robinson responds to "Christianism" by reclaiming religious experience as the true nucleus of religion. Her nuanced account of religious experience allows her to counter the Christian right in two ways. First, focusing on religious experience enables her to circumvent doctrinal dispute and cultivate an ecumenical spirit. Second, it enables her to affirm the historical and necessary influence of Christianity on democracy while supporting pluralism and avoiding sectarianism. Even as Robinson's work can be placed within the recent Christian resurgence, her defense of Christianity's political significance is radically innovative. Rather than claiming that America should be officially Christian, Robinson couches democracy itself as a religious practice and enjoins all Americans to commit to it for the sake of the nation's future. Robinson unites Christianity and democracy through a focus on the practice of receptivity, with the ultimate end being a diverse, and therefore aesthetically superlative, body of "believers" whose imaginative love for each other signals a kind of transcendence.

RELIGIOUS EXPERIENCE

In her fiction and essays, Robinson dwells on the central role of personal experience in religion, often appealing to Calvin and other Reformed theologians. Robinson affirms that we can only know ourselves in relation to the transcendent, but she adds that we can come to know God by "descending into ourselves" (*GOT* 227). She plaits transcendence and immanence in a way that makes her a very transcendentalist kind of Calvinist. Robinson's fiction luminously depicts the whole of life as potentially sacramental by subtly dissolving the dichotomy between the spiritual and the material. Anthony Domestico has shown how Glory in Robinson's *Home* redeems mundane tasks as forms of spiritual discipline: "For Glory, the way to grace is through hospitality, through caring even for those who resist her care. . . . [B]anal activities—cooking dinner, bathing her father—become ways of acknowledging the sacredness of this world and of her difficult family" (16). Robinson sees the religious sense as fundamentally aesthetic and posits a strong correlation between spiritual attunement and material quality of life.

In *Gilead*, an epistolary novel "written" by aging father John Ames to his young son Robbie, Ames writes that "it is religious experience above all that authenticates religion, for the purposes of the individual believer" (145). Reverend Ames (like Robinson herself) thinks the attempt to defend God by logical proofs is generally fruitless and misguided:

> I have had a certain amount of experience with skepticism and the conversation it generates, and there is an inevitable futility in it. It is even destructive. Young people from my own flock have come home with a copy of *La Nausée* or *L'Immoraliste*, flummoxed by the possibility of unbelief, when I must have told them a thousand times that unbelief is possible. And they are attracted to it by the very books that tell them what a misery it is. And they want me to defend religion, and they want me to give them "proofs." I just won't do it. It only confirms them in their skepticism. Because nothing true can be said about God from a posture of defense. (*GL* 177)

Lived experience, firsthand knowledge of the sacramental dimension of earthly life, trumps any written apologia. Religion is justified by its bearing on one's quality of life. In his fulsome epistle, Ames recurs often to experiences in which the transcendent emanates through the material. Knowing his years are numbered, Ames dwells on "the gift of physical particularity and how blessing and sacrament are mediated through it," writing, "I have been thinking lately how I have loved my physical life" (*GL* 69). Existence itself provokes wonder; Ames tells his son, "It's your existence I love you for, mainly. Existence seems to me now the most remarkable thing that could ever be imagined" (*GL* 53). Ames is not objectifying his son but rather marveling at the sheer gratuitousness of familial love. Earthly life is so exquisite that Ames believes the world must exceed itself, and he imagines that any sort of heaven must surpass earthly life without annihilating it.

As physical creatures, anything we can really know of the spiritual *must* come to us through the material world, and thus spiritual growth requires the cultivation of an aesthetic sensibility. In another passage, Ames describes glimpsing a profusion of fireflies as an occasion for thinking about the reflexive connection between materiality and spirituality:

> There were more fireflies out there than I had ever seen in my life . . . just drifting up out of the grass, extinguishing themselves in midair. We sat on the steps a good while in the dark and the silence, watching them. Finally Boughton said, "Man is born to trouble as the sparks fly upward." And really, it was that night as if the earth were smoldering. Well, it was, and it is. An old fire will make a dark husk for itself and settle in on its core, as in the case of this planet. I believe the same metaphor may describe the human individual, as well. Perhaps Gilead. Perhaps civilization. Prod a little and the sparks will fly. I don't know whether the verse put a blessing on the fireflies or the fireflies put a blessing on the verse, or if both of them together put a blessing on trouble, but I have loved them both a good deal ever since. (*GL* 72)

Ames's thoughts evoke Emerson and Whitman in their attention to the spiritual resonance of the natural world. As we'll see, this is characteristic of Robinson's personal view as well.

In *Lila*, too, experience is the measure of religion's credence. Lila emerges from a world vastly different than Ames's religion-saturated heartland town. Largely uneducated, she was rescued from an abusive family by a kind drifter. She spent her youth as a migrant laborer and her adult life working odd jobs to get by, including, briefly, prostitution. Gilead is for Lila only a wayside stop, and she enters Ames's church just to escape the rain. As she absorbs Gilead's religious atmosphere, Lila is frustrated by Ames's sacramental outlook and mentally interrogates him: "What do you ever tell people in a sermon except that things that happen mean something? Some man dies somewhere a long time ago and that means something. People eat a bit of bread and that means something. Then why won't you say how you know that? Do you just talk that way because you're a preacher?" (*LA* 34). Lila's judgment of Ames's religious practices from an outsider's perspective serves to corroborate Robinson's postulate that such things can only be understood through experience. Once Lila begins to think through her own lived history, she concludes that if existence itself can be gratuitous yet meaningful, then religious belief and practice, though extraneous and even unreasonable from the perspective of her own past, may be meaningful after all:

> So if you don't need to exist, then there is no reason to think about other things you don't need as if they didn't matter. You don't need somebody standing beside you. You don't, but you do. Take away every pleasure—but you couldn't, because there can be pleasure in a sip of water. A thought. There was no reason for Doane to tie a ribbon on Marcelle's wrist, and that was why she laughed when he did it, and loved him for it. Why they all loved them both. There was no reason to let an old man dip his hand in water and touch it to your forehead, as if he loved you the way people do who would touch your face and your hair. You'd have thought those babies were his own. All right, she thought. All right. (*LA* 76)

There are, Lila concludes, different types of necessity. She comes to a decision about baptism based on a cornpone sort of natural theology, tentatively affirming the gratuitous love of God and of the pastor as analogs of the gratuitous love of two nonreligious acquaintances. Her contemplation of the sacrament of baptism proceeds from her own experience, which Ames has insisted is the ultimate test of a thing's truth. Lila sees that there's a purity of intention and a spiritual weight to the act that imbues yet also transcends the act itself. She wrestles with the concept of sacrament as she attempts to wash off her baptism not long after the event, feeling uncertain of what she's committed herself to. Ames later affirms what she's already intuited, that baptism cannot be washed off precisely because of its spiritually freighted nature.

Lila brings this same homespun discrimination to her reading of Scripture. To improve her literacy, she works through the only book she has, a Bible swiped surreptitiously from Ames's church, and is surprised "to find so many things she already knew about written down in a book" (*LA* 176). Scripture is, initially at least, descriptive rather than normative for Lila. And her dialogic reflection on her own past heightens her awareness of the awe and blessedness that mark life along with the sorrow and misfortune. Lila arrives at the insight that "It could be that the wildest, strangest things in the Bible were the places where it touched earth" (*LA* 226–27). This "biblical strangeness" comes to include her own life: her sorrows and tragedies as well as the unexpected joy of marriage and procreation. When the strangest passages of the Bible make perfect sense in light of one's experience, the "supernatural" becomes to the attentive observer no more implausible than mundane life.

Religious experience validates belief, but it also highlights the provisionality of belief and thus reminds us of our fallibility. In the following passage in *Gilead,* Ames finds himself feeling inadequate and intellectually cornered in a conversation about American Christianity and its shortcomings:

> I was sitting there in my church. . . . And I felt, as I have often felt, that my failing the truth could have no bearing at all on the Truth itself, which could never conceivably be in any sense dependent on me or on anyone. And my heart rose up within me—that's exactly what it felt like—and I said, "I have heard any number of fine sermons in my life, and I have known any number of deep souls. I am well aware that people find fault, but it seems to me to be presumptuous to judge the authenticity of anyone's religion, except one's own. And that is also presumptuous."
>
> And I said, "When this old sanctuary is full of silence and prayer, every book Karl Barth ever will write would not be a feather in the scales against it from the point of view of profundity, and I would not believe in Barth's own authenticity if I did not also believe he would know and recognize the truth of that, and honor it, too." (172–73)

Here again, individual experience is the measure of religious truth, but the experience of failure and inadequacy is also the basis for practicing humility and generosity when evaluating others' beliefs and practices.

Robinson's emphasis on the centrality of individual experience in religion has drawn criticism, and the scene quoted above is one of the passages cited as problematic. Ames is responding in the passage to an earnest inquiry by his estranged godson Jack, who asks about the truth of Christianity: "Do you ever wonder why American Christianity always seems to wait for the real thinking to be done elsewhere?" (*GL* 172). *Gilead* contains a number of episodes, including conversations with Jack, in which Ames adamantly refuses to argue about the truth of Christianity, redirecting to experience instead as the proper litmus test. Jack is a tormented soul who earnestly desires to be intellectually convinced that Christianity is *true,* but, as Amy Hungerford notes, Ames fails to address Jack's inquiry because the two men are thinking in different registers (118). If Christianity can only be authenticated through experience, it cannot be criticized or debated on the level of logical argument and empirical proof, which leaves earnest seekers like Jack unconvinced and piqued at the perceived refusal to be taken seriously.

On account of Robinson's promotion of religious experience above doctrinal beliefs, critics have charged her with making religion interior, therapeutic, and insulated from criticism. This charge, made variously by Hungerford, Haddox, and Douglas, finds ample support in her novels. In his analysis of *Gilead,* Christopher Douglas contends that by downplaying belief, Robinson "treats religion as a form of cultural identity" or "a kind of memory to be recalled or repressed" (85, 93). As a cultural identity, it cannot be communicated to outsiders but can only be relived and experienced. In spite of the homonymy, Douglas's definition of Christianity-as-cultural-identity (influenced by multiculturalism) differs from the benighted Christianity-as-identity or Christianism that Robinson denounces. Cultural identity on the multicultural model is neither divorceable from ethics and normative behaviors nor reducible to an ideological evocation of an "unnameable essence." Nevertheless, Douglas finds Robinson's account of Christianity problematic because it "removes religion from being a set of ideas about eternal and universal truths" (100). So cloistered, religion is unavailable for rational debate. Douglas rightly interprets Robinson's emphasis on experience as a form of "opposition to the doctrinal certainty characterizing much of the conservative Christian resurgence" (98). Conveniently, Robinson can insist that *authentic* Christianity is more in line with, and somewhat responsible for, the liberal values shared by many of her readers, without having to demonstrate logically or empirically that her account is truer than the fundamentalism she opposes. Douglas readily acknowledges that Robinson never discredits Christian ideas, but he insists that *Gilead*'s readers are "gently dissuaded from thinking too closely about Christian ideas or theology" by its reluctance "to take up questions of doctrine and beliefs" (98). Thomas Haddox similarly suggests that Robinson's Christianity lacks religious distinctiveness. Haddox argues that the problem with Ames's outright refusal to enter theological debate, particularly on the doctrine of predestination, which Ames says is best left to mystery (*GL* 150), is that there's little to distinguish Christianity from any other experientially grounded spirituality: "If readers take Robinson and Ames at their word when they emphasize the irrefragability of religious experience, then this would include non-Christian religious experience as well and thereby frame her entire project within the discourse of the 'spiritual'" (200).

Douglas faults Robinson also for tendentious historical revisionism, claiming that *Gilead* offers a disingenuous account of the history of American Christianity. By positioning individual experience, not ideas, as the essence of Christianity, Robinson makes possible "the formation of a liberal white Christian identity that 'forgets' about the complexity of actual Christian history" in which Christians used the Bible to support slavery (Douglas 95). Robinson's history omits arguments between Christians about slavery, assuming a monolithic narrative of Christian antislavery whose primacy can be upheld more or less faithfully but never contravened. In other words, Robinson secures the identity of authentic Christianity beyond the pale of argument, which allows her to categorize all historical and present forms of Christianity that don't measure up as regression or perversion, as *ideology* rather than authentic religion. She is thus open to the charge of using Christianity to further liberal values in a way that's methodologically equivalent to the right-wing use of it for nationalistic purposes.

These are serious, potentially devastating criticisms of Robinson's work. A few things should be noted in response. First, we have to ask to what extent Robinson is accountable for doctrinal debate. Douglas is doing literary genealogy, chronicling "how American literature has responded to the contemporary Christian resurgence" (105). He is right to point out that Robinson's rendering of Christianity in *Gilead* has a polemical dimension. But I'm not convinced it's entirely fair to accuse Robinson, based on her novel, of "dishonestly cleansing 'true' Christianity of its history by 'forgetting' unsavory aspects" (Douglas 105). It's true that a "more comprehensive map of Christian practice" would include Christian slavery (which Robinson's nonfiction acknowledges), but why it's incumbent upon Robinson to provide this in a work of fiction, I'm not sure. Moreover, there's a semantic issue here: Douglas seems to define "true" Christianity according to historicity—the range of historical expressions of Christianity—whereas Robinson defines "true" in a prophetic sense, by authenticity. And Robinson's definition has plenty of historical precedent—much of the Christian Scriptures recount conflict over what "true" religion should look like. Finally, Robinson is much more disposed to discuss Christian ideas in her essays. Much of Douglas's criticism is warranted based on her novel, but we need to look to her nonfiction before rendering any final judgment.

AMERICAN CALVINIST: A TAUTOLOGY

Robinson openly engages Christian ideas in many of her essays. But here, too, some have charged Robinson with subordinating her religion to liberal values in the effort "to highlight what she perceives as a suppressed link between political liberalism and Christian faith" (Haddox 166). Todd Shy argues that Robinson's depiction of Calvinism is "ironically modern," framed by democratic concerns: equality, social justice, and generosity. Her modern approach is typified by the transferal of attention "away from the majestic heights of Calvin-style revelation to the local authenticity of the individual" (Shy 254). Noting that Robinson "emphasizes the deficiencies of contemporary life that might be remedied if Christianity were taken more seriously," Haddox raises the most pressing question: whether Robinson offers "a use of orthodoxy more than a commitment to it" (188). Before we can begin to answer this question, we must understand that Robinson thinks about orthodoxy very differently than the fundamentalists she criticizes.

Even in her essays, Robinson is clear that she does "not propose to argue for the truth of religion by storming the heavens, by arguing from design or offering ontological proofs. These things are meaningful only to those who are predisposed to finding them meaningful" (*WDH* 214). Robinson repeatedly condemns logical positivism and repudiates any form of apologetics that proceeds along similar lines, preferring the "older thought" of the Puritans in which "readers are implicitly invited to consult with themselves as to the persuasiveness of the description of the inward life that is offered to them" (*WDH* 199). Persuasiveness, for Robinson, is rooted in aesthetic power rather than rational argument.

Ray Horton has argued that Robinson's *Gilead* is best understood by recognizing that Christianity provides a theopoetics by which the characters process their mundane experiences. This theopoetics is "less propositional than phenomenological. It is exhibited less by the creeds Robinson's characters proffer than by the way their theology mobilizes background—the interpretive horizon for her characters' concerned modes of being in the world" (Horton 120–21). I contend that this theopoetics is also key to understanding how Robinson sees the relation of Puritanism to democracy. Robinson believes that democracy, as she envisions it, is fundamentally characterized by a Christian aesthetic, and so, for her, it seems to matter not so much what Americans "believe . . . or . . . how they enact and negotiate belief" as "what conditions of possibility—what modes of seeing, perceiving, experiencing, and narrating—belief makes available" (Horton 121). Robinson conveys that although religion should never influence politics theocratically, religion does furnish the architecture of possibility and the grammar for describing politics (even if one does not accept religion as true). The moral vision and commitments essential to sustaining democratic life are in this sense fundamentally, though not sectarianly, religious, and we need a theopoetics to make democracy work.

When discussing Calvin and Puritanism, Robinson focuses typically on three things: divine sovereignty (including divine election), human depravity or sinfulness, and the *imago dei* in human beings, with greatest emphasis on the last. While Jesus occasionally enters Robinson's later essays, it is as "a statement about the sanctity of humankind" (Engebretson 127). She focuses on the Incarnation, seldom mentioning the cross.[4] The tenets of Calvinism

---

4. For a fuller treatment of Robinson's treatment of Jesus, see Engebretson 127.

that have been historically most contentious, namely depravity and predestination, are for Robinson the least interesting. An awareness of our sinfulness is healthy, not morbidly masochistic. She highlights the paradox that when Tocqueville pronounced that America was great because Americans were good, those "good" Americans held a higher view of sin (*DOA* 157). Robinson rues that Americans have dispensed with original sin and reckons we've sought to liberate ourselves from the doctrine for fear that it's a self-fulfilling prophecy. The result, she argues, is a hopeless reliance on the meretricious power of positive thinking. Lacking a doctrine of sin, a bewildered pessimism takes over because we anticipate perfection yet inexplicably continue to err. Depravity, claims Robinson, is a democratic leveler of persons, just as the doctrine of election should be a source of liberation, not anxiety. Predestination is but an attempt to articulate the sense of divine mystery that comports with human experience (*DOA* 157). The mystery implicit in the conviction that our fate rests with God alone and that all rely on grace inculcates generosity and humility: "The belief that we are all sinners gives us excellent grounds for forgiveness and self-forgiveness, and is kindlier than any expectation that we might be saints, even while it affirms the standards all of us fail to attain" (*DOA* 157).

Robinson is keen to emphasize that human beings are remarkable not for our sinfulness but because we bear God's image, which depravity may tarnish but never obfuscate. She appeals to Calvin unconventionally in support of her thoroughly humanistic vision of the relation between God and humanity, which she touts as a "theistic realism" that's "vastly more capacious [than Christian fundamentalism], and notoriously anthropocentric" (*WDH* 217–18). Robinson stresses that Calvin's account "of human depravity . . . is by far the most conventional aspect of his thought," while he "is unique . . . in rescuing out of the general ruin the whole human being, body, mind, and spirit" (*GOT* 227–28). As Haddox notes, Robinson offers a welcome corrective to the facile caricature Calvin has often been reduced to: the pessimist who delights in God's indiscriminate assignation of some souls to eternal perdition (187). Robinson unveils the Calvin who relishes the wonders of material existence and values individual religious experience. She recurs to Calvin's account of the *imago dei* as a source of aesthetic pleasure, as in the following:

> Calvin constantly distinguishes between merit, a theological concept important in his time that he and the Reformation vehemently rejected, and the objective fact that we are made a little less than God and crowned with glory and honor. To worship God in the Creation is to celebrate as well the fact that we ourselves are created, and strangely and wonderfully made. Our

honor and glory are not our own doing, and are only more precious, more to be enjoyed and explored, for this reason. (*GOT* 201)

This notion of *imago dei* is the cornerstone of Robinson's religious vision, underpinning charity, humility, and wonder. It enables communal life by securing the dignity of the individual and fostering equality. "We would not now have a sizable part of our own population walking around prepared to engage in homicidal violence," Robinson sharply remarks, "if they truly believed that that young man in the hoodie was an image of God" (*GOT* 170). (Her fiction reveals racism to be a more insidious problem, ensnaring otherwise upright men of the cloth.)

This theological anthropology is the crux of Robinson's thought, the necessary bedrock of human dignity as a transcendental principle. She cites the US Constitution as evidence that "lacking the terms of religion, essential things cannot be said," and asserts that Jefferson and the founders adopted Judeo-Christian language "to assert a particular form of human exceptionalism, one that anchors our nature, that is to say our dignity, in a reality outside the world of circumstance" (*WCR* 162–63). Absent a concept of *imago dei*, "we hardly seem to know what we are" (*WDH* 225).[5] Moreover, on this account she declares the denigration of humanity, sinful though we are, to be a sin. Religion alone confronts us with our Promethean pride while also enjoining us to greatness, and it is Calvin's aesthetic vision on which Robinson dwells most deliberately.

It emerges that Robinson turns to Calvin and the Puritans most often when Democracy (a proper noun for her) is really her subject. One reason is that she locates the democratic ethos within the Puritan tradition. She never tires of reiterating that "the Reformist tendencies that lie behind American achievements in the direction of democracy and—John Winthrop's term, of course—liberalism, have Puritanism in New England as fons et origo" (*WDH* 190). But Calvin is important to her, above all, because he connects the ontological reality of the *imago dei* to the aesthetic faculty by which we recognize it. Calvin's aesthetics enables Robinson to define democracy itself as religious without insinuating that America is a Christian nation.

Robinson conceives of democracy more in terms of love than justice: "Democracy, in its essence and genius, is imaginative love for and identifi-

---

5. Robinson repudiates the notion that religion is a primitive attempt to explain things better explained by science as a blatant confusion about the nature of religion. Without the grammar of religion, human experience cannot be accurately described because science cannot translate its findings into any moral frame. See *Absence of Mind* for her fullest critique of "scientism" and treatment of science and religion.

cation with a community with which, much of the time and in many ways, one may be in profound disagreement" (*WCR* 27–28). "Imaginative love" is, for Robinson, foundational for religious community and for democracy, and she is loath to separate the two. Robinson parallels the current condition of democracy and religion in America:

> There is a disturbing lack of confidence in democracy in the frightened resistance to the workings of democracy.... It resembles nothing so much as the disturbing lack of faith in Christianity that puts the darkest interpretation on social change, religious diversity, foreign influence, the implications of science, and so much else besides. If Christianity expresses the nature and will of God, and if Christ will be with us even to the end of the age, why all this fear? If the United States is the greatest country on earth, why so little respect for its culture and people? (*WCR* 138)

These are rhetorical questions directed at implied claimants, and Robinson has stated that she does not consider America fundamentally superior to other nations. Nonetheless, she remains invested in defending the American way of life. In an essay on the civil rights movement (which she notably calls the "Third Great Awakening"), Robinson invokes an "essential America" characterized by "generosity and optimism." The "essential America" is envisioned by the Declaration of Independence, a statement full of "explicitly religious language [but which] functions as a powerful ethical statement for vast numbers of Americans who have no investment whatever in the authority of Scripture" (*GOT* 95–96). This essential America is not always actual America. The civil rights movement, as experienced at the time by a younger Robinson, was "an essential America bursting the bonds that had distorted and constrained it" (*GOT* 97–98). Robinson understands the civil rights movement as religious and suggests that when the "essential America" emerged, there existed an authentic and benignant American civil religion:

> If American civil religion can be said to have a congregation, I was a member in good standing—until certain shifts became apparent in the meaning and effect of religion in America. These changes made me realize that I had indeed allowed my culture to instruct me in my religion—to my benefit, during a period that was singularly worthy of the confidence I placed in it. This is to say, it was worthy as other periods, quite reliably, are not. (*GOT* 97–98)

Robinson's "essential America" is a kind of transcendent vision of receptive human beings practicing imaginative love for one another. As a civil religion, it has little to do with any notion of election or exceptionalism (evident in her implicit rebuke of nationalistic fundamentalists). Robinson addresses a nation she thinks has betrayed its better nature. The salient point here, for my purposes, is that she remains invested in what Sacvan Bercovitch calls "federal eschatology" (*Puritan* 161), and this is where her affinity to transcendentalism shines through. (*Federal* here applies less to the nation-state than to something like the demos.) Emerson's call to self-reliance was also tied to federal eschatology; it wasn't a summons to *individualism* but to democratic individuality.

I submit that in Robinson's view, the ultimate importance of religion to democracy is that religion provides the essential vision of hope and love without which we would lack the courage and moral resources to pursue the virtually impossible task of forming a better society. Religion is an aesthetics that inspires an ethics. What makes Robinson a transcendentalist is the way she links divine immanence and personal experience with federal eschatology. Democracy does not simply happen, and Robinson worries that Americans lack the moral resources to sustain it. It is no mean feat to coexist peacefully with others with whom one may agree on nothing save a commitment to representative government. For Robinson, "essential America" must affirm pluralism and diversity yet compel Americans to unity. She turns to Puritanism for a vision that is compelling yet nonsectarian. As we'll see, Robinson's account of religious experience centers on aesthetic fullness, which requires a disciplined faculty of receptivity. By democratizing the *imago dei* and connecting it to aesthetic pleasure, Robinson can insist that the very pluralism of democracy contributes to its richness as an aesthetic vision. Robinson employs the Puritan tradition to situate democracy within the register of religion and to present receptivity as a nonsectarian religious practice, one that, ultimately, requires no theistic belief. While Calvin and, more recently, Edwards remain her unrivaled saints, Robinson regularly invokes Emerson and Whitman also. She never uses the term *transcendentalist*, however, preferring to think of them as Puritans.

THE TRANSCENDENTALIST ROBINSON

Acknowledging the unorthodoxy of her view, Robinson avers that the striking feature of the transcendentalists is their fidelity to, not departure from, Puritanism. Robinson rightly highlights that both Emerson and Whitman were immersed in the Puritan tradition (although so were most of their peers). That Whitman "was a Quaker and he wrote like one" is true but lacking much warranted qualification (*WCR* xiii). And Emerson apparently intended to write a book on the salutary influence of Calvinism in New England (Bercovitch, *Puritan* 166). But I want to suggest that Robinson venerates these particular nineteenth-century American luminaries because they embody precisely what she wants to install as most vital (and agreeable to modern Americans) in Puritanism:

> Whatever else might be part of a Puritan worldview, the exalted mind is central for them as it is for all these writers. Emerson, Thoreau, Whitman ... share a fascination with the commonest elements of life as they are mediated and entertained by perception and reflection. The Puritans spoke of their religion as experimental, that is, experiential. Sacredness is realized in the act of attention because reality is communicative and the mind is made, grace assisting exquisite effort, to experience its meaning.... The absence of shrines and rituals and processions that interpreted the world and guided understanding of it in England and Europe reflected, as absence, a sense of immanence that gave theological meaning to anything in itself in the moment of perception—a buzzing fly, a blade of grass. The exalted mind could understand the ordinary as visionary, given discipline and desire. (*WDH* 294–95)

Robinson carefully composes a profile of Puritanism marked by personal experience and divine immanence. (That "whatever else" she initially mentions—the other stars in the Puritan constellation—would include total depravity and predestination, which, as we've seen, Robinson acknowledges sanguinely.) Robinson's account of the Puritan legacy encapsulates her conception of Christianity's importance to American political culture. Crucial here is that "discipline and desire" are requisite to perceiving divine immanence: A developed faculty of receptivity is central, in her view, to both Christianity and democracy.

Robinson highlights the Puritan character of transcendentalism; I want to highlight the transcendentalist character of her Puritanism. Transcendentalism was fundamentally a religious movement originating in the Unitarian church. While it was also an aesthetic movement, its art and aesthetics were tied to its theology. Religious views and fervor varied widely within the movement. Some members remained Unitarians, a few, like Theodore Parker and W. H. Channing, as ministers. Orestes Brownson eventually converted to Catholicism. Thoreau and Emerson were heterodox by the most liberal of estimates. What united them was their belief in a "higher Reason" and their emphasis on the centrality of personal experience in communing with the divine. According to Lawrence Buell, transcendentalism's central principle was "the affirmation of man's ability to experience God firsthand," and its "central message . . . [was] divine immanence" (*Transcendentalism* 45). In Emerson and Whitman, this focus on immanence became the cornerstone for a seminal vision of American political culture. In what follows, I further examine Robinson's work alongside that of Emerson and Whitman to establish how a certain adaptation of Puritanism results in a vision of democratic transcendence. At stake is the cogency of Robinson's position because thinkers like Jeffrey Stout and George Kateb, who share Robinson's political concerns, have adopted Emerson's and Whitman's politics analogously while excising Christianity entirely.

Emerson and Religious Experience

Emerson is renowned for his emphasis on the supreme authority of individual experience, especially in religious matters. But how did he understand the divine? Given the centrality of religious experience to Emerson's thought, it's an important question. Buell, after comprehensively surveying Emerson's statements about God, concludes, "Emerson's god is an immanent god, an indwelling property of human personhood and physical nature, not located in some otherworldly realm" (*Emerson* 162). On this account, divine immanence seems like a pantheistic transmutation of the Puritan concept of the inner light. But Emerson didn't understand the divine as wholly delimited by human conscience and subjectivity: He preserves an element of transcendence in his notion of divine "impersonality."

Buell identifies a dichotomy in Emerson's thought that scholars have never fully reconciled. In his "most contrarian act of intellectual radicalism," Emerson insists "both on a God-in-me and on the 'impersonality' of the divine" (*Emerson* 162). Emerson simultaneously affirmed a monism and an individualism that were interdependent, and thus, "what counted most for him was individual spiritual experience, but 'impersonality' was what authenticated it" (164). William James, an acolyte of Emerson's, offers an enlightening account of this paradox:

> [Emerson's] metaphysics consisted in the platonic belief that the foundation of all things is an overarching Reason. Sometimes he calls this divine principle the Intellect, sometimes "the Soul," [elsewhere] the One. Whate'er we call it, we are at one with it so far as our moments of insight go. But no one moment can go very far, and no one man can lay down the law for oth-

ers, for their angles of vision may be as sacred as his own. (qtd. in Buell, *Emerson* 163)

These two poles of Emerson's thought—absolute monism and radical individualism—are evident in his journal: "The height of Culture, highest behavior, consist[s] in the identification of the Ego with the universe," but such a one "shall be able continually to keep sight of his biographical *ego*," indenturing it "as rhetoric, fun, or footman, to his grand & public *ego*, without impertinence or ever confounding them" ("Natural"). Emerson's belief in this higher reason, his monism, was ultimately a safeguard against the "whim" he fancies of writing on his doorpost in *Self-Reliance* (Buell, *Emerson* 169). Emerson's monism allows him a means of exhorting everyone to her genius; it is the standard for his "perfectionism." Thus Stanley Cavell writes,

> Emersonian perfectionism—place it as the thought that "the main enterprise of the world for splendor, for extent, is the upbuilding of a man"—is not an elitist call to subject oneself to great individuals . . . but to the greatness, the thing Emerson calls by the ancient name of the genius, in each of us; it is the quest he calls "becoming what one is" and, I think, "standing for humanity." (184)

Emerson thought that in realizing one's potential, one "stands for humanity" and thereby proves the potential latent in us all. So, when he celebrates individual genius in "The American Scholar," he envisions an "image not of isolated heroes but of a nation of men in which 'each believes himself inspired by the Divine Soul which also inspires all men'" (Buell, *Emerson* 62–63). For Emerson, this call to greatness was bound up with American destiny (federal eschatology); in correlating the individual and the collective, Emerson ties individual citizens to America as a nation. This connection, which Bercovitch calls the "Emersonian triad [of] American nature, the American self, and American destiny" (*Puritan* 178), rests upon a democratization of the Calvinist notion of predestination. The "elect" no longer refers to a certain segment of humanity or to a religious group but to all Americans and thereby America as a nation. Emerson's religious vision and his political vision are intimately connected. Emerson has been reasonably accused of elitism. Yet he adheres to his own version of *imago dei*, something "spheral and infinite in every man," which deters us from denigrating others: "Rightly, every man is a channel through which heaven floweth, and, whilst I fancied I was criticising him, I was censuring or rather terminating my own soul" ("Nominalist"). Crucial here is the emergence of a link between aesthetics and ethics:

the idea of a common sacredness and potential that must be respected and nurtured. Receptivity becomes both a moral obligation and a means of aesthetic pleasure.

Like Emerson, Robinson turns to religion for a framework that affirms the worth and potential of every human being while also positing ontological interdependency and a collective destiny, and this religious framework is used to ratify democratic practice. Under the auspices of Calvinism, Robinson is able to reconcile more coherently the dichotomy that characterizes Emerson's thought—radical immanence and transcendent, unchanging divinity. While it would appear that Robinson is just returning to the more orthodox Calvinist position that furnished the framework underlying Emerson's heterodox Unitarianism, Robinson democratizes divine election analogously to Emerson. As Emerson's monism was the stay against utter antinomianism and "whim," Robinson appeals to the God of Calvinist theology—sovereign, ineffable, and unknowable, an utter mystery—to distinguish between authentic religious experience and indiscriminate mysticism or commodified spirituality.[6] And yet, precisely because God is radically transcendent, we only know God through our personal, intrinsically limited experience. Robinson nullifies any clear separation of transcendence and immanence: The notion "that every human being is an image of God . . . makes trivial any attempted distinction between the this-worldly and the transcendent" (*WCR* 78). Robinson, like Emerson, also connects personal experience to the human soul.

> My particular saint, John Calvin, says that our brilliance, our inventiveness, our imagination . . . are unmistakable proofs of the existence of the soul. He says that in descending into ourselves we find God, we being the products of such exquisite workmanship. In his praise of humankind, of God therefore, he makes no distinction between the body's intricacy and adeptness and the mind's or soul's agility and fluency. (*GOT* 227)

Robinson holds that the intuitive perception of the divine is an aesthetic sensibility of the soul, adducing Jonathan Edwards's concept of "divine taste" (*WDH* 198). Then citing Calvin's conviction that "the very sinews of reality" bespeak divine wisdom, Robinson posits a reciprocal, sacramental relationship between "the knowledge of God and the knowledge of ourselves" (*GOT*

---

6. Robinson gives a scathing appraisal of "seminaries that make a sort of Esperanto of world religions and transient pieties, a non-language articulate in no vision that anyone can take seriously," and "consumer-friendly mysticisms that have contributed so largely to the banality of our time" (*GOT* 104, 216).

143). We may encounter the divine by turning inward and by being receptive to one another. The *imago dei* is present in everyone but reflected diversely, which grounds our common humanity *and* exhorts us to cherish difference. Whereas a dogmatic focus on orthodoxy (defined by propositional belief) may engender a defensive posture, religious experience encourages humility and broadens our sympathies. It is thus a keystone for building community.

If religion consists of the practices by which we make the divine present (as I've proposed), and if the divine permeates the physical world and our very selves, then honing an aesthetic sensibility with which we scrutinize the world *is* a religious practice. Immanence and transcendence collapse here, as "participat[ing] so deeply in ultimate reality" is accomplished by a "heightening of consciousness" of the world around us (*WDH* 215).

However, these glimpses of the divine always occur through a glass darkly, and our experiences are always conditioned. Robinson affirms "the [William] Jamesian view" of the relation of experience to knowledge, concurring "that what we know about anything is determined by the way we encounter it, and therefore we should never assume that our knowledge of anything is more than partial" (*GOT* 229). Individual experience, over time, validates religious truth, but it also enlightens us to its own inexhaustibility. We can never exhaust the meaning of our experience; it is permanently under revision. Mystery abides, as long as one resists the temptation to pass off a limited perspective for universal truth. In *Gilead,* Ames, reflecting on a memory of sharing an ash-covered biscuit with his father, explains to his son how over time the memory of an experience accrues layers of significance, as well as nuance and distortions. Ames writes, "You never do know the actual nature even of your own experience. Or perhaps it has no fixed and certain nature" (*GL* 95). The fluid nature of experience allows for the rousing character of memory, but it also gives warrant for modesty in light of our proclivity for making experience conform to our flawed notions. This fact enjoins us to humility and tempers any inclination to condemn or repudiate others, however radically they differ from us.

Robinson's account of religious experience grounds a dual ethical obligation: We must develop the habit of paying others sustained and careful attention, while consistently exercising charity and grace in our judgments of them. This, for Robinson, is a fundamental Christian obligation. But it isn't the sole territory of Christians; it's also central to a functional democracy, and Robinson exhorts all Americans to this mode of life. As we see in Whitman, Robinson appeals to the Puritan tradition in order to arrive at a notion of democratic individuality.

Whitman and the Soul

Robinson begins *When I Was a Child I Read Books* by excerpting Whitman's *Democratic Vistas*: "America, if eligible at all to downfall and ruin, is eligible within herself. . . . [T]hese savage, wolfish parties alarm me" (qtd. in *WCR* ix). This quotation sets the tone for the volume: Robinson intends to persuade Americans that responsibility for the current cultural regression rests upon them, and she believes, like Whitman during the Gilded Age, that we live now "in a political environment characterized by wolfishness and filled with blather" (qtd. in *WCR* x). However, it's not only demagogues and talking heads who are to blame, but all Americans.

Robinson isn't alone in turning to Whitman as a prophetic voice to address our fractious political culture. Political thinkers like George Kateb and Jeffrey Stout have looked to Whitman and Emerson as profound political philosophers. Kateb identifies Whitman, along with Emerson and Thoreau, as a founding philosopher of American democratic culture. This transcendentalist trio accomplished "the invaluable work of glimpsing evidences of democratic extraordinariness and democratic transcendence in the United States (then the only democracy), and of proceeding to theorize them in order to encourage them" (*Inner* 32). They conceived of democracy as a thoroughgoing mode of life, which Kateb calls "democratic individuality."

It is Whitman's account of the human soul that most interests Kateb because it is the cornerstone of his democratic ethos. Whitman's conception of the soul is remarkably congruent to that which Robinson locates in Calvin and Edwards: The soul *is* our receptivity, the experiential nexus of transcendence and immanence. Both Robinson and Kateb turn to the soul to anchor democratic practice. Unlike Robinson, Kateb is an atheist who rejects all notion of an eternal soul, which has implications for Robinson's claims for the indispensability of Puritanism to American culture.

Robinson aims to rehabilitate the notion of soul. She blames our lack of reverence for the natural world and for the worth of the individual self on the long-standing divorce of soul from body, which she argues "has spiritualized the soul out of meaningful existence and de-spiritualized the world into an object of contempt at worst, or, more typically, a thing defined by its difference from anything called spiritual, which includes . . . almost everything that is distinctively human" (*GOT* 232). *Soul* functions as a way of recognizing both individual selfhood and universal humanity: "The concept 'soul' allows us to acknowledge the richness and variety of the experience of the self" and signals "an experience that I think we do share" (*GOT* 228). Robinson, following

Calvin, cites personal experience as witness to the soul's existence and posits an inverse correlation between belief in the reality of the soul and solipsism. By abandoning belief in the soul, we forfeit a fundamental source of interconnectedness. Robinson is reluctant to conjecture about the afterlife but modestly proposes that to affirm the soul is to affirm a higher moral order: "Surely no skeptic could doubt that a sound intuition lies behind the recognition of a profounder moral reality than any we have attained to. Grant it reality in an ontological sense—is there another one?—and there are important interpretive consequences, cosmologically speaking" (*GOT* 234). The pivotal point here is that we *intuit* the existence of this "moral reality," based on personal experience and the acknowledgment of individual worth. A democratic politics is, Robinson believes, the closest we can come to embodying this moral reality on a large scale.

Whitman, too, persistently recurs to the soul as the nexus between individuality and commonality. Soul has for Whitman both a secular and a religious sense, which at times overlap. The secular soul is basically human potentiality, the vast catalogue of all that one might do, believe, become, and desire. In its religious sense, as Kateb explains, "soul is unique and unalterable individual identity; one's genius or 'eidolon'; the 'real Me.' . . . It seems to be untouched by experience, and it survives death to find numberless incarnations" ("Whitman" 24). The body is of greatest value in both conceptions, but the secular soul especially is inextricably connected to the body. The self (the ego), for Whitman, is the author of personality. It "is active self-consciousness and disciplined creative energy" that "realizes one or another potentiality of the soul (and body)" (Kateb, "Whitman" 24–25). What others see in an individual is her personality, one particular expression (though others are possible) of the soul.

Whitman's poetry abounds with references to the soul, which is, moreover, its very organizing principle. In "Starting from Paumanok," the poet declares he will never write a line of verse that does not refer to the soul, "Because having look'd at the objects of the universe, I find there is no one nor any particle of one but has reference to the soul" (176). Whitman posits a correspondence between the soul, which is common to all human beings as a reservoir of potentiality, and everything in the universe. A later movement of the poem offers a similar view:

> Was somebody asking to see the soul?
> See, your own shape and countenance, persons, substances, beasts,
>   the trees, the running rivers, the rocks and sands.

> All hold spiritual joys and afterwards loosen them;
> How can the real body ever die and be buried?
> . . . .
> Behold, the body includes and is the meaning, the main concern,
>   and includes and is the soul;
> Whoever you are, how superb and how divine is your body, or any
>   part of it! (177–80, 187–88)

Again, the soul is linked both to the body and to all that one experiences that is outside the self. In *Song of Myself*, the interconnectedness of human beings enjoins individuals to mutual respect: "I believe in you my soul, the other I am must not abase itself to you, / And you must not be abased to the other" (82–83). In his great catalogue of Americana, Whitman's aim is not simply to reveal the elusive beauty of all things as a safeguard of equal dignity, but to disabuse us of the belief that there is *anything* outside ourselves to which we are not connected. All of it is part of our soul. Thus, "the unbeautiful are not just unbeautiful and . . . the wicked are not just wicked," because both are integrally connected to the beautiful and the good (Kateb, "Whitman" 32). In *Song of Myself*, Whitman links body and soul, and well as oneself and all other selves, by defining them in terms of each other:

> I have said that the soul is not more than the body,
> And I have said that the body is not more than the soul,
> And nothing, not God, is greater to one than one's self is,
> And whoever walks a furlong without sympathy walks to his own
>   funeral drest in his shroud,
> And I or you pocketless of a dime may purchase the pick of the
>   earth,
> And to glance with an eye or show a bean in its pod confounds
>   the learning of all times,
> And there is no trade or employment but the young man following
>   it may become a hero,
> And there is no object so soft but it makes a hub for the wheel'd
>   universe,
> And I say to any man or woman, Let your soul stand cool and
>   composed before a million universes. (1269–77)

Though Whitman places the self at the pinnacle of worth, any self deficient in sympathy is no self at all; the unsympathetic individual is *essentially* lacking. Whitman's "secular" soul harbors all human potentiality, and while the individual personality that one becomes constitutes only a single, limited expression of potentiality, one understands that *all* human beings are selective expressions of the same vast human soul. Whitman's conception of the soul implies two crucial ideas: "All the personalities that I encounter, I already am: That is to say, I could become or could have become something like what others are; that necessarily means, in turn, that all of us are always indefinitely more than we actually are. I am potentially all personalities, and we equally are infinite potentialities" (Kateb, "Whitman" 25). Put another way, we meet ourselves, or our potential selves, coming and going. We cultivate receptivity by acknowledging mutual correspondence; we understand the actions, choices, and instincts of others to be our own, in that we recognize the possibility of having proceeded likewise even if we've done otherwise.

As a philosopher of democratic culture, Whitman envisions a form of individuality that resists individualism. Kateb identifies Whitman's "secular" soul as the basis for democratic individuality, which is defined by three tenets: "self-expression, resistance in behalf of others, and receptivity or responsiveness (being 'hospitable') to others" ("Whitman" 20). Kateb venerates Whitman for fostering a vision of individuality characterized *essentially* by receptivity. Receptive living is contingent upon an understanding of our common potentiality or, in other words, a sense of the (secular) soul possessed by all. The particular virtue of such receptivity (or responsiveness) is that it inspires a "connectedness [that] is not the same as nationhood or group identity" ("Whitman" 21). Unlike ideology, receptivity unites individuals without requiring an antagonist. This has decisive ramifications for democratic life, as "the deepest moral and existential meaning of equal rights is this kind of equal recognition granted by every individual to every individual. Democratic connectedness is mutual acceptance. Rejection of any other human being, for one reason or another, for apparently good reasons as well as for bad ones, is self-rejection" ("Whitman" 26). This receptivity imbues our judgment of others with clemency and tempers the desire to punish. In Whitman, aesthetics and ethics are inextricable.

Robinson is invested in fostering precisely this kind of democratic connectivity and receptivity. Note the congruence of her description of the soul with Whitman's: "The soul, being both radically individual and universal among human beings, is an inexhaustible revelation of one's own nature and of the nature of every other soul who has lived, lives, and will live. The concept of the soul is the profoundest possible bond among us, an unshakable basis for compassion, recognition, and love" (*WDH* 214–15). Both Robinson and Whitman see an integral connection between experience and equal recognition. Our common soul establishes receptivity as a moral duty, but receptivity is also a source of aesthetic pleasure. In *Gilead*, Robinson gives us a picture of the receptivity engendered by this understanding of soul, as Ames speaks of the "incandescence" he senses in others, especially during vulnerable conversations like confession or "unburdening":

> When people come to speak to me, whatever they say, I am struck by a kind of incandescence in them, the "I" whose predicate can be "love" or "fear" or "want," and whose object can be "someone" or "nothing" and it won't really matter, because the loveliness is just in that presence, shaped around "I" like a flame on a wick, emanating itself in grief and guilt and joy and whatever else. But quick, and avid, and resourceful. To see this aspect of life is a privilege of the ministry which is seldom mentioned. (44–45)

Robinson understands religious experience is the supreme form of aesthetic experience, a view that turns upon the Puritan conception of the soul as "suited to the reception of ultimate truth and ultimate beauty" (*WDH* 193). And if ultimate beauty is a kind of religious experience, democratic individuality is a religious mode of life, and receptivity to others a religious practice.

At the same time, a view to our composite nature bestows a concomitant sense of one's own strangeness. One becomes somewhat alien or "unknowable" to oneself because one's own personality is so incomplete a picture of the soul. The more one realizes himself to be composite, the stranger he becomes to himself. But this, too, serves the moral end of "open[ing] oneself to a kinship to others that is defined by receptivity or responsiveness to them" (Kateb, "Whitman" 31). Robinson likewise emphasizes this mystery of human life. She claims, "There is at present a dearth of human imagination for the integrity and mystery of other lives" (*WCR* 45), and she believes this lack of imagination, connected with a paucity of other-regard, contributes to our cultural decline. Robinson maintains that one reason Puritan theology is conducive to democracy is its recognition "that we live in and with our minds differently from one another" and "experience our own minds differently from one moment to the next" (*WDH* 199). That there are "variable responses to the essential and immutable," even within the same individual, should inspire humility and a recognition of unknowability.

Whitman and Robinson believe that democratic individuality is a heroic way of life because "to live democratically, to live receptively and responsively, is risky, and therefore the invitation to it is easily resisted" (Kateb, "Whitman" 32). Democratic individuality differs sharply from liberal individualism in positing that all democratic individuals are radically connected; there is contingency that requires courage to sustain. Robinson writes, "Western society at its best expresses the serene sort of courage that allows us to grant one another real safety, real autonomy, the means to think and act as judgment and conscience dictate. It assumes that this great mutual courtesy will bear its best fruit if we respect, educate, inform, and trust one another" (*WCR* 44–45). Robinson and Whitman both affirm a religious conception of the soul that mitigates the risk involved in democratic living and offers a sense of stability. Kateb (begrudgingly) writes that Whitman isn't satisfied that the whole of one's identity consists in "the simple fact that one's stream of consciousness—the mingling of self and soul on the terms of neither—is one's own and no one else's"; rather, as a guarantor of individual uniqueness, "Whitman wants to affirm his faith that deep down in the person is something that is both distinctive and unchanging. What is involved is a religious conception of soul as unique and unalterable identity, whether immortal or not" ("Whitman" 35).

Yet Kateb argues that Whitman's religious notion of the soul is not only extraneous but also inimical to his radically democratic vision:

> I think that such substantialist talk about the person or the soul gets in the way of Whitman's most democratic teaching. I much prefer to stay with his idea that what is left inside oneself when one is filling a function or playing a part is an infinite reservoir or, better, repertoire. Unexpressed potentiality rather than an indestructible core (that must remain hidden or can show itself only specially) suits the idea of "a great composite democratic individual," which is the idea to be preserved. ("Whitman" 36)

Kateb favors dispensing with the religious dimension of the soul. He contends that the receptivity so central to democratic individuality can be inculcated without religion, at least without theism. One need not agree with Kateb's views on religion to accept that he, like Jeffrey Stout, finds the resources for democratic life in a secular version of Emersonian perfectionism.[7]

DEMOCRACY WITHOUT DIVINITY

I emphasize these similarities at length because the later reception of Emerson's and Whitman's work has implications for how Robinson's work should be

---

7. See Stout, especially 21–41.

received. Democratic individuality (founded upon Emersonian perfectionism) is characterized by its insistence on profound equality and the immeasurable worth of every living being, which, as we've seen, are Robinson's primary concerns. According to Kateb, it is "a belief in radical equality made aesthetic," which beholds the other (human or not) with generosity and is unique in "the conviction that one can make the sense of one's infinitude a bridge to other human beings and perhaps to the rest of nature" (*Inner* 33–34). This mode of existence aspires to a form of transcendence:

> Beyond the experience [of connectedness] at even the extraordinary level lies a rare moment, mood, or episode of transcendence. This highest level is contemplative and consequently only impersonal: an evanescent loss of the sense of one's unique self in favor of everything outside it. I think that on all its levels democratic individuality is not egocentric, that the democratic ego is not sharply defined, grasping for more than its share, sure of its identity and therefore sure of its wants and desires. . . . But democratic transcendence makes this tendency to free self-loss qualitatively different [from Plato or Tocqueville]. (*Inner* 34–35)

Yet, while drawing heavily from Whitman and Emerson, and affirming a form of transcendence, democratic individuality is, by Kateb's measure, a thoroughly secular way of life:

> Emerson, Thoreau, and Whitman all give voice to the need to bless existence in its entirety, not only to bless particulars as they come along. . . . I try to understand this need and to connect it to the will to take the moral and existential meanings of democracy seriously. But that will is too religiously dependent. All these writers are given to religiousness, unorthodox as it is, for they do not appear to take the last step and renounce the will to have supernatural sponsorship and authentication. . . . For me, Emersonian religiousness cannot be allowed to spoil a transcendence that the Emersonians inspire and that requires no more-than-human agency above or behind the world as it is. . . . These three writers deliver formulations that can be severed from their religiousness and set up as the consummation of democratic individuality. (*Inner* 34–35)

Jeffrey Stout differs from Kateb in that he believes democratic individuality is not incompatible with religion, but Stout agrees that it does not require supernatural backing.[8]

---

8. See Stout 9–11.

Kateb insists the "consummation of democratic individuality" comes when it is shorn of religion. But his democratic individuality *is,* by William James's definition and mine, religious. Its moments of transcendence demand from the individual a forfeiture of self to the whole and a clear form of discipline. And the striking similarities between his view and Robinson's makes the latter's problematic. What becomes "godlike" is democracy itself, or the demos perhaps. The transcendent, then, is this great human web. The transcendence that Kateb envisions is *not* reducible to vulgar nationalism. It is rather a radical vision of human connectedness and equality. But it is a religious expression, and one that is inextricably bound up with national politics. If Robinson's Calvinist Christianity bears a strong resemblance to Kateb's religion, then questions arise regarding how tied to political practice Robinson's religion is.

Robinson proceeds from the assumption that "the distinction between civic and religious is never clear" (*GOT* 95). But she assumes there is *some* distinction, because only in religious terms can the ideals necessary for civic life be adequately articulated:

> The Right is more than happy to be excused from these ideals [wisdom, courage, generosity, personal dignity], standards that have, historically, been invoked in order to mitigate the uglier impulses, greed prominent among them. The Left cannot account for the civic virtues in theoretical or ideological terms and feels awkward speaking of them in religious terms. This is only truer because the Right has made religious language toxic by putting it to uses that offend generosity and dignity. (*WDH* xii–xiii)

Robinson thus turns to a theopoetics that allows for pluralism and diversity to become a source of aesthetic fullness. My openness to and acceptance of others contributes to my own spiritual satisfaction. If democracy is a form of imaginative love, then navigating the difficult and contentious mundane mechanics of democracy with grace and charity is a religious mode of life. Imaginative love for others is, by Robinson's logic, a way of loving God, as my fellow Americans all carry the *imago dei.* To create community, to bring out the best in human beings, is to engender a pleroma—a divine fullness. Receptivity to others is a spiritual discipline, and so living democratically is a religious practice. This has the effect of suggesting that it is incumbent upon Christian fundamentalists, *as Christians,* to be more receptive to other points of view and other commitments. It is also nonsectarian enough to appeal to non-Christians. And yet, how to avoid the notion that there's no clear necessity for organized religion? The point I wish to make is that Robinson's Calvinism is virtually identical to a vision of democratic individuality that, while noble and compelling, requires no theism for its poetics.

Kateb argues that democratic individuality attains to a kind of transcendence of its own, with no supernatural backing. Robinson contends that democratic life does require religious or supernatural backing, but the resources that she claims are offered (exclusively, in some cases) by Calvinism are not, according to Kateb and others, found only there. And since her religious vision so closely resembles that of Whitman and Emerson, I contend that Robinson's account of transcendence, which she conflates at times with immanence, is much closer to Kateb's than she thinks. By conceiving of the *imago dei* as she does, and emphasizing the soul as experience, Robinson makes it virtually impossible to distinguish between the divine as a transcendent God and the divine as manifest in a human congregation who, through their imaginative love for one another, achieve an aesthetic/religious plenitude. Robinson ultimately fails to offer a compelling account of transcendence that's distinct from the transcendence that Kateb describes. There's no remainder to Robinson's Calvinism; it is wholly invested in democratic practice. The danger, I would suggest, lies in its loss of all capacity to speak prophetically.

Robinson offers a cogent and timely caution to Christian groups who seek political power for the sake of legally installing America as a Christian nation, and she offers a political vision eminently preferable to the antagonistic ideology she so disdains. And in her fiction we see clear instances where she depicts the dangers of a culturally encrusted Christianity. She shows through the characters of Jack and Glory Boughton, by engaging the issues of race and patriarchy, how susceptible Christianity is to becoming culturally encrusted and how it loses its prophetic power and influence when this occurs.[9] But from a broad perspective, it seems, in the end, that in the attempt to reach a broad audience and offer a Christian vision more capacious and compelling than that of the antagonistic Christian right, Robinson produces a theological legerdemain that loses all religious distinctiveness.

I close with Robinson because she introduces a fruitful tension. All the authors I focus on present practice and discipline as the essential core of religion. Of course, these can never be utterly divorced from religious ideas and beliefs, if religion is to avoid becoming but another form of consumerism. The focus on practice draws attention to the role of religion in shaping who we become—what kind of people we are. And practices, unlike propositional beliefs, are ineluctably and essentially public and cannot be shielded from

---

9. See Tanner for an excellent treatment of patriarchy and domesticity in Robinson's fiction.

debate and criticism. Robinson raises the question of how and if democracy can survive and flourish without religious commitments, and how we can insist on the necessity of religion and affirm pluralism. Her own solution is thoughtful and rather original, but it cannot be normative. Defining her as a transcendentalist raises important questions about internal consistency and, especially, about whether her vision of democracy requires a civil religion of the kind that, as I discussed in the introduction, tends to result in just the sort of tepid religious monoculture Robinson detests. Furthermore, does her account result in a religion without remainder, one without sufficient ground left for prophetic purchase?

Certainly Robinson does not personally share Matthew Arnold's tormented skepticism of the truth of Christianity, but there's the danger that her essays implicitly affirm a conviction similar to that of Arnold and others in his day: that religion is needed most for its sweetness and light, for its social leaven. We're left with a paradox: Religion, at its best, offers moral resources that benefit a society, but as soon as religion is deemed valuable *for that reason,* it loses something essential. Robinson insists, "It is the absence of divinity that dehumanizes nature. There is nothing paradoxical in this thought" (*WDH* 79). But if divinity is but a name for a higher moral reality, for an ontological fullness, what is left of Christianity if democracy ever lives up to its potential?

WORKS CITED

Alarcón, Daniel Cooper. "Literary Syncretism in Ana Castillo's *So Far from God.*" *Studies in Latin American Popular Culture*, no. 23, 2004, pp. 145–52.

Aldama, Frederick Luis. *Postethnic Narrative Criticism: Magicorealism in Oscar "Zeta" Acosta, Ana Castillo, Julie Dash, Hanif Kureishi, and Salman Rushdie.* U of Texas P, 2003.

Allen, Glen Scott. "The End of Pynchon's Rainbow: Postmodern Terror and Paranoia in DeLillo's *Ratner's Star.*" *Critical Essays on Don DeLillo*, edited by Hugh Ruppersburg and Tim Engles, G. K. Hall, 2000, pp. 115–34.

Anzaldúa, Gloria. *Borderlands/La Frontera*. 4th ed., Aunt Lute, 2012.

Asad, Talal. *Genealogies of Religion: Discipline and Reasons of Power in Christianity and Islam.* Johns Hopkins UP, 1993.

Baker, Jeff. "Plucking the American Albatross: Pynchon's Irrealism in *Mason & Dixon.*" Horvath and Malin, pp. 167–88.

Basseler, Michael. "Narrative Empathy in George Saunders's Short Fiction." Coleman and Ellerhoff, pp. 153–72.

Bawer, Bruce. "Don DeLillo's America." *The New Criterion*, vol. 3, no. 8, 1985, pp. 34–42.

Bellah, Robert N. "Civil Religion in America." *Daedalus*, vol. 134, no. 4, 2005, pp. 40–55.

Bellah, Robert N., and Phillip E. Hammond. *Varieties of Civil Religion*. Harper and Row, 1980.

Bennett, Tanya Long. "No Country to Call Home: A Study of Castillo's *Mixquiahuala Letters.*" *Style*, vol. 30, no. 3, 1996, pp. 462–78.

Benton, Graham. "Daydreams and Dynamite: Anarchist Strategies of Resistance and Paths for Transformation in *Against the Day.*" Severs and Leise, pp. 191–213.

Bercovitch, Sacvan. *The American Jeremiad*. Anniversary ed. U of Wisconsin P, 2012.

———. *The Puritan Origins of the American Self.* Yale UP, 2011.

———. *The Rites of Assent: Transformations in the Symbolic Construction of America.* Routledge, 1993.

Blackford, Holly. "The Spirit of a People: The Politicization of Spirituality in Julia Alvarez's *In The Time of the Butterflies*, Ntozake Shange's *Sassafrass, Cypress & Indigo*, and Ana Castillo's *So Far from God*." *Things of the Spirit: Women Writers Constructing Spirituality*, edited by Kristina K. Groover, U of Notre Dame P, 2004, pp. 224–55.

Boddy, Kasia. "'A Job to Do': George Saunders on, and at, Work." Coleman and Ellerhoff, pp. 1–22.

Branch, Lori. "The Rituals of Our Re-secularization: Literature between Faith and Knowledge." *Religion & Literature*, vol. 46, no. 2/3, 2014, pp. 9–33.

Bryant, Paula. "Discussing the Untellable: Don DeLillo's *The Names*." *Critical Essays on Don DeLillo*, edited by Hugh Ruppersburg and Tim Engles, G. K. Hall, 2000, pp. 157–70.

Buell, Lawrence. *Emerson*. Belknap Press of Harvard UP, 2003.

———. *Literary Transcendentalism: Style and Vision in the American Renaissance.* Cornell UP, 1973.

Caminero-Santangelo, Marta. "'The Pleas of the Desperate': Collective Agency versus Magical Realism in Ana Castillo's *So Far from God*." *Tulsa Studies in Women's Literature*, vol. 24, no. 1, 2005, pp. 81–103.

Carson, Benjamin D. "The Chicana Subject in Ana Castillo's Fiction and the Discursive Zone of Chicana/o Theory." *Bilingual Review / La Revista Bilingüe*, vol. 28, no. 2, 2004, pp. 109–26.

Castillo, Ana. *The Guardians.* Random House, 2008.

———. *Massacre of the Dreamers: Essays on Xicanisma.* Twentieth anniversary updated ed. U of New Mexico P, 2014.

———. *The Mixquiahuala Letters.* Bilingual Press / Editorial Bilingüe, 1986.

———. *Peel My Love Like an Onion.* Double Day, 1999.

———. *Sapogonia: An Anti-Romance in 3/8 Meter.* Anchor, 1990.

———. *So Far from God.* W. W. Norton & Company, 1993.

Cavanaugh, William. *Being Consumed: Economics and Christian Desire.* Eerdmans, 2008.

Cavell, Stanley. *Emerson's Transcendental Etudes.* Edited by David Justin Hodge, Stanford UP, 2003.

Coffman, Christopher K. "Bogomilism, Orphism, Shamanism: The Spiritual and Spatial Grounds of Pynchon's Ecological Ethic." Severs and Leise, pp. 91–114.

Coleman, Dawn. "The Spiritual Authority of Literature in a Secular Age." *Christianity & Literature*, vol. 67, no. 3, 2018, pp. 519–30.

Coleman, Philip, and Steve Gronert Ellerhoff, editors. *George Saunders: Critical Essays.* Palgrave Macmillan, 2017.

Conte, Joseph M. "Conclusion: Writing amid the Ruins: 9/11 and *Cosmopolis*." Duvall, pp. 179–92.

Cowart, David. "The Lady Vanishes: Don DeLillo's *Point Omega*." *Contemporary Literature*, vol. 53, no. 1, 2012, pp. 31–50.

———. *The Physics of Language.* U of Georgia P, 2002.

———. *Thomas Pynchon & the Dark Passages of History*. U of Georgia P, 2011.

Cusack, Carole M. *Invented Religions: Imagination, Fiction and Faith*. Ashgate, 2010.

Dalsgaard, Inger H., et al., editors. *The Cambridge Companion to Thomas Pynchon*. Cambridge UP, 2011. *Cambridge Companions Online*, https://dx.doi.org/10.1017/CCOL9780521769747.013.

DeCurtis, Anthony. "The Product: Bucky Wunderlick, Rock 'n Roll, and Don DeLillo's *Great Jones Street*." Lentricchia, *Introducing*, pp. 131–42.

De La Torre, Miguel A. *Latina/o Social Ethics: Moving beyond Eurocentric Moral Thinking*. Baylor UP, 2010.

Delgadillo, Theresa. "Forms of Chicana Feminist Resistance: Hybrid Spirituality in Ana Castillo's *So Far from God*." *Modern Fiction Studies*, vol. 44, no. 4, 1998, pp. 888–916.

———. *Spiritual Mestizaje: Religion, Gender, Race, and Nation in Contemporary Chicana Narrative*. Duke UP, 2011.

Del George, Dana. "Ghosts and Theme Parks: The Supernatural and the Artificial in George Saunders's Short Stories." Coleman and Ellerhoff, pp. 121–36.

DeLillo, Don. *Americana*. Houghton-Mifflin, 1971.

———. *Cosmopolis*. Scribner, 2003.

———. "Dangerous Don DeLillo." Interview with Vince Passaro, *New York Times*, 19 May 1991, pp. 6:34–36, 38, 76–77.

———. "Don DeLillo: 'I'm Not Trying to Manipulate Reality—This Is What I See and Hear.'" Interview with Robert McCrum, *The Guardian*, 7 Aug. 2010, https://www.theguardian.com/books/2010/aug/08/don-delillo-mccrum-interview.

———. *End Zone*. Houghton-Mifflin, 1972.

———. *Falling Man*. Scribner, 2008.

———. "An Interview with Don DeLillo." Interview with Antonio Aiello, *PEN America*, 15 Sept. 2010, https://pen.org/an-interview-with-don-delillo/.

———. "In the Ruins of the Future: Reflections on Terror and Loss in the Shadow of September." *Harper's*, Dec. 2001, pp. 33–40, https://harpers.org/archive/2001/12/in-the-ruins-of-the-future/.

———. *Libra*. Viking, 1988.

———. *Mao II*. Penguin, 1992.

———. "An Outsider in This Society." Interview with Anthony DeCurtis, Lentricchia, *Introducing*, pp. 43–66.

———. *Players*. Vintage, 1989.

———. *Point Omega*. Scribner, 2010.

———. *Underworld*. Scriber Paperback, 1998.

———. *White Noise*. Penguin Classics, 2009.

———. "'Writing as a Deeper Form of Concentration': An Interview with Don DeLillo." Interview with Maria Moss, *Sources: Revue d'Etudes Anglophones*, no. 5, 1999, pp. 82–97.

Dewey, Joseph. *Beyond Grief and Nothing: A Reading of Don DeLillo*. U of South Carolina P, 2006.

———. "The Sound of One Man Mapping: Wicks Cherrycoke and the Eastern (Re)solution." Horvath and Malin, pp. 112–31.

Domestico, Anthony. "Blessings in Disguise: The Unfashionable Genius of Marilynne Robinson." *Commonweal Magazine*, 3 Nov. 2014, pp. 12–17.

Douglas, Christopher. *If God Meant to Interfere: American Literature and the Rise of the Christian Right*. Cornell UP, 2016.

Dreyfus, Hubert, and Sean Dorrance Kelly. *All Things Shining*. Free Press, 2011.

Duncan, Byard. "George Saunders: Life Coach of the Year 2013." *GQ*, 5 Dec. 2013, https://www.gq.com/story/george-saunders-men-of-the-year-life-coach.

Dupré, Louis K. *Passage to Modernity: An Essay in the Hermeneutics of Nature and Culture*. Yale UP, 1993.

———. *Religion and the Rise of Modern Culture*. U of Notre Dame P, 2008.

———. *Transcendent Selfhood: The Loss and Rediscovery of the Inner Life*. Seabury, 1976.

Duvall, John N., editor. *The Cambridge Companion to Don DeLillo*. Cambridge UP, 2008. *Cambridge Companions Online*, https://doi.org/10.1017/CCOL9780521870658.

Eagleton, Terry. *Culture and the Death of God*. Yale UP, 2014.

———. *Hope without Optimism*. U of Virginia P, 2015.

Elias, Amy J. "Plots, Pilgrimage, and the Politics of Genre in *Against the Day*." Severs and Leise, pp. 29–46.

Emerson, Ralph Waldo. "The Natural History of Intellect." *The Complete Works of Ralph Waldo Emerson*, https://www.rwe.org/the-natural-history-of-intellect/.

———. "Nominalist and Realist." *The Complete Works of Ralph Waldo Emerson*, https://www.rwe.org/viii-nominalist-and-realist/.

Engebretson, Alex. *Understanding Marilynne Robinson*. U of South Carolina P, 2017.

Ferris, Joshua. Introduction. *CivilWarLand in Bad Decline*, Random House, 2016, pp. xi–xviii.

Fessenden, Tracy. *Culture and Redemption: Religion, the Secular, and American Literature*. Princeton UP, 2007.

———. "The Problem of the Postsecular." *American Literary History*, vol. 26, no. 1, 2014, pp. 154–167.

Foster, Dennis. "Alphabetic Pleasures: *The Names*." Lentricchia, *Introducing*, pp. 157–74.

Franke, William. *A Philosophy of the Unsayable*. U of Notre Dame P, 2014.

Freer, Joanna. *Thomas Pynchon and American Counterculture*. Cambridge UP, 2014.

Frohlich, Mary. "Spiritual Discipline, Discipline of Spirituality: Revisiting Questions of Definition and Method." *Minding the Spirit: The Study of Christian Spirituality*, edited by Elizabeth A. Dreyer and Mark S. Burrows, Johns Hopkins UP, 2005, pp. 65–78.

Frow, John. "The Last Things before the Last: Notes on *White Noise*." Lentricchia, *Introducing*, pp. 175–92.

García-Caro, Pedro. *After the Nation: Postnational Satire in the Works of Carlos Fuentes and Thomas Pynchon*. Northwestern UP, 2014.

Geertz, Clifford. "Religion as a Cultural System." *The Interpretation of Cultures: Selected Essays*, Fontana Press, 1993, pp. 87–125.

Gillman, Laura, and Stacey M. Floyd-Thomas. "*Con Un Pie a Cada Lado* / With a Foot in Each Place: Mestizaje as Transnational Feminisms in Ana Castillo's *So Far from God*." *Meridians—Feminism, Race, Transnationalism*, vol. 2, no. 1, 2001, pp. 158–75.

Gleason, Paul. "Don DeLillo, T. S. Eliot, and the Redemption of America's Atomic Waste Land." *Critical Essays on Don DeLillo*, edited by Hugh Ruppersburg and Tim Engles, G. K. Hall, 2000, pp. 130–43.

Greiner, Donald J. "Thomas Pynchon and the Fault Lines of America." Horvath and Malin, pp. 73–83.

Haddox, Thomas F. *Hard Sayings: The Rhetoric of Christian Orthodoxy in Late Modern Fiction*. The Ohio State UP, 2013.

Hall, David D. *Lived Religion in America: Toward a History of Practice*. Princeton UP, 1997.

Hayes-Brady, Clare. "Horning In: Language, Subordination and Freedom in the Short Fiction of George Saunders." Coleman and Ellerhoff, pp. 23–40.

Heide, Markus. "The Postmodern 'We': Academia and Community in Ana Castillo's *So Far from God* and Denise Chávez' *Face of an Angel*." *U. S. Latino Literatures and Cultures: Transnational Perspectives*, edited by Francisco A. Lomelí and Karin Ikas, C. Winter, 2000, pp. 171–80.

Heim, S. Mark. *The Depth of the Riches: A Trinitarian Theology of Religious Ends*. William B. Eerdmans, 2003.

Hewitt, John P. *Dilemmas of the American Self*. Temple University Press, 1989.

Horton, Ray. "'Rituals of the Ordinary': Marilynne Robinson's Aesthetics of Belief and Finitude." *PMLA*, vol. 132, no. 1, 2017, pp. 119–34.

Horvath, Brooke, and Irving Malin, editors. *Pynchon and* Mason & Dixon. U of Delaware P, 2000.

Howe, Daniel Walker. *Making the American Self: Jonathan Edwards to Abraham Lincoln*. Harvard UP, 1997.

Hume, Kathryn. "The Religious and Political Vision of *Against the Day*." Severs and Leise, pp. 167–90.

Hungerford, Amy. *Postmodern Belief: American Literature and Religion since 1960*. Princeton UP, 2011.

James, William. *The Varieties of Religious Experience. Writings, 1902–1910*, edited by Bruce Kuklick, Library of America, 1987, pp. 1–478.

Johnson, Kelli Lyon. "Violence in the Borderlands: Crossing to the Home Space in the Novels of Ana Castillo." *Frontiers: A Journal of Women Studies*, vol. 25, no. 1, 2004, pp. 39–58.

Johnston, John. "Generic Difficulties in the Novels of Don DeLillo." *Critique*, vol. 30, no. 4, 1989, pp. 261–75.

Kateb, George. *The Inner Ocean: Individualism and Democratic Culture*. Cornell UP, 1992.

———. "Walt Whitman and the Culture of Democracy." *A Political Companion to Walt Whitman*, edited by John E. Seery, UP of Kentucky, 2011, pp. 19–46.

Kavadlo, Jesse. *Don DeLillo: Balance at the Edge of Belief*. Peter Lang, 2004.

Keesey, Douglas. *Don DeLillo*. Twayne, 1993.

Kellman, Steven G. "Don DeLillo's Logogenetic *Underworld*." *UnderWords: Perspectives on Don DeLillo's* Underworld, edited by Joseph Dewey et al., U of Delaware P, 2002, pp. 68–78.

Kelly, Adam. "Language between Lyricism and Corporatism: George Saunders's New Sincerity." Coleman and Ellerhoff, pp. 41–58.

Knight, Christopher J. *Omissions are Not Accidents: Modern Apophaticism from Henry James to Jacques Derrida*. U of Toronto P, 2010.

Knight, Peter. "DeLillo, Postmodernism, Postmodernity." Duvall, pp. 27–40.

———. "Everything Is Connected: *Underworld*'s Secret History of Paranoia." *MFS: Modern Fiction Studies*, vol. 45, no. 3, 1999, pp. 811–36.

Kohn, Robert. "Seven Buddhist Themes in Pynchon's *The Crying of Lot 49*." *Religion & Literature*, vol. 35, no. 1, 2003, pp. 73–96.

Lanza, Carmela Delia. "Hearing the Voices: Women and Home and Ana Castillo's *So Far from God*." *MELUS*, vol. 23, no. 1, 1998, pp. 65–79.

———. "'A New Meeting with the Sacred': Ana Castillo's *So Far from God*." *RLA: Romance Languages Annual*, vol. 10, no. 2, 1998, pp. 658–63.

Larkin, Lesley. "Reading as Responsible Dialogue in Ana Castillo's *The Mixquiahuala Letters*." *MELUS*, vol. 37, no. 3, 2012, pp. 141–66.

Latour, Bruno. *Reassembling the Social: An Introduction to Actor-Network-Theory*. Oxford UP, 2005.

Lee, Richard. "Narrative Point of View, Irony and Cultural Criticism in Selected Short Fiction by George Saunders." *Short Story*, vol. 18, no. 1, 2010, pp. 81–94.

LeMahieu, Michael. *Fictions of Fact and Value: The Erasure of Logical Positivism in American Literature, 1945–1975*. Oxford UP, 2013.

Lensing, Dennis M. "Postmodernism at Sea: The Quest for Longitude in Thomas Pynchon's *Mason & Dixon* and Umberto Eco's *The Island of the Day Before*." *The Multiple Worlds of Pynchon's* Mason & Dixon: *Eighteenth-Century Contexts, Postmodern Observations*, edited by Elizabeth Jane Wall Hinds, Camden House, 2005, pp. 125–43.

Lentricchia, Frank, editor. *Introducing Don DeLillo*. Duke UP, 1991.

Lewis, R. W. B. *The American Adam: Innocence, Tragedy, and Tradition in the Nineteenth Century*. U of Chicago P, 1955.

Lofton, Kathryn. *Consuming Religion*. U of Chicago P, 2017.

Lovell, Joel. "'Stay Open, Forever, So Open It Hurts.'" *The New York Times Sunday Magazine*, 6 Jan. 2013, pp. 22–47.

Lynch, Joy M. "'A Distinct Place in America Where All Mestizos Reside': Landscape and Identity in Ana Castillo's *Sapogonia* and Diana Chang's *The Frontiers of Love*." *MELUS*, vol. 26, no. 3, 2001, pp. 119–44.

Madsen, Deborah L. *Understanding Contemporary Chicana Literature*. U of South Carolina P, 2001.

Mailer, Norman. *St. George and the Godfather*. Signet, 1972.

Maltby, Paul. *Dissident Postmodernists: Barthelme, Coover, Pynchon*. U of Pennsylvania P, 1991.

Manríquez, B. J. "Ana Castillo's *So Far from God*: Intimations of the Absurd." *College Literature*, vol. 29, no. 2, 2002, pp. 37–49.

Mazur, Eric Michael, and Kate McCarthy. *God in the Details: American Religion in Popular Culture*. Routledge, 2011.

McCann, Sean, and Michael Szalay. "Do You Believe in Magic? Literary Thinking after the New Left." *The Yale Journal of Criticism*, vol. 18, no. 2, 2005, pp. 435–68.

McClure, John A. "DeLillo and Mystery." Duvall, pp. 166–78.

———. *Partial Faiths: Postsecular Fiction in the Age of Pynchon and Morrison.* U of Georgia P, 2007.

———. "Postmodern Romance: Don DeLillo and the Age of Conspiracy." Lentricchia, *Introducing,* pp. 99–116.

Mermann-Jozwiak, Elisabeth. "Gritos Desde La Frontera: Ana Castillo, Sandra Cisneros, and Postmodernism." *MELUS,* vol. 25, no. 2, 2000, pp. 101–18.

Michael, Magali Cornier. *New Visions of Community in Contemporary American Fiction: Tan, Kingsolver, Castillo, Morrison.* U of Iowa P, 2006.

Millen, Alex. "Affective Fictions: George Saunders and the Wonderful-Sounding Words of Neoliberalism." *Critique: Studies in Contemporary Fiction,* vol. 59, no. 2, 2018, pp. 127–41.

Miller, Adam S. *Speculative Grace: Bruno Latour and Object-Oriented Theology.* Fordham UP, 2013.

Moore, Gillian Elizabeth. "'Hope That, in Future, All Is Well': American Exceptionalism and Hopes for Resistance in Two Stories by George Saunders." Coleman and Ellerhoff, pp. 59–76.

Morgan, C. E. "I Want Soul." Interview with Anthony Domestico, *Commonweal,* 8 July 2016, pp. 16–19.

Morris, Laura. "Beyond Irony: Reconsidering the Post-Postmodernism of Dave Eggers and George Saunders." *Narratives at the Beginning of the 3rd Millennium,* edited by Jessica Homberg-Schramm et al., Cambridge Scholars, 2016, pp. 117–30.

Naydan, Liliana M. "Media Violence, Catholic Mystery, and Counter-Fundamentalism: A Post-9/11 Rhetoric of Flexibility in Don DeLillo's *Point Omega*." *Critique: Studies in Contemporary Fiction,* vol. 56, no. 1, 2015, pp. 94–107.

———. *Rhetorics of Religion in American Fiction.* Bucknell UP, 2016.

Neeper, Layne. "'To Soften the Heart': George Saunders, Postmodern Satire, and Empathy." *Studies in American Humor,* vol. 2, no. 2, 2016, pp. 280–99.

Nel, Philip. "DeLillo and Modernism." Duvall, pp. 13–26.

Olster, Stacey. "White Noise." Duvall, pp. 79–93.

Orsi, Robert A. *Between Heaven and Earth: The Religious Worlds People Make and the Scholars Who Study Them.* Princeton UP, 2005.

Osteen, Mark. *American Magic and Dread.* U of Pennsylvania P, 2000.

Parrish, Timothy. "Pynchon and DeLillo." *UnderWords: Perspectives on Don DeLillo's* Underworld, edited by Joseph Dewey et al., U of Delaware P, 2002, pp. 79–92.

Patell, Cyrus K. *Negative Liberties: Morrison, Pynchon, and the Problem of Liberal Ideology.* Duke UP, 2001.

Pearce-Gonzales, Bryan R. "Sabotaging Patriarchy: La Locura as Feminist Countersociety in Ana Castillo's *So Far from God.*" *Label Me Latina/o,* no. 3, 2013, pp. 1–14.

Pérez, Gail. "Ana Castillo as Santera: Reconstructing Popular Religious Praxis." *A Reader in Latina Feminist Theology: Religion and Justice,* edited by María Pilar Aquino et al., U of Texas P, 2002, pp. 53–79.

Pynchon, Thomas. *Against the Day.* Penguin, 2006.

———. *Bleeding Edge.* Penguin, 2014.

———. "The Deadly Sins/Sloth: Nearer, My Couch, to Thee." *The New York Times,* 6 June 1993, https://www.nytimes.com/books/97/05/18/reviews/pynchon-sloth.html.

———. *Gravity's Rainbow*. Penguin Classics, 2006.

———. *Inherent Vice*. Penguin, 2009.

———. "Is It O. K. to Be a Luddite?" *The New York Times*, 28 Oct. 1984, https://www.nytimes.com/books/97/05/18/reviews/pynchon-luddite.html.

———. *Mason & Dixon*. Picador, 1997.

———. *V.* Harper Perennial Modern Classics, 2005.

———. *Vineland*. Penguin, 1997.

Quintana, Alvina E. "Ana Castillo's *The Mixquiahuala Letters*: The Novelist as Ethnographer." *Criticism in the Borderlands: Studies in Chicano Literature, Culture, and Ideology*, edited by Héctor Calderón and José David Saldívar, Duke UP, 1991, pp. 72–83.

Rando, David. "George Saunders and the Postmodern Working Class." *Contemporary Literature*, vol. 53, no. 3, 2012, pp. 437–60.

Robinson, Marilynne. *Absence of Mind: The Dispelling of Inwardness from the Modern Myth of the Self*. Yale UP, 2011.

———. *The Death of Adam: Essays on Modern Thought*. Houghton Mifflin, 1998.

———. *Gilead*. Picador, 2006.

———. *The Givenness of Things: Essays*. Picador, 2016.

———. *Home*. Picador, 2009.

———. *Lila*. Picador, 2015.

———. *What Are We Doing Here?* Farrar, Straus and Giroux, 2018.

———. *When I Was a Child I Read Books*. Farrar, Straus and Giroux, 2012.

Rose, Jane E. "Negotiating Work in the Novels of Ana Castillo: Social Dis-ease and the American Dream." *CLA Journal*, vol. 54, no. 4, 2011, pp. 387–409.

Sacks, Sam. "George Saunders's Gospel of Compassion." *The Wall Street Journal*, 10 Feb. 2017, https://www.wsj.com/articles/george-saunderss-gospel-of-compassion-1486761004.

Saltzman, Arthur. "'Cranks of Ev'ry Radius': Romancing the Line in *Mason & Dixon*." Horvath and Malin, pp. 63–72.

Sauer, Michelle M. "'Saint-Making' in Ana Castillo's *So Far from God*: Medieval Mysticism as Precedent for an Authoritative Chicana Spirituality." *Mester*, no. 29, 2000, pp. 72–91.

Saunders, George. *The Brief and Frightening Reign of Phil*. Riverhead, 2005.

———. *CivilWarLand in Bad Decline*. Random House, 2016.

———. "George Saunders by Sam Lipsyte." Interview with Sam Lipsyte. *BOMB Magazine*, 15 Mar. 2017, https://bombmagazine.org/articles/george-saunders/.

———. "George Saunders on How Art Can Inspire Empathy in the Trump Era." Interview with Alexander Bisley, *Vox*, 18 Mar. 2017, https://www.vox.com/conversations/2017/3/18/14957294/george-saunders-trump-empathy.

———. "George Saunders's Advice to Graduates." *The New York Times*, 31 Jul. 2013, https://6thfloor.blogs.nytimes.com/2013/07/31/george-saunderss-advice-to-graduates/.

———. *In Persuasion Nation*. Riverhead, 2006.

———. "Interview with George Saunders." Interview with Todd Leopold, *Goodreads*, 6 Feb. 2017, https://www.goodreads.com/interviews/show/1217.George_Saunders.

———. *Lincoln in the Bardo*. Random House, 2017.

———. *Pastoralia*. Riverhead, 2000.

———. *Tenth of December*. Random House, 2013.

———. "Why Fiction Matters: An Interview with George Saunders." Interview with Kevin Spinale, *America Magazine*, 22 Mar. 2013, https://www.americamagazine.org/arts-culture/2013/05/22/why-fiction-matters-interview-george-saunders.

Schmidt, Leigh Eric. *Restless Souls: The Making of American Spirituality*. Harper San Francisco, 2005.

Sells, Michael A. *Mystical Languages of Unsaying*. U of Chicago P, 1994.

Severs, Jeffrey, and Christopher Leise, editors. *Pynchon's Against the Day: A Corrupted Pilgrim's Guide*. U of Delaware P, 2011.

Shy, Todd. "Religion and Marilynne Robinson." *Salmagundi*, no. 155/156, 2007, pp. 251–64.

Sirias, Silvio, and Richard McGarry. "Tradition and Rebellion in Ana Castillo's *So Far from God* and Sylvia López-Medina's *Cantora*." *MELUS*, vol. 25, no. 2, 2000, pp. 83–100.

Smith, Christian. *Religion: What It Is, How It Works, and Why It Matters*. Princeton UP, 2017.

Smith, Rachel Greenwald. *Affect and American Literature in the Age of Neoliberalism*. Cambridge UP, 2015.

Socolovsky, Maya. "Borrowed Homes, Homesickness, and Memory in Ana Castillo's *Sapogonia*." *Aztlán: A Journal of Chicano Studies*, vol. 24, no. 2, 1999, pp. 73–94.

Stout, Jeffrey. *Democracy and Tradition*. Princeton UP, 2005.

Szeghi, Tereza M. "Indigeneity and Mestizaje in Ana Castillo's *The Mixquiahuala Letters* and Leslie Marmon Silko's *Almanac of the Dead*." *Comparative Literature*, vol. 65, no. 4, 2013, pp. 429–49.

Tanner, Laura E. "Uncomfortable Furniture: Inhabiting Domestic and Narrative Space in Marilynne Robinson's *Home*." *Contemporary Women's Writing*, vol. 7, no. 1, 2013, pp. 35–53.

Taylor, Charles. *A Secular Age*. Belknap Press of Harvard UP, 2007.

Thoreen, David. "The Fourth Amendment and Other Modern Inconveniences: Undeclared War, Organized Labor, and the Abrogation of Civil Rights in *Vineland*." *Thomas Pynchon: Reading from the Margins*, edited by Niran Abbas, Fairleigh Dickinson UP, 2003, pp. 215–33.

Trussler, Michael. "Everyday Zombies: Ethics and the Contemporary in 'Sea Oak' and 'Brad Carrigan, American.'" Coleman and Ellerhoff, pp. 205–20.

Walter, Roland. "The Cultural Politics of Dislocation and Relocation in the Novels of Ana Castillo." *MELUS*, vol. 23, no. 1, 1998, pp. 81–97.

Weisenburger, Steven. "Gravity's Rainbow." Dalsgaard et al., pp. 44–58.

Whitman, Walt. *Leaves of Grass and Other Writings*. Edited by Michael Moon, W. W. Norton, 2002.

Will, George F. "Shallow Look at the Mind of an Assassin." *The Washington Post*, 22 Sept. 1988, p. A25.

Williams, J. P. *Denying Divinity: Apophasis in the Patristic Christian and Soto Zen Buddhist Traditions*. Oxford UP, 2000.

Williams, Rowan. *Faith in the Public Square*. Bloomsbury, 2012.

Wilson, Robert Cameron. "'Third-Person Ventriloquism': Microdialogues and Polyphony in George Saunders's 'Victory Lap.'" Coleman and Ellerhoff, pp. 221–36.

Wood, James. "Atoms of Paranoia." Review of *Underworld*, by Don DeLillo, *The Guardian*, 8 Jan. 1998, pp. 11.

Woodiwiss, Catherine. "George Saunders on Trump, Mystery, and Why He Rejects Social Media." *Sojourners*, 30 Aug. 2016, https://sojo.net/articles/george-saunders-trump-mystery-and-why-he-rejects-social-media.

Wuthnow, Robert. *After Heaven: Spirituality in America Since the 1950s*. U of California P, 1998.

Yardley, Jonathan. "Don DeLillo's American Nightmare." Review of *White Noise*, by Don DeLillo, *The Washington Post Book World*, 13 Jan. 1985, p. 3.

Yoder, John Howard. "Civil Religion in America: A Radical Protestant Perspective." *Civil Religion and Transcendent Experience*, edited by Ralph C. Wood and John E. Collins, Mercer UP, 1988, pp. 1–23.

Žižek, Slavoj. *The Puppet and the Dwarf: The Perverse Core of Christianity*. MIT P, 2003.

INDEX

Against the Day (Pynchon): election myth and, 103–4; environmental destruction in, 120; penance in, 112–13; pilgrimage in, 126–30; renunciation in, 114–20; shamanistic journeying in, 123–25

agnosticism vs. apophasis, 46

Alarcón, Daniel, 75n13, 79–80

Allen, Glen Scott, 39n9

American dream: Castillo and, 63–64, 69–75; DeLillo and, 28; Pynchon and, 99, 101–2; Saunders and, 138–39, 150–52

American myth, 3–5, 28–30, 138

American revolution, 108–9

apophatic discourse: about, 45–47; *The Cloud of Unknowing*, 47–50; DeLillo and, 27–28, 43–45, 47–57; postmodernity and, 48. *See also* negative theology

apophatic theory, 46

Aquinas, Thomas, 45

Arnold, Matthew, 201

Asad, Talal, 18

assimilation, 62–63, 71, 72

atheism, 10, 74, 99, 172n2, 192

attunement, 120–25, 176

authenticity: Castillo, Chicanx spirituality, and, 62–63, 75, 79–80; De La Torre on Latinx spirituality and, 76–77; DeLillo and, 43, 56, 59; Pynchon and, 114; Robinson and, 168, 176, 179–81, 185, 190; Saunders and, 140; spirituality vs. religion and, 14

Baker, Jeff, 110n8

baptism, 178

Barth, Karl, 179

baseball, 12, 30, 37–38

Basseler, Michael, 136, 137

Bawer, Bruce, 28n4

belief: in Castillo, 76, 84; conviction vs. indeterminacy of, 22; in DeLillo, 26–27, 35–43, 51–52; discipline and practice vs., 2, 10–12, 24, 201–2; Emerson and, 188–89; Heim on pluralism and, 110; ideology and, 5; in linear progress, 1; lived religion scholarship and, 21; in Pynchon, 104, 105, 110–11, 119, 129, 131; religion and, 18–20; in Robinson, 169, 171–72, 176, 178–83, 186; in Saunders, 140–41, 143, 150, 161, 165; in the soul, 193–94

213

Bellah, Robert, 5–8

Bercovitch, Sacvan: "American Jeremiads," 23; on Emerson, 189; on federal eschatology, 186; on Puritans, 3–5, 29; on representative self, 30, 70, 105; on third-person sensibility, 31n6

Bible, Robinson on, 178

Blackford, Holly, 66

Bloch, Ernst, 17

body-spirit dualism, 76, 78

borderlands state (*nepantla*), 61–63, 77, 94–95

Branch, Lori, 22

Bryant, Paula, 44n10

Buddhism: apophasis in, 46; Nirvana vs. Christian salvation, 110; Pynchon and, 112, 112n10; Saunders and, 136, 153, 161; Shambhala pilgrimage in Pynchon's *Against the Day*, 126–30

Buell, Lawrence, 188–89

Calvin, John, 190, 192–93

Calvinism, 176, 181–86, 190, 199–200

Caminero-Santangelo, Marta, 65–66

Carson, Benjamin, 66n7

Castillo, Ana: American Dream as nightmare, 69–75; borderlands state, Chicanx subjectivity, and, 61–64, 77, 94–95; Chicana literature and, 64–67; Chicana spirituality and, 67–68, 78–81; *lo cotidiano* (everyday particularity) and, 77–83, 93; ethics *para joder* (trickster ethics) and, 77–79; holy *joderones* (bandit saints) of, 75–76, 78–94; indigenous spirituality and, 81–87; *jodiendo en conjunto* (the particular and the communal) and, 79–81; liberation theology and, 76–77; on spirituality vs. religion, 67; telenovela conventions, appropriation of, 65

—works: *The Guardians*, 87–94; *Massacre of the Dreamers*, 82, 87; *The Mixquiahuala Letters*, 66, 81–83; *Peel My Love Like an Onion*, 69–70; *Sapogonia*, 70–72, 83–87. See also *So Far from God*

Catholicism: Castillo and, 67–68, 79–81, 83, 88–92; DeLillo and, 28–29, 36–37, 41–43, 53; Pynchon and, 112–13; Saunders and, 136, 153, 161

Cavanaugh, William, 32

Cavell, Stanley, 189

Chicanx spirituality and subjectivity, 61–65, 67–68, 78–82. See also Castillo, Ana

choice, individual: belief-focus and, 18; culture vs. religion and, 11; freedom of, in Saunders, 147; impact on others, in Saunders, 161; religion reduced to, 18, 22; third-person self and, 31

"Christianism," 173, 175

Christianity: Castillo on dualisms in, 76; civil religion and, 7–8; as cultural identity, 180; fundamentalism/right-wing, Robinson on, 171–75; as identity vs. ethic, in Robinson, 173–75; Pynchon's counterbalance to, 114; superseded by nationalism in Saunders, 152. See also Catholicism; Puritans and Puritanism

"city upon a hill," 5, 30, 103–4, 148

civil religion, 5–9, 185–86

civil rights movement, 185

Cloud of Unknowing, The, 47–50

Cold War, 29–30, 33–37, 39n9

compassion: Pynchon and, 114–15, 117; Saunders and, 135–38, 153, 160, 163–65

complicity, Pynchon on, 98

consensus, rhetoric of, 3–4

Constitution, US, 184

consumerism and consumer spirituality: in Castillo, 63, 72; in DeLillo, 28, 30–35, 37; Dreyfus and Kelly and, 20; Robinson on mysticism and, 190n6; in Saunders, 138, 147–54; seeker spirituality and, 14; universal third person and, 30–35; Wuthnow on authentic spirituality vs., 14

Conte, Joseph M., 29n5

conversions, 9, 111

covenantal theology, 8, 143, 148

Cowart, David, 32, 43, 44, 48, 58, 112n10

culture: American monoculture, assumption of, 170–73; as debates, 3; religion as overlapping/distinguished from, 11; Robinson on culture wars, 169; self-help culture in Saunders, 154–58

De La Torre, Miguel, 61, 64, 71, 75–79, 89, 91, 93–94

Declaration of Independence, 185

Deleuze, Gilles, 44n10

Delgadillo, Theresa, 68, 79, 81

DeLillo, Don: American mythology and, 28–30, 36–38; apophatic discourse and, 27–28, 43–45, 47–57; Catholicism and, 28–29, 36–37, 41–43, 53; consumer culture and universal third person in, 30–35; language, approach to, 27, 44–45; moral and spiritual development of characters, 38; mystery and mysticism in, 39–44, 48–51, 56; terrorism and transcendence, 50–55; transcendence, belief, and practice in, 25–27

—works: *Americana*, 28, 30–31; *Cosmopolis*, 25n1, 41–42; *End Zone*, 25, 50; *Falling Man*, 50–56, 59; *Libra*, 36; *Mao II*, 25, 39–41, 51–52; *The Names*, 41, 58; *Players*, 25; *Point Omega*, 31–32, 48n15; *Running Dog*, 25n1; *White Noise*, 30, 47. See also *Underworld*

democracy: DeLillo's "The American People" and, 29; globalization and, 29n5; Puritanism and, 182–83, 184, 196; Robinson on, 170–71, 173, 175, 182–83, 184–86, 196

democratic individuality, 192, 196–200

depravity, 183

deus absconditus (the hidden God), 49–50

development, moral and spiritual: American literature and, 22; apophasis and, 46, 48, 50; in Castillo, 78–80; in DeLillo, 38; the home and, 68; narrative time and, 22; in Pynchon, 118, 123, 127–29

Dewey, Joseph, 27, 40, 44n13, 57, 110n8, 111, 114n12

Diaz, Porfirio, 94

dignity: Robinson on, 184; in Saunders, 133–34, 152–53, 154–58, 160

disciplines, spiritual. See spiritual disciplines

Domestico, Anthony, 176

Douglas, Christopher, 8–9, 21, 168–69, 180–81

Dreyfus, Hubert, 20

Dupré, Louis, 15–17, 20, 24, 26, 58–59, 108–9

Eagleton, Terry, 5, 151n1

Edwards, Jonathan, 190, 192

Egan, Jennifer, 134

election, American: American culture and, 3; "city upon a hill," 5, 30, 103–4, 148; civil religion and, 7–9; in DeLillo, 30; Emerson and, 189; Puritan underpinnings of, 104; in Pynchon, 100–108; in Robinson, 182–83, 190

Eliade, Mircea, 15n8, 109

Emerson, Ralph Waldo, 177, 186–87, 188–91, 197–98

empathy: in Castillo, 85; in DeLillo, 38; in Saunders, 134–38, 163

enlightenment: apophasis and, 51; in Castillo, 79; DeLillo and, 45, 56; Nirvana, 110; in Pynchon, 114; search for meaning and, 14

Enlightenment rationalism, 110–11, 110n8

environment, relationship with: in Castillo, 66, 80–81, 87–88, 92; Pynchon's attunement, 120–25; Robinson on, 167

equality: American myth and ideal of, 4; in Castillo, 68, 86; Emerson on, 198; in Pynchon, 103; in Robinson, 184, 198

eschatology, federal, 186, 189

ethics *para joder* (trickster ethics), 64, 77–79

exceptionalism, American: academic view of, 2; civil religion and, 5–9, 185–86; as poor substitute for transcendence, 24; Puritan rhetoric of consensus, the American myth, and, 2–4. See also *specific authors*

experience, religious: apophasis and, 45–47, 54, 55; in Castillo, 79; in DeLillo, 38, 43, 44n13; Emerson and, 188–91; Latinx theology and, 77; mystical experience and feeling-centered view of religion, 19–20; in Pynchon, 116–17, 127; Robinson on religious experience, 175–81, 190–91, 196; the sacred as category of interpretation vs. experience, 16–17; "spirituality" and, 13

federal eschatology, 186, 189

feng shui, 120–23

Ferris, Joshua, 134

Fessenden, Tracy, 8, 13, 19–20, 22

forbearance, 114–15

formation. See development, moral and spiritual

Foster, Dennis, 44n10

fragmentary narrative, 66

Franke, William, 26n2, 46, 47
freedom: American myth and, 4; in Castillo, 71; of choice, 147, 172; democracy as "freedom on the march," 29n5; nonintegrated self and, 16; in Pynchon, 99, 101–2, 105; Saunders and denial of, 142–43; seeker spirituality and, 14
Frothingham, Octavius, 13–14
Frow, John, 44n10
fundamentalism, Robinson on, 171–75

García-Caro, Pedro, 102
Geertz, Clifford, 11
globalization, 29, 29n5
Gnosticism, 108, 114
God: Castillo on, 76; *deus absconditus* (the hidden God), 49–50; Emerson on, 188; *imago dei*, 183, 189, 191, 199–200; question of, in DeLillo's *Falling Man*, 51–54; Robinson on, 176
goddess worship, 82–87
grace: in Pynchon, 112n10, 113; in Robinson, 176, 183, 191; in Saunders, 134, 149, 152, 160, 161
gratitude, discipline of, 145–48
Greene, Graham, 163
Greiner, Donald J., 110n8

Haddox, Thomas, 180, 181–82
Hall, David, 21
Hammond, Phillip, 6–8
Hayes-Brady, Clare, 139
Heide, Markus, 74
Heim, S. Mark, 109–10
heroism, in Castillo, 74
Hewitt, John, 3
history, immunity to, 105–6
home in Chicana spirituality, 68
hopelessness, conditional, 78
Horton, Ray, 182
Hume, Kathryn, 112, 112n10, 114–15, 119, 127
Hungerford, Amy, 22, 40, 41, 43, 179–80
hybridity: Castillo and *mestizaje* (mixing), 61–62, 64–68, 78, 79, 87, 94; Chicana hybrid spirituality, in Castillo, 75, 78–85; Pynchon and, 109–11, 131

identity construction in Castillo, 66–67; power of, 1
ideology: of America, 5; in Castillo, 61, 63–64, 68, 74–75; consumerism and, in DeLillo, 32; defined, 5; in DeLillo, 25–38, 49, 51, 55, 59; in Pynchon, 98–100, 102–9, 112, 131; receptivity vs., 195; Robinson on, 167–68, 169–73, 181; in Saunders, 138–40, 142, 150–52; secular, lived as religious, 22; situatedness, 23n9. *See also* political ideology
idol worship, 84, 85
imago dei, 183, 189, 191, 199–200
immanence: consumption and, 32; Dupré on selfhood and, 16, 58–59; Emerson on, 188; meaning-making and, 18–19; Robinson and, 176, 186–88, 190–92, 200; secular immanent framework, 17; transcendence and, 53, 176, 191, 200
indigenous spirituality: in Castillo, 81–87; in Pynchon, 123–25
individualism: in Castillo, 70, 78; compassion and, 153; democratic individuality vs., 186; Emerson and, 186, 188–89; Pynchon's "True Faith" and, 105; Reaganism and, 104; Saunders and, 138, 153–55, 162; Whitman on, 193, 195
interconnectedness: Kateb on transcendence and, 199; Robinson on soul and, 193; in Saunders, 137–38, 158, 161, 162
intersubjectivity, 133–34, 138, 162, 165
Islam: apophasis in Sufism, 45; in DeLillo, 51, 55; Pynchon and, 106, 114; Robinson on, 168

James, Henry, 48
James, William, 11, 188–89, 191, 199–200
Jameson, Fredric, 44
Jefferson, Thomas, 184
Jewish tradition, 45

Kabbalah, 45
kataphatic statements, 47, 52
Kateb, George, 188, 192–200
Kellman, Steven, 44n10
Kelly, Adam, 149
Kelly, Sean Dorrance, 20
Knight, Christopher J., 48
Knight, Peter, 39n9, 44

Kristeva, Julia, 44n10

language: bilingualism in Castillo, 65; in DeLillo, 26–28, 40, 43–47; Robinson on founders and Judeo-Christian language, 184–85. *See also* apophatic discourse
Larkin, Lesley, 66
Latinx theology, 76–77. *See also* Castillo, Ana
Latour, Bruno, 12
Lee, Richard, 136
LeMahieu, Michael, 45
Lentricchia, Frank, 28n4, 30, 39n9
Lewis, R. W. B., 3
liberation theology, 68, 76–77
lived religion scholarship, 21
Lofton, Kathryn, 33
Lovell, Joel, 134

Madsen, Deborah, 62
magical realism, 65–66
Mailer, Norman, 1–2
Maltby, Paul, 101
Manichaeanism, 119
Manifest Destiny: Castillo and, 62, 75; DeLillo and, 30; Pynchon and, 110n8, 123
Manríquez, B. J., 66n7
mapping, 103, 122–23
martyrdom: Castillo's *So Far From God* and, 74–75, 87; Pynchon's *Against the Day* and, 119n14, 120; Saunders's "Sea Oak" and, 151
Mary, the Blessed Virgin, 88–91
McClure, John, 9–10, 36, 100, 109, 111, 114n12
meaning: civil religion and, 6; located in mind, 16; meaning-making, 18–19; stable meanings, desire for, 58–59
Mermann-Jozwiak, Elisabeth, 65, 67n8
Miller, Adam, 19
miracles: in Castillo, 66; in DeLillo, 56; in Pynchon, 102–3
monism of Emerson, 189–90
monoculture, 170–73
moral development. *See* development, moral and spiritual

Morris, Laura, 136
mujerista theology (women's liberation theology), 76
mystery and mysticism: apophasis and, 46; in Castillo, 91; in DeLillo, 27, 36, 38–44, 47–51, 54–59; DeLillo on Latin mass and, 28; feeling-centered view of religion, 19–20; in Pynchon, 108, 115, 123–28; Robinson on, 171–72, 183, 190–91, 196; in Saunders, 146; spirituality vs. religion and, 13
myth, American, 3–5, 28–30, 138. *See also* American dream

nationalism: academic assumptions about, 2; American ideology vs., 5; Bellah on, 8; in DeLillo, 29–30, 34; Kateb's transcendence vs., 199; in Pynchon, 101, 106, 107, 130; Robinson on, 168, 172–75, 186; in Saunders, 146, 152
nativism, 1, 169–70
Naydan, Liliana, 10, 48n15
Neeper, Layne, 137
negative theology, 116, 119. *See also* apophatic discourse
neoliberalism, 33, 143, 149
Nirvana, 110

ontotheological synthesis, 15–17, 24, 26, 108
ontotheology, 26n2
Orsi, Robert, 18, 22
Osteen, Mark, 36

paranoia, 36–37, 39n9
Patell, Cyrus, 98
patience, discipline of, 116
Paz, Octavio, 62
penance, in Pynchon's *Against the Day*, 112–13
Pérez, Gail, 75, 75n13, 87
pilgrimage, in Pynchon's *Against the Day*, 126–30
Plotinus, 45
pluralism, religious: apophatic discourse and, 47; civil religion and, 6; Heim on, 109–10; Pynchon and, 109–11; religion as vital thing and, 19; Robinson and, 168–69, 175, 186, 199

political ideology: Castillo and, 63; DeLillo and, 26, 28–31, 34–35; Pynchon and, 100; Robinson and, 169; Saunders and, 142–43
positive thinking: Robinson on, 183; in Saunders, 146, 151–52, 154–55
postmodernism: apophasis and postmodern consciousness, 48; Buddhism and, 114; Castillo and, 66n7; Chicana literature and, 66–67; DeLillo and, 39n9, 44, 48; Dupré and Pynchon on reality and, 108; pilgrimage and, 127n16; Pynchon and, 98, 108, 114, 127n16; Saunders and, 137, 161
postsecularism and postsecular studies: on immanent framework, 17; McClure on "partial faiths" and, 9; monolithic view of religion in, 19; transcendence and, 15, 24
practice, religious: definition of religion based on, 10–11; DeLillo and, 27; lived religion scholarship and, 21; Robinson and, 200–201; spiritual disciplines vs., 15. See also ritual; spiritual disciplines
prayer: in Castillo, 74, 79–80, 83–84, 89–92; in DeLillo, 27, 49; in Pynchon, 117, 127; in Saunders, 141, 153
predestination, 183, 189
Protestant work ethic, 151
Puritans and Puritanism: Bercovitch on, 3–5, 29; in Pynchon, 102–4; Robinson and, 167, 184, 186–88, 196; Saunders and, 143; transcendentalism and, 186–88
Pynchon, Thomas: Allen on paranoia and, 39n9; on American dream and political ideology, 99–100; on American exceptionalism and religious hybridity, 108–11; attunement, discipline of, 120–25; on complicity, 98; myth of American election in, 100–107; penance, discipline of, 112–13; pilgrimage, discipline of, 126–30; on power, transcendence, and integration, 97–99; renunciation, discipline of, 114–20; on Sloth, 131; terror and security in, 107
—works: *Bleeding Edge*, 97, 105–6, 120, 130–31; *Gravity's Rainbow*, 100–101, 110n8; *Inherent Vice*, 98, 101–2; "Is It O. K. to Be a Luddite?," 99, 103; *Mason & Dixon*, 102–3, 110n8, 114n12, 121–23; *V.*, 99; *Vineland*, 97–98, 104–5, 114n12, 120. See also *Against the Day*

Quintana, Alvina, 82

Rando, David, 149–50, 152
rationalism, 76–77, 110
Reaganism, 104–5
receptivity, 192, 195–96, 199
redemption: Bercovitch on "American" and, 4; in DeLillo, 33, 43–44; in Pynchon, 112–13; in Saunders, 144, 150–53, 161
religion: belief-centered view of, 18–19; definitions of, 10–12, 21–22; feeling-centered view of, 19–20; James on religion as private, 11; McClure on "partial faiths" and, 9–10, 19; monolithic view of, 19
renunciation, in Pynchon's *Against the Day*, 114–20
representative selfhood, 3–4, 30, 70, 73, 105
right-wing Christianity, Robinson on, 171–75
ritual: American exceptionalism and, 23; in Castillo, 68, 80–81, 87; civil religion and, 7; cultural, as spiritual disciplines, 15; definitions of religion and, 6, 11–12; DeLillo on, 41; dissent as, 23; in Pynchon, 107, 127; terrorism responses and, in Pynchon, 107. See also practice, religious; spiritual disciplines
Robinson, Marilynne: as Calvinist, 176, 181–86, 190, 199–200; on Christian identity vs. ethic, 173–75; democratic individuality and, 192, 196–200; Emerson and, 188–91; on ideology and monoculture, 167–68, 169–73; overview, 167–69; on religious experience, 175–81, 196; theopoetics of, 182, 199; transcendentalism, Puritanism, and, 186–88; Whitman, the soul, and, 192–98
—works: "Fear," 168; *Gilead*, 176–77, 179–82, 191, 196; *Home*, 176; *Lila*, 177–78; *Mother Country*, 62, 167; *What Are We Doing Here?*, 174n3; *When I Was a Child I Read Books*, 192
Rose, Jane, 69

sacrament, concept of, 178
sacred, the: Castillo and, 68, 79; as category of interpretation vs. experience, 16–17; Fessenden on feeling and, 20; in Pynchon, 103, 127; "transcendent" vs., 15

saints: Castillo's holy *joderones* (bandit saints), 75–76, 78–94; suffering, in Saunders, 150

salvation: in Castillo, 71, 91; in DeLillo, 33; meanings of, 110n7; Nirvana vs., 110; in Pynchon, 103–4, 110–11, 116, 119n14; Robinson on "personal" salvation, 171; in Saunders, 139; Schmidt's "restless souls" and, 14

sanctification, 141

Saunders, George: dignified humanity in, 133–34; dignified suffering in, 159–61; empathy and compassion in, 135–38, 163–65; exceptionalism, varieties of, 138–41; gratitude, discipline of, 145–48; kindness in, 134–35; reputation of, 134; self-help culture and dignity as gift, 154–58; self-improvement, discipline of, 141–45; suffering, valorization of, 148–54; universality of suffering and seeing as seen, 162–65; vulnerability in, 158, 160

—works: "Al," 136; "Bounty," 139–41, 149, 153; "Brad Carrigan, American," 139; *The Brief and Frightening Reign of Phil*, 139; *Congratulations, By the Way*, 134–35; "The Falls," 145–47; "The 400-Pound CEO," 143–45; "Isabelle," 133–34; *Lincoln in the Bardo*, 161–65; "My Amendment," 141–43; "My Flamboyant Grandson," 147–48; "Offloading for Mrs. Schwartz," 153–54; "Pastoralia," 154; "Sea Oak," 149–53; "Tenth of December," 159–61; "Winky," 155–58

Schleiermacher, Friedrich, 19

Schmidt, Leigh Eric, 13–14

secularization: civil religion and, 7; progressive, 17, 20; Pynchon on, 99

secularization thesis, 9–10, 13

seeker spirituality, 13–14, 74, 126, 179

self-help culture, 154–58

selfhood: Castillo and, 61, 63–65, 82; Dupré on, 16, 26, 58–59; myth of self-made individual in Saunders, 139–40; representative, 3–4, 30, 70, 73, 105; third-person self, in DeLillo, 30–35

self-improvement as discipline, 141–45

self-integration, 17

self-sufficiency: in DeLillo, 47; in Saunders, 140, 142–44, 153, 156, 162

shamanistic practices, 123–25

Shambhala, 126–30

Shy, Todd, 181

slavery, 180–81

sloth, Pynchon on, 131

Smith, Christian, 10n6

Smith, Rachel Greenwald, 143

Smith, Zadie, 134

So Far from God (Castillo): American dream as nightmare, 72–75; epigraph for, 94; *The Guardians* compared to, 91; magical realism in, 65–66; the particular and the communal in, 79–81; *santera* (artisan who creates images of saints) in, 87

soul: in Castillo, 69–70, 84, 86, 92–93; in DeLillo, 42, 52; in Pynchon, 107, 115–17, 123–25, 131; religion and, 12–13; in Robinson, 179, 183, 188–90, 200; in Saunders, 157; Schmidt's "restless souls," 14; in Whitman and Robinson, 192–98

spiritual development. *See* development, moral and spiritual

spiritual disciplines: in Castillo, 84, 92; practices vs., 15; Pynchon and alternative forms of, 111–12; Pynchon on political ideology and toxic forms of, 100. *See also* practice, religious; ritual; specific disciplines, such as gratitude

spirituality: Castillo on, 67–68; Chicana hybrid spirituality in Castillo, 78–81; consumer, 14; dichotomy of religion and, 13–14; materiality vs., in Robinson, 177; practice-based, 14–15; seeker, 14; syncretism vs. hybridity, 109; transcendence and, 15–17

Stout, Jeffrey, 188, 192, 197, 198

success stories, 70, 140, 143–44

suffering, in Saunders: dignified, 159–61; shared, 161; universality of, 162–65; valorization of, 148–54

sweat lodges, 74

Szeghi, Tereza, 81

Taylor, Charles, 17, 23, 109

telos, sacred, 3–4

terrorism: 9/11 attacks, 10, 29, 50–51, 58–59, 106–7; in DeLillo's *Falling Man*, 50–56, 59; in Pynchon's *Bleeding Edge*, 106–7

theopoetics of Robinson, 182, 199
third person, universal, 30–35
Thoreau, Henry David, 187, 198
Thoreen, David, 105
Tocqueville, Alexis de, 183
transcendence: American exceptionalism as poor substitute, 24; America's claim to, 23; apophatic tradition and, 43–44, 46; consumerism and, in DeLillo, 32–33; definition of, 10n6, 15; definition of religion and, 10–11, 19–20; in DeLillo, 25, 28, 32–33, 38, 45, 50–55, 58–59; democratic individuality and democratic transcendence, 188, 192, 198–200; Dupré's ontotheological synthesis, 15–17, 24, 26; Emerson on, 188, 198; immanence and, 53, 176, 191, 200; Pynchon on, 97–99, 105, 109–10, 126; Robinson on, 175–76, 190–91, 200; stable meanings and, 58–59
transcendentalism: Emerson, Robinson, and, 188–91; Puritanism and, 186–88; religion vs. spirituality and, 13; Robinson and, 169, 186–97; Whitman, Robinson, and the soul, 192–98
tribalism, 173–75
Trussler, Michael, 137, 153
Turner, Victor, 127n16

Underworld (DeLillo): American exceptionalism as religion in, 36–38; apophasis in, 47, 49–50, 56–58; Cold War in, 30; consumer culture and universal third person in, 32–35; Dewey on religious dimension of, 44n13; integrated characters in, 25n1; mystery in, 39, 42; religious language in, 27
utopianism, 101, 131

Vattimo, Gianni, 9
Virgen de Guadalupe, 82, 88–89

Walter, Roland, 65, 71, 94
waste, redemptive qualities of, 33
Weisenburger, Steven, 98n3
Whitman, Walt, 177, 186–87, 192–98
—works: *Song of Myself,* 194; "Starting from Paumanok," 193–94
Will, George F., 28n4
will and willpower, in Saunders, 143, 145
Williams, J. P., 45–47
Williams, Rowan, 21, 158, 163–64
Wilson, Robert Cameron, 137–38
Winthrop, John, 148, 184
Wood, James, 39n9
Wuthnow, Robert, 14–15

Yardley, Jonathan, 28n4
Yoder, John Howard, 7

LITERATURE, RELIGION, AND POSTSECULAR STUDIES
LORI BRANCH, SERIES EDITOR

Literature, Religion, and Postsecular Studies publishes scholarship on the influence of religion on literature and of literature on religion from the sixteenth century onward. Books in the series include studies of religious rhetoric or allegory; of the secularization of religion, ritual, and religious life; and of the emerging identity of postsecular studies and literary criticism.

American Exceptionalism as Religion: Postmodern Discontent
  JORDAN CARSON

Missionary Cosmopolitanism in Nineteenth-Century British Literature
  WINTER JADE WERNER

Constructing Nineteenth-Century Religion: Literary, Historical, and Religious Studies in Dialogue
  EDITED BY JOSHUA KING AND WINTER JADE WERNER

Good Words: Evangelicalism and the Victorian Novel
  MARK KNIGHT

Enlightened Individualism: Buddhism and Hinduism in American Literature from the Beats to the Present
  KYLE GARTON-GUNDLING

A Theology of Sense: John Updike, Embodiment, and Late Twentieth-Century American Literature
  SCOTT DILL

Walker Percy, Fyodor Dostoevsky, and the Search for Influence
  JESSICA HOOTEN WILSON

The Religion of Empire: Political Theology in Blake's Prophetic Symbolism
  G. A. ROSSO

Clashing Convictions: Science and Religion in American Fiction
  ALBERT H. TRICOMI

Female Piety and the Invention of American Puritanism
  BRYCE TRAISTER

Secular Scriptures: Modern Theological Poetics in the Wake of Dante
  WILLIAM FRANKE

Imagined Spiritual Communities in Britain's Age of Print
  JOSHUA KING

Conspicuous Bodies: Provincial Belief and the Making of Joyce and Rushdie
  JEAN KANE

Victorian Sacrifice: Ethics and Economics in Mid-Century Novels
  ILANA M. BLUMBERG

Lake Methodism: Polite Literature and Popular Religion in England, 1780–1830
  JASPER CRAGWALL

Hard Sayings: The Rhetoric of Christian Orthodoxy in Late Modern Fiction
  THOMAS F. HADDOX

Preaching and the Rise of the American Novel
  DAWN COLEMAN

Victorian Women Writers, Radical Grandmothers, and the Gendering of God
  GAIL TURLEY HOUSTON

Apocalypse South: Judgment, Cataclysm, and Resistance in the Regional Imaginary
  ANTHONY DYER HOEFER

www.ingramcontent.com/pod-product-compliance
Lightning Source LLC
Chambersburg PA
CBHW020651230426
43665CB00008B/399